THE ELECTRONIC LIBRARY

THE ELECTRONIC LIBRARY

Edited by
KUSUM VERMA

AKANSHA PUBLISHING HOUSE
NEW DELHI - 110 002 (INDIA)

AKANSHA PUBLISHING HOUSE
R-37B, Vani Vihar, Uttam Nagar
New Delhi-110 059
E-mail: ektabooks@yahoo.com

Showroom:
4649/21B, Ansari Road,
Daryaganj, New Delhi-110 002
Phone: 9212065579, 9811582579

The Electronic Library

First Published, 2004
Reprint, 2007

ISBN 81-87606-71-1

PRINTED IN INDIA

Published by M.P. Misra for Akansha Publishing House, New Delhi-110 002 and Printed at Tarun Offset Press, Delhi.

Preface

Libraries have always adopted newer technologies for fulfilling their basic commitments, and the adoption of digital technology in libraries is a part of this historical process. With the emergence of electronic media the potential to store large quantities of information has increased, with an advantage of accessing and transferring it to any place and from anywhere in the world through electronic means using the advanced network facilities which is a boon to libraries. Surprisingly, the technology for electronic transfer of information has also advanced so rapidly that it is now possible for electronic publishing, electronic storage, processing and delivery of information including text and images.

The term electronic libraries refers to a new way of carrying out the functions of libraries encompassing new types of electronic information resources, new approaches to acquisition, especially more access to other libraries collection and sharing it. It also undertake new methods of storage and preservation, new approaches to classificatior. and cataloguing, especially of electronic data, intensive use of electronic system and networks, and dramatic shifts in intellectual, organisational and electronic practices. It may have several provisions to access documents, which are of high value, mostly from outside the organisation. All the libraries in developed nations have totally shifted to electronic environment and those of them in the developing countries are in the process of marching towards the new electronic environment to find their place and fit into the changing information society with all its limitations.

The roles, responsibilities and potentials of electronic libraries are elaborately described in the present volume. It will serve as a highly informative reference tool to practising librarians and students and teachers of library science.

Editor

Contents

1

Documentation of Electronic Library

A library is an organization, rather than a building or a collection, than the requirement for institutional commitment for electronic information to have more than a fleeting existence. The organization of libraries is already changing as electronic information increasingly becomes part of their charge. Most research libraries have had substantial systems departments which maintain infrastructures while the librarians take on more and more digital information responsibilities.

Some libraries locate the responsibility for electronic information distinctly from that for print. Most libraries are coming to see the forms as inseparable and include digital responsibilities along with artifactual responsibilities in assignments for collection development, cataloging and public service. As libraries move more into the electronic environment the historic tripartite division of libraries into public services, technical services and collection development continues functionally but in more fluid arrangements. In addition, the need for consortial activity has become evident both for provision and preservation of digital information.

People who combine bibliographic understanding, problem-solving abilities, negotiating skills and process orientation will be needed throughout libraries; such staff will take on the demanding new technical, collection and service responsibilities for long-term support of digital collections. The permanent existence of a digital research library will require assured continuity in operational funding. Almost any other library activity can survive a funding hiatus of a year or more.

Acquisitions, building maintenance, and preservation can be suspended, or an entire staff can be dispersed and a library shut down for several years, and the artifactual collections will more or less survive. But digital collections, like the online catalog, require continual maintenance if they are to survive more than a very brief interruption of power, environmental control, backup, migration and related technical care. Online catalog maintenance costs have reached a rough steady state, and the capital costs for new OPACs are decreasing relative to the capabilities provided. The catalog size will continue to increase, but catalog records are small relative to the information to which they refer.

Digital collections, however, as a proportion of the library's supply of information, will grow for the foreseeable future, and the quantity of information requiring care will become considerable. Unit costs of storage are likely to continue falling for some time, which may make the financial burden manageable. Long term funding will be required to assure long term care. Libraries and their parent institutions will need to develop new fiscal tools and use familiar fiscal tools for new purposes. Public institutions, usually constrained to annual funding, will have particular difficulties, but existing procedures for capital or plant funding may provide precedents.

One familiar technique is the endowment. It has been difficult to obtain private funding for endowments of concepts and services rather than books and mortar, but it is possible. Institutions might also build endowments out of operating funds over periods of time. Some revenue streams associated with digital research libraries may be practical. Consortial arrangements may allow for lease or purchase of shares in a digital collection. Shorter-term access might be provided to other institutions on a usage basis. Access could be sold to certain classes of users, e.g. businesses, non-local clienteles, or specific information projects.

New relations with publishers, presently difficult to perceive through the miasmic fog rising from intellectual property, might provide income for storage of electronically published materials during the copyright lifetime in which publishers collect usage fees. With commitment and imagination long term fiscal tools will be found. All these are instrumental means of accomplishing the greatest requirement, that of conscious, planned institutional commitment to preserve that part of human culture which will flower in electronic form. While museums preserve artifacts, often beautiful, that embody information, libraries preserve information that — until now — has been embedded in artifacts.

The advent of electronic information will accentuate the difference between these roles as libraries take the responsibility for the preservation of information in non-artifactual forms. For the past century most research libraries have been associated with universities, and this connection seems likely to continue in the immediate future. Whatever the governance structure, an institution wishing to benefit from electronic information will have to make a conscious commitment to providing resources. Where the role of a library is to facilitate access to information, its mission is to support the mission of its parent institution. One can extend this to understand that if a university wishes to continue gaining support for its mission from its library, it will have to make commitments to the library's role.

In the electronic environment, this means new longstanding financial commitments which the library and university together must identify and accomplish. The commitment will have to be clearly and publicly made if scholars and other libraries are to have confidence that a given digital collection is indeed likely to exist for the long term. It is essential that guidelines or standards be established defining what is meant by a long term commitment, and defining what electronic repositories of data can qualify to be called a digital research library.

Just as donors of books, manuscripts and archives look for demonstration of long term care and commitment, so too will scholars and publishers as they create digital information which requires a home. The progress in digital archiving was strikingly international, and it was unevenly distributed around the globe. Trends in major developed nations are described below.

In US, the Digital Libraries Federation (DLF) has now been in existence for several years, but remains opaque to external observers. A coalition of about 20 libraries, it has developed some brief broad strategic outlines of proposed activity but has been silent as to actual projects within member libraries. In early DLF statements digital archiving was listed as one of three main priorities; more recently it is an "other" priority, with pre-eminent place given to user authentication and authorization matters. Details of the digital archival commitment being made by the project are unclear, and in its beginnings the project appears to have been subordinated to the specific content respository created for it on marriage and law in the 19th century. OCLC—the largest library utility—is well placed to create and provide archiving services, for it has readily available both the financial and intellectual capital to do so.

In 1997 it committed to archiving e-journals on behalf of its members subscribers and bravely included a commitment to technological migration. However it has remained silent on details of how it intends to achieve this goal, and has not yet had to come through with this commitment in any specific instance. Also, it has included the statement that it will migrate digital objects "at its discretion," presumably depending upon the degree of difficulty. Though in practice perhaps such a statement is always implied, its unqualified emphasis so early does not add to the confidence one wishes in such a project. The Canadian Initiative on Digital Libraries began work in 1997, but to date has shown little emphasis on digital archiving. On the other hand, many Canadian libraries are members of USA consortia (e.g. OCLC and RLG) whom they may count upon to act in their behalf. The commonwealth tradition of national planning and initiative appears in strong contrast to the fragmented, non-governmental activities in North America.

It remains to be seen which approach will generate the optimal and broadly exploited archiving technologies that are needed. However one can wish from the outset that the USA groups were more communicative about what they are doing, and in particular that they would coordinate their efforts with one another; to date there is little evidence that they do so. But it is notable that regardless of where digital archiving investigation is going on, it is in consortial activity. There is uniform recognition that digital archiving is not a matter soluble by individual institutions, whether for collection reasons or for technological reasons.

PADI (Preserving Access to Digital Information) is headed by an officer of the National Library of Australia, has an office and a budget and has developed statements of vision, goals and objectives. PADI maintains strong links between the library and archive communities. Its Statement of Principles on Preservation of Australian Digital Objects reflects an early achievement of national consensus. It has been followed by reports attempting to deal with location of responsibilities, definitions of how digital information is to be preserved, and the likely costs over time of digital archiving. Archives serve a variety of different functions in the larger society and even within the smaller scholarly community.

Research libraries in particular serve to support education, continuous learning and research for their designated constituents. The focal points of this type of collection are intellectual artifacts generally in textual and graphic formats. An increasingly significant amount of the intellectual content is published and distributed in electronic journals. Functionally, the archive is designed to render text and still images and other formats as practically possible with no significant loss in intellectual content.

The archive reserves the right to freely manipulate the internal format of the manifestation over time as long as the plain meaning of the intellectual content is preserved. In general, archiving takes place at a semantic level, not a syntactic one. This allows the archive to be constructed around the principle of data format migration, rather than access system emulation. Since the notion of issue-less journals represents a major shift in serials publishing practice and is unsupported by current library systems and scholarly practice of citation, the project team have decided to retain the concept of the issue as central to the design and implementation of the Archive.

However, they retain some flexibility in this matter by allowing a loose definition of issue as a publisher-specified aggregation of content items without necessary regard for fixed publication patterns. This issue-centric focus is central to the design and implementation of the Archive. Many think of e-journal archiving only in terms of preserving articles. However, e-journals actually contain a complex range of components. The target for preservation is defined in this project as the electronic version of the journal. At this early experimental stage, it was deemed best to preserve as much as possible in the categories of components and functionality.

To determine what components and functionality of e-journals exist, twenty-one journals were examined. This sample included eleven titles from the publishing partners and ten titles from other sources. They covered a wide range of disciplines and represented titles available in print and electronic formats as well as titles only available electronically. For all journals with printed versions, information about both the printed and electronic versions is available in the electronic version. All journal sites have basic descriptive information such as scope and purpose, subject coverage, and copyright statement.

Advertisements present a particular challenge for archiving. First, it is not uncommon for Web advertisements to be served from an organization other than the content publisher so that archiving agreements would not necessarily cover their deposit. Second, advertisements are frequently "dynamic," changing from day to day. The same page viewed on different days can have different advertisements. The advertisement seen in one country may be different from that seen in the same context in another; drug advertisements, for instance, are regulated at the national level and therefore vary with the country of receipt. Web advertisements will be an important source for documenting contemporary business, society, design, and technology.

However, they represent a minor type of content for scholarly e-journals. One of the great powers of digital journal articles is that they are not limited to linear text and static pictures. Increasingly, articles include "supplementary materials," digital files of many types. These files can include digital materials used in the research described or materials that expand on or illustrate topics. These supplementary files represent a significant resource but also a significant challenge to the Archive. In general, there is little control over the technical formats for supplementary files, no guidance to authors about good practices in the creation of such files, and little editorial analysis of the file content.

The technical heterogeneity of these materials could introduce a wide and ever-growing range of formats into the Archive, significantly increasing the complexity of the preservation task. The lack of guidelines and quality control means that unlike the case of articles themselves, the Archive is faced with objects of unknown virtue and potentially troublesome content. One of publishing partners suggested that it would be very useful to publishers if archives could provide guidance on preferred technical formats and practices that are well suited for preservation and archiving.

In the current environment, there is nothing to suggest to authors how to create digital objects with a greater chance of long-term viability. Many authors and their editors are very concerned about the longevity of their publications and if given guidance, may well be willing to change practices in ways that will reduce the complexity of preserving supplementary article content. Most articles offer internal linking among components within the HTML version of the full text. External links are also common and link out to authors' email addresses, author-provided URLs, citations in external indexing resources, other articles by the same author, and related articles. Linking is a fast-changing area in e-journals and represents one of the great value-added features of electronic over paper publishing. However, links pose significant challenges in archiving. The largest application of links today is for references, allowing a user to navigate automatically from one article to a related cited article.

Most publishers, however, do not simply insert static links in references. Most links today are in the form of Digital Object Identifiers (DOIs), a type of persistent link or "name" that remains valid even if the cited work moves between systems or publishers. Frequently publishers keep a database of references and only determine the DOI for a citation — a costly process — once. This allows the DOI to be reused each time the same work is cited. While the majority of links found in e-journals today are for references, there is every reason to expect linking to become richer with time.

There is already significant growth in links to "knowledge bases" such as GenBank. As these new types of links occur they will be added by automated means to existing articles. Because links are dynamic and are expected to grow with time for already archived articles, it is unclear whether an archive should attempt to capture those links available at the point an article is ingested. All journal Web sites include browsing functionality and most include search capability. All journals except one include help features. While considering the components of electronic journals which should be archived and how much of the look and feel of an e-journal should be preserved, there were concerns that costs would prohibit comprehensive archiving.

It is clear that all articles, reports, columns, editorials, communications, abstracts, errata, and correspondence must be archived. It is less clear which other components should be preserved and how nontraditional components — such as links, threaded discussions, data sets, and data simulations — should be handled. One of the criteria to be met by this archive design is to make preserved information available to libraries under conditions negotiated with the publisher. Policies governing access to the Archive must address three questions: who can access the Archive, under what circumstances, and how will access be obtained.

An archive intending to restrict access to only those who have had a past subscription to the archived content would bear considerable expense to gather the required licensee information and to build and operate the appropriate access management system. Rather than pursue this option, Harvard believed that the increasingly wide-spread adoption of the "moving wall" concept in the scholarly journal environment suggested a more practical approach. After deposit, archived materials would enter an initial "dark" period chronologically bounded by the trigger events defined in the submission agreement.

Economic issues are paramount in planning for archiving. In the paper environment, many of the costs of archiving are buried in library budgets. Much of what is done to preserve print journals is the same activity needed to provide day to day access to the literature. In the e-journal environment libraries are moving to an architecture which separates archiving from daily service, making archiving costs painfully apparent. Further, it is unlikely the libraries will have or need the same large-scale redundancy in e-journal archiving that they have had for paper journals. It is more likely that the operating costs of archiving will be centered in only a few places, raising obvious issues of how to spread costs fairly.

Building an archiving program over a larger digital library environment, activities (preservation monitoring), organization (computer operations), and technical infrastructure (a digital repository) already in place can be used to support the archiving activity. Second, applying smart automation to the process of adding content to the Archive can be used to reduce labor, and thus the cost, of ongoing Archive operation. Even if an archive is successful in controlling costs, the ultimate question remains "who pays."

Some options for support of archiving are inappropriate for Harvard's Archive. The institution will not simply bear the cost of archiving on its own as a national library might. Certainly Harvard would expect to contribute to the cost of archiving, but it will be difficult to convince university administrators that the institution should simply dedicate resources at this level for the common good. Some have suggested an archive should support itself, at least in part, by providing services others would pay to use based on the archived content.

The intent of the proposal was that the community that benefits from the Archive also assumes some share of the cost of archiving. The archiving fee would be composed of two elements: 1) An "ingestion" fee to pay the operating costs of day to day receipt, quality control, and archival preparation of new content. 2) An amount to be added to the Archive endowment to cover the long-term cost of storage and preservation activity. Endowment is a very appealing model to pay for a long-term commitment such as archiving.

The core component of this infrastructure is the Digital Repository Service (DRS), an Oracle-based repository for digital objects. Within the DRS, object content streams are stored along with their associated administrative and structural metadata. The DRS, now in its second production release, currently maintains over 240,000 objects with a total size of 120 gigabytes. The DRS is responsible only for the managed preservation of the objects deposited within it; resource discovery and delivery are handled through independent systems. Digital objects are delivered out of the DRS through media type-specific delivery applications. Delivery applications are available for simple objects, those atomically composed of a single physical content stream, such as a raster image file; and complex objects, logical aggregations of intellectually or structurally related content streams, such as an electronic monograph structurally delivered in a page turning navigational environment.

Digital objects stored in the DRS can be given persistent identifiers registered with and resolved by the Name Resolution Service (NRS). NRS identifiers and their resolution mechanism are compatible with IETF recommendations for URNs. The NRS is composed of two subsystems: an Oracle-based administrative system that maintains the mappings between URNs and URLs, and a THTTP-based resolution server. Archived e-journal components will be named in the NRS at a level of granularity corresponding to that of discovery and delivery, that is, at the issue and item level. Descriptive metadata useful for resource discovery is contained in catalog systems external to the DRS.

Issue-level catalog metadata will also include an actionable link in the form of an NRS persistent identifier to a dynamically generated, issue-specific Web page, providing table-of-contents-like access to individual e-journal issue items. Item-level metadata will be managed in a new item-level catalog, implemented either as a separate database in the ILS, or as a stand-alone XML database. It will provide a mechanism for search and browsing and will include actionable links to dynamically generated Web pages displaying individual journal items. The design of the Archive was conceived in relation to the OAIS reference model, with its six main archival functions: ingest, data management, archival storage, preservation, access, and administration.

Large portions of the operational aspects of the Archive are amenable to automation, including areas such as publisher registration and profiling, Submission Information Package (SIP) submission, ingest validation at a syntactic level, SIP-to-AIP (Archival Information Package) transformation, archival storage deposit, preservation migration, routine reporting, and handling and responding to access requests. This degree of automation is achievable through a strict requirement of publisher compliance to formal standards for SIPs and the definition of a small set of normative data formats.

The resulting uniformity of the Archive input stream and the canonical nature of internal archive storage practices provides the opportunity to rely upon automated systems to perform routine ingest, archival storage, data management, and access functions. Through the collaborative development of community standards, there is good potential for the sharing of common infrastructure components between archiving projects and institutions. Dependent upon the implementation details of a new ILS currently undergoing installation, serial check-in and claiming operations may also be amenable to automation. The primary remaining tasks that will require manual intervention include ingest validation at a semantic level; preservation planning, primarily the monitoring of the technical obsolescence of data formats; and ongoing periodic auditing of archived materials.

The unit of submission to the Archive is the e-journal issue. Physically, the SIP will take the form of a three-level file system hierarchy corresponding to the e-journal title, issue, and items. The title-level directory is empty and is present only to provide a common structural parent. The issue-level directory contains a METS file encapsulating all issue-level metadata and pointers to issue-level content files and to the item-level directories, each of which in turn has a METS file containing all item-level metadata and pointers to item-level content. Content object technical metadata stored in the METS files provides the necessary representation information to facilitate archival preservation activities and content delivery.

A preliminary draft specification of the SIP is undergoing public review and comment. One of the core concepts of the Archive is the use of a common archival item-level schema for articles and "article-like" content. The design of this schema will begin with an investigation of existing common schemas, such as the ISO 12083 and the PubMedCentral Document Type Definitions (DTDs), for possible use as is or as the basis for additional development. If a new schema should be necessary, in whole or in part, the design and documentation of it may be contracted out to an appropriate consultant and developed with coordinated input from the larger community.

As will be set out in the Archive submission agreement, when practical it will be the responsibility of content providers to transform their journal content from its internal native form into compliance with the Archive's schema when the publisher has content marked up in SGML or XML. In order to transform content to this schema, participating publishers will need a significant level of internal technical expertise or access to external technical expertise and the resources to implement the transformation workflow. It is clear that not all publishers of scholarly content will have these assets. Since digital preservation activities are performed on a type-specific basis, minimizing the number of acceptable data formats can reduce the complexity and cost of archive operations. To place this on a formal basis, the Archive will define a small set of preferred normative formats.

In general, a single normative format will be defined for each functional category of content: for example, XML for metadata, XML for full-text, TIFF for raster still images, XML/ SVG for vector still images, etc. Data submitted in non-normative formats will be transformed upon ingest into an analogous normative format whenever possible without significant loss of intellectual meaning. For example, submitted JPEG files will be transformed into their analogous TIFF representations. Content objects submitted to the Archive in non-normative formats that are not susceptible to transformation into a normative analogue will be accepted, but only under the proviso that they may be preserved only at the bit level — i.e., in the form of the initially deposited bit stream — and that their usefulness over time may become problematic. Long-term archival preservation requires the initial capture of intellectual content at the highest possible resolution, finest possible granularity, and most abstract representation.

Additional criteria for the selection of normative formats include open standards, mature and robust technology, long-term viability, prevalence of commercial grade tools, and the potential for instantiated data objects to be created as far upstream as possible in publishers' production processes. The composition of the set of normative formats will undergo periodic review to insure they remain appropriate for archival purposes with regard to continual technological advances. During Harvard's initial evaluation of the PDF format with regard to its inclusion in the set of archival normative formats, several undesirable characteristics of PDF were discovered.

Foremost, perhaps, is the fact that PDF is a proprietary rather than an open standard. Although Adobe has published the specifications, this is a matter of company policy and subject to unpredictable change. The built-in extensibility of PDF allows it to provide a structural envelope into which content can be placed in a variety of base formats. For example, PDF files can be composed partially or entirely of raster page images rather than the actual text.

Internal PDF content streams can be formatted or compressed using completely private schemas, some or all of which may be resistant to archival preservation. Also, PDF is most generally encoded in a binary rather than an ASCII form which tends to increase the complexity if not the difficulty of processing.

All online content providers rely to a greater or lesser extent upon the high degree of domain expertise of their users in detecting semantic errors. After SIP validity has been confirmed, issue and item-level descriptive metadata is extracted from the issue and item-level METS files of the SIP, and transmitted to the Data Management function for storage and later use in archive administration and resource discovery. For the most part, SIP components are deposited as is. The METS files are rewritten to include additional internal archive-specific administrative metadata, and to change the references to content files from file references valid within the SIP file system hierarchy to DRS inter-object references. Some of the technical metadata existing in the METS files may be duplicated in internal DRS storage structures in order to facilitate ongoing archive administration and preservation activities.

The Data Management function is responsible for maintaining descriptive information about archival holdings and administrative data necessary to the internal management of the Archive. Issue and item-level descriptive metadata is received from the Ingest function. E-journal content is modeled within the Archive at both an issue level and an item level. Issues are defined loosely as primarily publisher-specified aggregations of individual items, with some additional issue-level, and generally non-citable, content such as masthead, editorial board, cover image, etc.

Items are defined as indivisible pieces of citable content such as articles, editorials, reviews, letters, errata, etc. For purposes of internal administration of the Archive as well as for end-user content discovery and delivery, bibliographic control of journal content is necessary at both issue and item levels. This two level modeling scheme is explicitly issue-centric. Naming is the process of assigning unique, persistent identifiers to resources. Uniqueness insures an unambiguous mapping between an identifier for a resource as described in a discovery service and the instantiation of that resource as delivered to the user.

sPersistence is required when identifiers for archived content are publicly visible and thus, susceptible to being captured and used in external systems outside the control of the Archive. A "bookmarked" name should always resolve to the correct named content object regardless of the passage of time or changes to the underlying architecture or implementation of the Archive. Within the Archive, naming needs to occur at the level of granularity of the discovery and delivery services, that is, at the issue and item levels. The Digital Object Identifier (DOI) mechanism is the most widely used naming scheme for electronic journal articles. However, DOIs resolve to resource instantiations defined by the registering body for those DOIs, in this case, by the publishers.

Therefore, an article DOI will resolve to that article in the publisher's content delivery service. There is no widely implemented mechanism to interrupt the DOI resolution process and substitute resolution to a local "appropriate copy" such as the Archive. Thus, it is necessary for an Archive-specific identifier to be given to named issue and item-level content components.

The Archival Storage function of the Archive is provided by the extant DRS. The DRS batch loading process requires that each physical data stream be available as a separate file, along with an additional XML-encoded control file specifying loading and storage options. This proscribes the form of the AIP within the DRS as the complete set of SIP components with each issue and item-level METS metadata and content file deposited as individual digital objects. The Ingest function is responsible for transforming the SIP into the AIP prior to DRS deposit.

After successful deposit of an AIP into the DRS, the Archive will generate and transmit an e-mail message of confirmation to the submitting content provider. The issuance of this confirmation constitutes the formal notice of the archive's assumption of archival responsibility for the deposited material. Issue and item-level METS metadata files contain internal pointers to their component content files. In addition, the DRS has its own explicit mechanism to maintain typed relationships between individual digital objects stored within it.

Thus, issue and item-level METS files will be stored within the DRS with an inter-level parent/child structural relationship. Similarly, METS metadata files and their component content files will be stored with an intra-level parent/child relationship. Because the purpose of this Archive is to preserve the significant intellectual content of journals — not the original form in which the content was authored or delivered — the Archive will most likely rely upon transformation to prevent obsolescence.

Preservation planning is an area of active development. Although much more analysis is needed, some key distinctions have emerged in considering the technical and operational implications of assuming responsibilities to monitor obsolescence and to migrate data. Harvard's expectation is that the Archive will offer multiple levels of service in which the highest level represents the Archive's commitment to monitor formats and associated technologies, to develop and execute migration strategies that attempt to preserve all of the format's native functions and semantic integrity, and to disseminate files (e-journal components) in formats that can be rendered by contemporary applications. The Archive will provide the highest level of preservation service for a limited set of preferred normative formats as discussed previously.

Objects submitted in non-normative formats are expected to fall into two categories: those that can be transformed upon ingest into an analogous normative format and those that cannot. Objects in this latter category will receive fewer services. At a minimum, objects will receive "bitstore service" in which they are refreshed and can be disseminated from the Archive to members of the designated community or to "digital archaeologists" committed to investing the resources needed to re-render the objects with contemporary applications.

The implication of instituting a preservation policy with multiple service levels is that all objects associated with an e-journal item can be deposited to, and accepted by, the Archive, but those integral to the item's semantic meaning should when at all possible be deposited in normalized, repository-compliant formats for full preservation service. The Access function encompasses both e-journal resource discovery and delivery.

XML-encoded full-text content items are dynamically transformed into HTML using XSLT. Other item content media types are delivered via the appropriate DRS delivery applications. Rather than browsing or searching these Archive catalogs for relevant content, a user may possess a priori appropriate citation information for the desired content, such as author and title, chronology and enumeration, or a DOI uniquely identifying an item. A valid access request to the Archive can be made by using this citation information in a properly formed OpenURL which encodes the citation data into an actionable URL.

The Archive will implement an OpenURL service to accept such requests and respond with the appropriately displayed item. Access authorization is a binary function. During the initial dark period following submission, e-journal content is available only to Archive staff for internal administrative and maintenance purposes, and to auditors as described in the Administration function. Once content is lit up in consequence of an appropriate trigger event, that content is available to the general public.

Authorization is enforced only at the point at which the delivery of actual issue or item-level content is requested; cataloging metadata for all content is always available to the public. Delivery of raw e-journal issue data can be requested and returned as an OAIS Dissemination Information Package (DIP). At least one form of the DIP should be equivalent to a Submission Information Package (SIP) so that a DIP delivered from a compliant archive can be ingested directly by another archive.

The Archive will consider support for additional standard DIP formats as they emerge in the future. For the wholesale batch dissemination of archived content, that content will be transformed from its internal Archival Information Package (AIP) form to a DIP. The handling of and response to requests for a DIP will be an off-line, asynchronous operation. It is highly desirable that the archiving community cooperates in the development of standard definitions of the DIP to facilitate the transformation of archival materials between participating institutions. The Administration function is responsible for the routine operation of the Archive. The primary responsibilities of the Archive staff with regard to technical issues are the initial development, ongoing maintenance, and future enhancement of Archive systems.

Additionally, the expertise of the staff will be helpful in monitoring technical innovation and obsolescence with regard to normative data formats and potential preservation migration transformations. This activity would be performed in cooperation with the Archive preservation manager and collection curators. All technical work will be performed using accepted industry standards and processes for technical management, design, implementation and testing methodologies, configuration management, and documentation. The Archive architecture relies heavily on efficiencies achieved by compliance to common standards, e.g., SIP structure and the archival schema.

Widespread compliance is best achieved by insuring that these standards are developed in an open collaborative process. Archive staff will be responsible for the coordination of these processes and the resultant timely publication of appropriate specifications. In traditional preservation, curators are responsible for ensuring that collections remain usable. While they may store collections in centralized, environmentally-controlled storage facilities, or partner with conservators and preservation technologists to repair or copy materials, curators are ultimately fully responsible to account for the extent, condition, and usability of their collections. The inherent fragility and complexity of digital collections require a shift in preservation responsibilities.

To ensure that items do not become obsolete, curators and other owners need to delegate preservation responsibilities to technical staff with the expertise and the tools. In this new model, preservation technologists assume perpetual rather than temporary custody of the physical objects in their care. They must monitor the items as well as the environment. Because obsolescence is inevitable for all digital formats, they must be able to develop and present migration strategies to the curators and owners, then implement the strategy the owner prefers.

In traditional preservation, curators have ongoing custodial responsibility and preservation technologists intervene infrequently. In the preservation model for digital archiving, repository managers assume the ongoing custodial responsibility and curators are consulted as necessary to make decisions about migration and other issues. Archive itself has a variety of partners and stakeholders.

Additionally, the Archive must have a relation with the broader community. The brighter the Archive, the more governance a publisher should have; the more services offered, the more governance a publisher should have. In addition to the stakeholder community with its representative input, there is the necessity for an external auditing service.

Such a service might be part of a broader confederation of archival organizations and stakeholders. Such a confederacy might be charged with establishing registries for content and format types; certifying policies, practices and procedures; and supporting the ongoing development of digital archiving. Digital and network technologies are rapidly changing the nature of scholarly communication. Scholars increasingly use the electronic medium to publish their research results.

In this medium, new knowledge can be disseminated extremely quickly by anyone with access to the Internet, and accessed at any time from anywhere with a network connection. Costs to reproduce and disseminate information — though not necessarily the costs to produce, review, and edit it — can be greatly reduced online, thus enabling organizations that could not afford to publish scholarly information to do so. The nature of the electronic medium also supports new modes of publishing. Freed from the constraints of print, scientists can publish long, complex data sets along with their articles.

Sound, video, and interactive programs can be published along with text and still images. Search and linking facilities can be added to electronic versions of journals and monographs making it substantially easier for researchers to locate and use relevant research. The interconnectedness of the Internet also allows the nature of journals to change from a set of issues with a static set of articles, to more dynamic collections and databases of published research. While electronic journals offer new benefits, they also bring new risks.

Researchers depend not only on current journals, but on the centuries-old back files of journals that they can use for scholarship. However, electronic journals are not easily preserved. Unlike print journals they live on fragile media, rely on rapidly changing technology and computing environments for their presentation, and depend on the policies and fortunes of their copyright holders for their disposition.

The new types of content supported by electronic journals, the advanced search and linking facilities, and the rapid access that electronic journal readers are accustomed to, further complicate the preservation problem. Despite the complexities of the preservation problem, though, libraries cannot afford to ignore it. Electronic versions of scholarly journals are in many cases becoming the versions of record, with important scholarly communication not included in print publications.

Creating Electronic Texts

Creating and processing electronic texts was one of the earliest areas of computational activity, and has been going on for at least half a century. When combined with an intimate knowledge of the non-electronic source material, readers should be able to decide for themselves which approach—and thus which combinations of hardware and software, techniques and design philosophy—will be most appropriate to their needs and the needs of any other prospective users. Although every functional aspect of computers is based upon the distinctive binary divide evidenced between 1's and 0's, true and false, presence and absence, it is rarely so easy to draw such clear distinctions at the higher levels of creating and documenting electronic texts.

The digitization of texts is not simply making groups of words available to an online community; it involves the creation of an entirely new object. This is why achieving a sense of what it is that you are creating is critical. The blueprint for construction will allow you to define the foundation of the project. It will also allow you to recognise any problems or issues that have the potential to derail the project at a later point. Document analysis is all about definition - defining the document context, defining the document type and defining the different document features and relationships. At no other point in the project will you have the opportunity to spend as much quality time with your document. This is when you need to become intimately acquainted with the format, structure, and content of the texts.

One of the first tasks to perform in document analysis is to define the goals of the project and the context under which they are being developed. This could be seen as one of the more difficult tasks in the document analysis procedure, as it relies less upon the physical analysis of the document and more upon the theoretical positions taken with the project. This is the stage where you need to ask yourself why the document is being encoded. It is also important to take into consideration the external influences on the project. Often the bodies that oversee digitization projects, either in a funding or advisory capacity, have specific conditions that must be fulfilled. They might for example have markup requirements or standards that must be taken into account when establishing an encoding methodology. Also, if you are creating the electronic text for scholarly purposes, then it is very likely that the standards of this community will need to be adhered to.

Again, it must be remembered that the electronic version of a text is a distinct object and must be treated as such. Just as you would adhere to a publishing standard of practice with a printed text, so must you follow the standard for electronic texts. The most stringent scholarly community, the textual critics and bibliographers, will have specific, established guidelines that must be considered in order to gain the requisite scholarly authority. Therefore, if you were creating a text to be used or approved by this community their criteria would have to be integrated into the project standards, with the subsequent influence on both the objectives and the creative process taken into account.

If the digitization project includes image formats, then there are specific archiving standards held by the electronic community that might have to be met—this will not only influence the purchase of hardware and software, but will have an impact on the way in which the electronic object will finally be structured. External conditions are easily overlooked during the detailed analysis of the physical object, so be sure that the standards and policies that influence the outcome of the project are given serious thought, as having to modify the documents retrospectively can prove both detrimental and expensive. While you cannot satisfy each desire, trying to evaluate what information might be the most important to your audience will allow you to address the needs and concerns you deem most appropriate and necessary.

Also, if there are specific objectives that you wish users to derive from the project then this too needs to be established at the outset. If the primary purpose for the texts is as a teaching mechanism, then this will have a significant influence on how you choose to encode the document. Conversely, if your texts are being digitized so that users will be able to perform complex thematic searches, then both the markup of content and the content of the markup will differ somewhat. Regardless of the decision, be sure that the outcome of this evaluation becomes integrated with the previously determined project objectives. You must also attempt to assess what tools users will have at their disposal to retrieve your document.

The hardware and software capabilities of your users will differ, sometimes dramatically, and will most likely present some sort of restriction or limitation upon their ability to access your project. SGML encoded text requires the use of specialised software, such as Panorama, to read the work. Even HTML has tagsets that early browsers may not be able to read. It is essential that you take these variants into consideration during the planning stage. There might be priorities in the project that require accessibility for all users, which would affect the methodology of the project. However, don't let the user limitations stunt the encoding goals for the document.

Hardware and software are constantly being upgraded so that although some of the encoding objectives might not be fully functional during the initial stages of the project, they stand a good chance of becoming accessible in the near future. The first stage of document analysis is not only necessary for detailing the goals and objectives of the project, but also serves as an opportunity to examine the context of the document. This is a time to gather as much information as possible about the documents being digitized. The amount gathered varies from project to project, but in an ideal situation you will have a complete transmission and publication history for the document.

There are a few key reasons for this. Firstly, knowing how the object being encoded was created will allow you to understand any textual variations or anomalies. This, in turn, will assist in making informed encoding decisions at later points in the project. The difference between a printer error and an authorial variation not only affects the content of the document, but also the way in which it is marked up. Secondly, the depth of information gathered will give the document the authority desired by the scholarly community. A text about which little is known can only be used with much hesitation. While some users might find it more than acceptable for simply printing out or reading, there can be no authoritative scholarly analysis performed on a text with no background history. Thirdly, a quality electronic text will have a TEI header attached. The TEI header records all the information about the electronic text's print source.

The electronic document will provide you with an opportunity to develop the variant branches found within the text. Depending upon the decided project objectives, you are free to highlight, augment or furnish your users with as many different associations as you find significant in the text. Yet to do this, you must fully understand the ontology of the texts and then be able to delineate this textuality through the encoding of the computerised object. It is important to remember that the transmission history does not end with the publication of the printed document.

Tracking the creation of the electronic text, including the revision history, is a necessary element of the encoding process. The fluidity of electronic texts precludes the guarantee that every version of the document will remain in existence, so the responsibility lies with the project creator to ensure that all revisions and developments are noted. While some of the documentation might seem tedious, an electronic transmission history will serve two primary purposes. One, it will help keep the project creator(s) aware of what has developed in the creation of the electronic text.

If there are quite a few staff members working on the documents, you will be able to keep track of what has been accomplished with the texts and to check that the project methodology is being followed. Two, users of the documents will be able to see what emendations or regularisations have been made and to track what the various stages of the electronic object were. Defining the document type is a critical part of the digitization process as it establishes the foundation for the initial understanding of the text's structure. At this point you should have an idea of what documents are going to be digitized for the project. Even if you not sure precisely how many texts will be in the final project, it is important to have a representative sample of the types of documents being digitized. Examine the sample documents and decide what categories they fall under.

The structure and content of a letter will differ greatly from that of a novel or poem, so it is critical to make these naming classifications early in the process. Not only are there structural differences between varying document types but also within the same type. Deciding upon document type will give you an initial sense of the shape of the text. There are basic structural assumptions that come with classification: looking for the stanzas in poetry or the paragraphs in prose for example. Having established the document type, you can begin to assign the texts a more detailed structure. Without worrying about the actual tag names, as this comes later in the process, label all of the features you wish to encode. For example, if you are digitizing a novel, you might initially break it into large structural units: title page, table of contents, preface, body, back matter, etc.

Once this is done you might move on to smaller features: titles, heads, paragraphs, catchwords, pagination, plates, annotations and so forth. One way to keep the naming in perspective is to create a structure outline. This will allow you to see how the structure of your document is developing, whether you have omitted any necessary features, or if you have labelled too much. Once the features to be encoded have been decided upon, the relationships between them can then be examined. Establishing the hierarchical sequence of the document should not be too arduous a task—especially if you have already developed a structural outline. It should at this point be apparent, if we stick with the example of a novel, that the work is contained within front matter, body matter, and back matter. Within front matter we find such things as epigraphs, prologues, and title pages.

There are three basic categories to consider: structure, format and content. In terms of structure there are quite a few typical elements that are encoded. This is a good time to examine the structural outline to determine what skeletal features need to be marked up. In most cases, the primary divisions of text - chapters, sections, stanzas, etc.—and the supplementary parts—paragraphs, lines, pages—are all assigned tag names. With structural markup, it is helpful to know how detailed an encoding methodology is being followed. As you will discover, you can encode almost anything in a document, so it will be important to have established what level of markup is necessary and to then adhere to those boundaries. Some of the common elements relate to attributes such as bold, italic and typeface. Then there are other aspects that take a bit more thought, such as special characters.

Format issues also include notes and annotations (items that figure heavily in scholarly texts), marginal glosses, and indentations. Elements of format are easily forgotten, so be sure to go through the representative documents and choose the visual aspects of the text that must be carried through to the electronic object. The third encoding feature concerns document content. This is where you will go through the document looking for features that are neither structural nor format based. This is the point where you can highlight the content information necessary to the text and the user. Refer back to the decisions made about textual relationships and what themes and ideas should be highlighted. If, for example, you are creating a database of author biographies you might want to encode such features as author's name, place of birth, written works, spouse, etc.

Having a clear sense of the likely users of the project will make these decisions easier—and perhaps more straightforward. This is also a good time to evaluate what the methodology will be for dealing with textual revisions, deletions, and additions—either authorial or editorial. Again, it is not so critical here to define what element tags you are using but rather to arrive at a listing of features that need to be encoded. Once these steps have been taken you are ready to move on to the digitization process. Digitization is quite simply the creation of a computerised representation of a printed analog. There are many methods of digitizing and varied media to be digitized.

Digitizing other formats, audio and video for example, there are many thorough analyses of procedure. Peter Robinson's The Digitization of Primary Textual Sources covers most aspects of the decision making process and gives detailed explanations of all formats. In other words, recommendations for digitizing are constantly changing. As hardware and software develop, so does the quality of digitized output. The price cuts in storage costs allow smaller projects to take advantage of archival imaging standards.

The digitization chain is a concept expounded by Peter Robinson in his aforementioned publication. The idea is based upon the fundamental concept that the best quality image will result from digitizing the original object. If this is not an attainable goal, then digitization should be attempted with as few steps removed from the original as possible. Therefore, the chain is composed of the number of intermediates that come between the original object and the digital image - the more intermediates, the more links in the chain.

Scanning a copy of a microfilm of an illustration originally found in a journal is acceptable if it is the only option you have, but clearly scanning the image straight from the journal itself is going to make an immeasurable difference in quality. This is one important reason for carefully choosing the hardware and software. If you know that you are dealing with fragile manuscripts that cannot handle the damaging light of a flatbed scanner, or a book whose binding cannot open past a certain degree, then you will probably lean towards a digital camera. If you have text that is from an 18th-century book, with fading pages and uneven type, you will want the best text scanning software available.

The equipment ranges from scanners (flatbed, sheetfed, drum, slide, microfilm) to high-end digital cameras. In terms of standards within the digitizing community, the results are less than satisfactory. Projects tend to choose the most available option, or the one that is affordable on limited grant funding. However, two of the most common and accessible image capture solutions are flatbed scanners and high-resolution digital cameras. Flatbed scanners have become the most commonplace method for capturing images or text. Their name comes from the fact that the scanner is literally a flat glass bed, quite similar to a copy machine, on which the image is placed face down and covered.

The scanner then passes light-sensitive sensors over the illuminated page, breaking it into groups of pixel-sized boxes. It then represents each box with a zero or a one, depending on whether the pixel is filled or empty. The importance of this becomes more apparent with the discussion of image type below. As a result of their lowering costs and widespread availability, the use of quality flatbeds ranges from the professional digital archiving projects to the living rooms of the home computer consumer. One benefit of this increased use and availability is that flatbed scanning technology is evolving continually. This has pushed the purchasing standards away from price and towards quality.

In an attempt to promote the more expensive product, the marketplace tends to hype resolution and bit-depth, two aspects of scanning that are important to a project but are not the only concerns when purchasing hardware. While it is not necessarily the case that you need to purchase the most expensive scanner to get the best quality digital image, it is unlikely that the entry-level flatbeds will provide the image quality that you need.

However, while it used to be the case that to truly digitize well you needed to purchase the more high-end scanner, at a price prohibitive to most projects, the advancing digitizing needs of users have pushed hardware developers to create mid-level scanners that reach the quality of the higher range. As a consumer, you need to possess a holistic view of the scanner's capabilities. Not only should the scanner provide you with the ability to create archival quality images but it should also make the digitization process easier. Scanning hardware has the ability to provide this discernment for the user, so these intelligent automated features are a necessity to decrease task time. One of the disadvantages of a flatbed scanner is that to capture the entire image the document must lie completely flat on the scanning bed.

With books this poses a problem because the only way to accomplish this is to bend the spine to the breaking point. It becomes even worse when dealing with texts with very fragile pages, as the inversion and pressure can cause the pages to flake away or rip. A solution to this problem, one taken up by many digital archives and special collections departments, is to digitize with a stand-alone digital camera. Digital cameras are by far the most dependable means of capturing quality digital images. They can make images of very high resolution, unlike video cameras.

These benefits are most clearly seen in the digitization of manuscripts and early printed books - objects that are difficult to capture on a flatbed because of their fragile composition. The ability to digitize with variant lighting is a significant benefit as it won't damage the make-up of the work, a precaution which cannot be guaranteed with flatbed scanners. The high resolution and heightened image quality allows for a level of detail you would expect only in the original. As a result of these specifications, images can be delivered at great size.

The images can be seen at such a high-resolution that the faintest pencil annotations can be read on-screen. There are a few tools that are commonly seen in use with many digitization projects. There are a wide variety of text scanning softwares available, all with varying capabilities. As this software is optimised for laser quality printouts, projects working with texts from earlier centuries need to find a package that has the ability to work through more complicated fonts and degraded page quality.

While there is no standard, most projects work with Caere's OmniPage scanning software. In terms of image manipulation, there are more choices depending upon what needs to be done. For image-by-image manipulation, including converting TIFFs to web-deliverable JPEGs and GIFs, Adobe Photoshop is the more common selection. Electronic text creation primarily involves the digitization of text and images. Apart from re-keying, the best method of digitizing text is Optical Character Recognition (OCR). This process is accomplished through the utilisation of scanning hardware in conjunction with text scanning software.

OCR takes a scanned image of a page and converts it into text. Similarly, image capture also requires an image scanning software to accompany the hardware. However, unlike text scanning, image capture has more complex requirements in terms of project decisions and, like almost everything else in the digitization project, benefits from clearly thought out objectives. The first decision that must be made regarding image capture concerns the purpose of the images being created. The reason for this is simple: the higher quality the image need be, the higher the settings necessary for scanning. There are four main types of images:

— 1-bit blac —8-bit colour and

— 24-bit colour

A bit is the fundamental unit of information read by the computer, with a single bit being represented by either a '0' or a '1'. A '0' is considered an absence and a '1' is a presence, with more complex representations of information being accommodated by multiple or gathered bits. A 1-bit black and white image means that the bit can either be black or white. This is a rarely used type and is completely unsuitable for almost all images. The only amenable image for this format would be printed text or line graphics for which poor resulting quality did not matter.

Another drawback of this type is that saving it as a JPEG compressed image—one of the most prevalent image formats on the web—is not a feasible option. 8-bit greyscale images are an improvement from 1-bit as they encompass 256 shades of grey. It is often used for non-colour images and provides a clear image rather than the resulting fuzz of a 1-bit scan. While greyscale images are often considered more than adequate, there are times when non-colour images should be scanned at a higher colour because the finite detail of the hand will come through distinctly. Also, the consistent recommendation is that images that are to be considered preservation or archival copies should be scanned as 24-bit colour.

8-bit colour is similar to 8-bit greyscale with the exception that each bit can be one of 256 colours. The decision to use 8-bit colour is completely project dependent, as the format is appropriate for web page images but can come out somewhat grainy. Another factor is the type of computer the viewer is using, as older ones cannot handle an image above 8-bit, so it will convert a 24-bit image to the lower format. However, the factor to take into consideration here is primarily storage space. An 8-bit image, while not having the quality of a higher format, will be markedly smaller. If possible, 24-bit colour is the best scanning choice. This option provides the highest quality image, with each bit having the potential to contain one of 16.8 million colours.

The arguments against this image format are the size, cost and time necessary. Again, knowing the objectives of the project will assist in making this decision. If you are trying to create archival quality images, this is taken as the default setting. 24-bit colour makes the image look more photo-realistic, even if the original is greyscale. The thing to remember with archival quality imaging is that if you need to go back and manipulate the image in any way, it can be copied and adjusted. However, if you scan the image as a lesser format then any kind of retrospective adjustments will be impossible.

While a 24-bit colour archived image can be made greyscale, an 8-bit greyscale image cannot be converted into millions of colours. The second concern relates to the resolution of the image. The resolution is determined by the number of dots per inch (dpi). The more dots per inch in the file, the more information is being stored about the image.

Again, this choice is directly related to what is being done with the image. If the image is being archived or will need to be enlarged, then the resolution will need to be relatively higher. If, when using an imaging software program, you click on the 'save as' function to finalise the capture, you will see that there are quite a few image formats to choose from.

In terms of text creation there are three types fundamental to the process: TIFF, JPEG, and GIF. These are the most common image formats because they transfer to almost any platform or software system. TIFF (Tagged Image File Format) files are the most widely accepted format for archival image creation and retention as master copy. More so than the following formats, TIFF files can be read by almost all platforms, which also makes it the best choice when transferring important images. Most digitization projects begin image scanning with the TIFF format, as it allows you to gather as much information as possible from the original and then saves these data. This touches on the only disadvantage of the TIFF format - the size of the image.

However, once the image is saved, it can be called up at any point and be read by a computer with a completely different hardware and software system. Also, if there exists any possibility that the images will be modified at some point in the future, then the images should be scanned as TIFFs. JPEG (Joint Photographic Experts Group) files are the strongest format for web viewing and transfer through systems that have space restrictions. JPEGs are popular with image creators not only for their compression capabilities but also for their quality.

While a TIFF is a lossless compression, JPEGs are a lossy compression format. This means that as a filesize condenses, the image loses bits of information. However, this does not mean that the image will markedly decrease in quality. If the image is scanned at 24-bit, each dot has the choice of 16.8 million colours - more than the human eye can actually differentiate on the screen. So with the compression of the file, the image loses the information least likely to be noticed by the eye. The disadvantage of this format is precisely what makes it so attractive - the lossy compression. Once an image is saved, the discarded information is lost. The implication of this is that the entire image, or certain parts of it, cannot be enlarged.

Additionally, the more work done to the image, requiring it to be re-saved, the more information is lost. This is why JPEGs are not recommended for archiving - there is no way to retain all of the information scanned from the source. Nevertheless, in terms of viewing capabilities and storage size, JPEGs are the best method for online viewing. GIF (Graphic Interchange Format) files are an older format that are limited to 256 colours. Like TIFFs, GIFs use a lossless compression format without requiring as much storage space. While they don't have the compression capabilities of a JPEG, they are strong candidates for graphic art and line drawings. They also have the capability to be made into transparent GIFs - meaning that the background of the image can be rendered invisible, thereby allowing it to blend in with the background of the web page. This is frequently used in web design but can have a beneficial use in text creation.

TIFFs would not be used for online delivery, but if you want your images to have any future use, either for archiving, later enlarging, manipulation, or printing, or simply as a master copy, then there is no other format in which to store the images. In terms of online presentation, then JPEGs and GIFs are the best method. JPEGs will be of a better calibre and smaller filesize but cannot be enlarged or they will pixelate. Yet in terms of viewing quality their condition will almost match the TIFF. How you use GIFs will depend on what types of images are associated with the project. However, if you are making thumbnail images that link to a separate page which exhibits the JPEG version, then GIFs are a popular choice for that task. Preservation imaging is defined as 'high-speed, 1-bit (simple black and white) page images shot at 600 dpi and stored as Group 4 fax-compressed files'. The results of this are akin to microfilm imaging.

While this does preserve the text for reading purposes, it ignores the source as a physical object. Archiving often presupposes that the objects are being digitized so that the source can be protected from constant handling, or as an international means of accessibility. However, this type of preservation annihilates any chance of presenting the object as an artefact. Archiving an object has an entirely different set of requirements. Yet, having said this, there is also a prevalent school of thought in the archiving community that the only imaging that can be considered of archival value is film imaging, which is thought to last at least ten times as long as a digital image. Nonetheless, the idea of archival imaging is still discussed amongst projects and funding bodies and cannot be overlooked..

However, many of the top international digitization centres recommend 600 dpi as an archival standard - it provides excellent detail of the image and allows for quite large JPEG images to be produced. The only restrictive aspect is the filesize, but when thinking in terms of archival images you need to try and get as much storage space as possible. Remember, the master copies do not have to be held online, as offline storage on writeable CD-ROMs is another option. TIFF files, with their complete retention of scanned information and cross-platform capabilities are really the only choice for archival imaging.

The images maintain all of the information scanned from the source and are the closest digital replication available. The size of the file, especially when scanned at 24-bit, 600 dpi, will be quite large, but well worth the storage space. You won't be placing the TIFF image online, but it is simple to make a JPEG image from the TIFF as a viewing copy. This information is provided with the caveat that scanning technology is constantly changing for the better. It is more than likely that in the future these standards will become passé, with higher standards taking their place. The goal of recognition technology is to re-create the text and, if desired, other elements of the page including such things as tables and layout.

Refer back to the concept of the scanner and how it takes a copy of the image by replicating it with the patterns of bits - the dots that are either filled or unfilled. OCR technology examines the patterns of dots and turns them into characters. Depending upon the type of scanning software you are using, the resulting text can be piped into many different word processing or spreadsheet programs. Caere OmniPage released version 10.0 in the Autumn of 1999, which boasts the new Predictive Optical Word Recognition Plus+ (POWR++) technology. As the OmniPage factsheet explains, POWR++ enables OmniPage Pro to recognize standard typefaces, without training, from 4 to 72 point sizes.

POWR++ recognizes 13 languages and includes full dictionaries for each of these languages.

However, OCR software programs (including OmniPage) are very up-front about the fact that their technology is optimised for laser printer quality text. The reasoning behind this should be readily apparent. As scanning software attempts to examine every pixel in the object and then convert it into a filled or empty space, a laser quality printout will be easy to read as it has very clear, distinct, characters on a crisp white background - a background that will not interfere with the clarity of the letters. However, once books become the object type, the software capabilities begin to degrade. This is why the first thing you must consider if you decide to use OCR for the text source is the condition of the document to be scanned.

If the characters in the text are not fully formed or there are instances of broken type or damaged plates, the software will have a difficult time reading the material. The implications of this are that late 19th and 20th-century texts have a much better chance of being read well by the scanning software. As you move further away from the present, with the differences in printing, the OCR becomes much less dependable. The changes in paper, moving from a bleached white to a yellowed, sometimes foxed, background creates noise that the software must sift through. Then the font differences wreak havoc on the recognition capabilities.

The gothic and exotic type found in the hand-press period contrasts markedly with the computer-set texts of the late 20th century. It is critical that you anticipate type problems when dealing with texts that have such forms as long esses, sloping descenders, and ligatures. Taking sample scans with the source materials will help pinpoint some of these digitizing issues early on in the project. While the advantages of exporting text in different word processing formats are quite useful if you are scanning in a document to print or to compensate for an accidentally deleted file, there are a few issues that should take priority with the text creator. Assuming you are using a software program such as OmniPage, you should aim for a scan that retains some formatting but not a complete page element replication.

In terms of text creation, and the long-term preservation of the digital object, you want to be able to control this markup. If possible, scanning at a setting that will retain font and paragraph format is the best option. Scanning at a mid-level of formatting will assist you if you have decided to use your own encoding. As you proofread the text you will be able to add the structural markup chosen for the project. Once this has been completed the text can be saved out in a text-only format. Therefore, not only will you have the digitized text saved in a way that will eliminate program-added markup, but you will also have a basic level of user-dictated encoding. Unfortunately for the text creator, there are still many situations where the documents or project preclude the use of OCR.

If the text is of a poor or degraded quality, then it is quite possible that the time spent correcting the OCR mistakes will exceed that of simply typing in the text from scratch. The amount of information to be digitized also becomes an issue. Even if the document is of a relatively good quality, there might not be enough time to sit down with 560 volumes of texts (as with the Early American Fiction project) and process them through OCR. The general rule of thumb, and this varies from study to study, is that a best-case scenario would be three pages scanned per minute - this doesn't take into consideration the process of putting the document on the scanner, flipping pages, or the subsequent proofreading. If, when addressing these concerns, OCR is found incapable of handling the project digitization, the viable solution is re-keying the text.

There are a few issues that come into play with in-house digitization. The primary concern is the speed of re-keying. Most often the re-keying is done by the research assistants working on the project, or graduate students from the text creator's local department. The problem here is that paying an hourly rate to someone re-keying the text often proves more expensive than out-sourcing the material. Also, there is the concern that a single person typing in material tends to overlook keyboarding errors - and if the staff member is familiar with the source material, there is a tendency to correct automatically those things that seem incorrect.

So while in-house digitization is an option, these concerns should be addressed from the outset. Again, as with most steps in the text creation process, the answers to these questions will be project dependent. The decisions made for a project that plans to digitize a collection of works will be markedly different from those made by an academic who is creating an electronic edition. It reflects back, as always, to the importance of the document analysis stage.

Markup is most commonly defined as a form of text added to a document to transmit information about both the physical and electronic source. Do not be surprised if the term sounds familiar; it has been in use for centuries. It was first used within the printing trade as a reference to the instructions inscribed onto copy so that the compositor would know how to prepare the typographical design of the document. There still seems to be some demarcation between the usage of the term for bibliography and for computing, but the boundary is really quite blurred.

The leap from markup as a method of labelling instructions on printer's copy to markup as a language used to describe information in an electronic document is not so vast. Therefore when we think of markup there are really three differing types. The first is the markup that relates strictly to formatting instructions found on the physical text, as mentioned above. It is used for the creation of an emended version of the document and, with the exception of the work of textual scholars, is rarely referred to again. Then there is the proprietary markup found in electronic document encoding, which is tied to a specific piece of software or developer.

This markup is concerned primarily with document formatting, describing what words should be in italics or centred, where the margins should be set, or where to place a bulleted list. There are a few things to note about this type of markup. The first is that being proprietary means that it is intimately tied to the software that created it. This does not pose a problem as long as the document will only remain within that software program; and as long as the creator recognises that in the future there is no guarantee that the software will exist. This is important, as proprietary software formats allow users to say where and how they want the document formatted, but then the software inserts its own markup language to accomplish this.

When users create documents in Word or a PDF file, they are unconsciously adding encoding with every keystroke. As anyone who has created a document in one software format and attempted to transfer it to another is aware, the encoding does not transfer - and if for some reason a bit of it does, it rarely means the same thing. The third type of markup is non-proprietary, a generalised markup language.

There are two critical distinctions between this markup and the previous two. Firstly, as it is a general language and not tied to a specific software/hardware, it offers cross-platform capabilities. This ensures that documents utilising this style of encoding will be readable many years down the line. Secondly, while a generalised markup language, as with the others, allows users to insert formatting markup in the document, it also allows for encoding based upon the content of the work. This is a level of control not found in the previous styles of markup. Here the user is able not only to describe the appearance of the document but the meanings found within it.

HyperText Markup Language (or HTML as it is commonly known) is a non-proprietary format markup system used for publishing hypertext on the World Wide Web. To date, it has appeared in four main versions (1.0, 2.0, 3.2, 4.0), with the World Wide Web Consortium (W3C) recommending 4.0 as the markup language of choice. HTML is a derivative of SGML - the Standard Generalised Markup Language. SGML allows you to create your own markup language but provides the rules necessary to ensure its processing and preservation.

HTML is a successful implementation of the SGML concepts, and, as a result, is accessible to most browsers and platforms. Along with this, it is a relatively simple markup language to learn, as it has a limited tagset. HTML is by far the most popular web-publishing language, allowing users to create online text documents that include multimedia elements (such as images, sounds, and video clips), and then put these documents in an environment that allows for instant publication and retrieval. There are many advantages to a markup language like HTML. While W3C recommends the usage of HTML 4.0, many of its features are simply not available to users with early versions of browsers. Unlike PDF which is extremely concerned with keeping the document and its format intact, HTML has no true sense of page structure and files can neither be saved nor printed with any sense of precision. Besides the benefit of a markup language that crosses platforms with ease, HTML attracts its many users for the simple manner with which it can be mastered.

For users who do not want to take the time to learn the tagset, the good news is that conversion-to-HTML tools are becoming more accessible and easier to use. For those who cannot even spare the time to learn how to use HTML-creation software, of which there are a limited quantity, they can sit down with any text creation program and author an HTML document. Then by using the 'Open File'; tool in a browser, the document can immediately be viewed. In contrast, the concise guidelines to HTML that are available on-line (and usually as a "help" option from the menu of a Web client) are a good introduction to some of the basic SGML concepts. This is of real value to the user. The notion of marking up a text is quite often an overwhelming concept. Most people do not realise that markup enters into their life every time they make a keystroke in a word processing program.

So for the uninitiated, HTML provides a manageable stepping-stone into the world of more complex encoding. Once this limited tagset is mastered, many users find the jump into an extended markup language less intimidating - and more liberating. However, one of the drawbacks to this easy authoring language is that many of the online documents are created without a DTD. A DTD is the abbreviation for a document type definition, which outlines the formal specifications for an SGML encoded document. Basically, a DTD is the method for spelling out the SGML rules that the document is following. It sets thc standards for what markup can be used and how this markup interacts with others.

So, for example, if you create an HTML document with a specific software program, say HoTMetaL PRO, the resulting text will begin with a document type declaration stating which DTD is being used. As it stands now, web browsers require neither a DTD nor a document type declaration. Browsers are notoriously lax in their HTML requirements, and unless something serious is missing from the encoded document it will be successfully viewed through a Web client. The impact of this is that while HTML provides a convenient and universal markup language for a user, many of the documents floating out in cyberspace are permeated with invalid code. The focus then moves away from authoring documents that conform to a set of encoding guidelines and towards the creation of works that can be viewed in a browser. This problem will become more severe with the increased use of Extensible Markup Language, or XML as it is more commonly known.

This markup language, which is being lauded as the new lingua franca, combines the visual benefits of HTML with the contextual benefits of SGML/TEI. However, while XML will have the universality of HTML; the web clients will require a more stringent adherence to markup rules. While documents that comply with the rules of an HTML DTD will find the transition relatively simple, the documents that were constructed strictly with viewing in mind will require a good deal of clean up prior to conversion. This is not to say that HTML is not a useful tool for creating online documents. As in the case of PostScript and PDF, the choice to use HTML should be document dependent. It is the perfect choice for static documents that will have a short shelf-life.

If you are creating course pages or supplementary materials regarding specific readings that will not be necessary or available after the end of term, then HTML is an appropriate choice. If, however, you are concerned about presentational and structural integrity, the markup of document content and/or the long-term preservation of the text, then a user-definable markup language is a much better choice.

2

Preservation of Electronic Library

The term 'digital preservation', means the planning, resource allocation, and application of preservation methods and technologies necessary to ensure that digital information of continuing value remains accessible and usable. The concept of digital preservation encompasses material that begins its life in digital form as well as material that is converted from traditional to digital formats. Recording media for digital materials are vulnerable to deterioration and catastrophic loss, and even under ideal conditions they are short lived relative to traditional format materials.

Although archivists have been battling acid-based papers, thermo-fax, nitrate film, and other fragile media for decades, the threat posed by magnetic and optical media is qualitatively different. They are the first reusable media and they can deteriorate rapidly, making the time frame for decisions and actions to prevent loss is a matter of years, not decades. More insidious and challenging than media deterioration is the problem of obsolescence in retrieval and playback technologies. Innovation in the computer hardware, storage, and software industries continues at a rapid pace, usually yeilding greater storage and processing capacities at lower cost. Devices, processes, and software for recording and storing information are being replaced with new products and methods on a regular three- to five-year cycle, driven primarily by market forces.

Records created in digital form in the first instance and those converted retrospectively from paper or microfilm to digital form are equally vulnerable to technological obsolescence. Another challenge is the absence of established standards, protocols, and proven methods for preserving digital information. With few exceptions, digital library research has focussed on architectures and systems for information organization and retrieval, presentation and visualization, and administration of intellectual property rights. The critical role of digital libraries and archives in ensuring the future accessibility of information with enduring value has taken a back seat to enhancing access to current and actively used materials.

As a consequence, digital preservation remains largely experimental and replete with the risks associated with untested methods; and digital preservation requirements have not been factored into the architecture, resource allocation, or planning for digital libraries. New technologies for mass storage of digital information abound, yet the technologies and methods for long-term preservation of the vast and growing store of digital information lag far behind. Strategies, methods, and technologies for long-term preservation of digital information that already exist or are being discussed, designed, and developed today have yet to demonstrate the technological or economic feasibility of operating on a mass scale.

In order to preserve digital materials on a scale commensurate with mass storage capabilities and in formats that are accessible and usable, it is necessary to articulate some basic requirements. There are two ways to examine digital preservation requirements: from the perspective of users of digital materials and from the view of libraries, archives, and other custodians who assume responsibility for their maintenance, preservation, and distribution. Libraries and archives will not accomplish their preservation missions if they do not satisfy the requirements of their users by preserving materials in formats that enable the types of analyses that users wish to perform. At the same time, libraries and archives are unlikely to be able to satisfy all requirements of all potential users primarily due to resource constraints.

By making explicit preservation requirements from both the users' and custodians' perspectives, libraries and archives will be better able to integrate digital preservation into overall planning and resource allocation. The potential uses of digital materials are varied, unpredictable, and almost endless. Any generalizations, even if restricted to one community of users such as humanities scholars, run the risk of overlooking and understating potential user needs. Precise requirements for presentation and analytical tools vary among disciplines, yet some basic requirements are likely to transcend fields and disciplines. The ability to establish the authenticity and integrity of a source is critical to users, whether it is generated by an individual, created in the conduct of institutional business, or produced through a formal publication process.

Mechanisms that will enable users to establish authenticity require archives and libraries to store much more than the content of digital documents. Attributes such as formal document structures, metadata that document the maintenance and use history of the document, time and date stamps, and a series of references among documents are essential for determining authenticity and for understanding the provenance of sources and placing them in a larger context.

Networking and access to digital sources will change all dimensions the scholarly work process, including identifying sources, communicating with colleagues, interpreting and analyzing data, disseminating research findings, and teaching. If their projections are correct, digital preservation programs must support a high degree of integration of source material into analytical processes by coupling research sources with the tools necessary to analyze them; by maintaining linkages between research results and the sources on which they are based; and by providing a means to incorporate primary sources into teaching.

Users will seek documents that are easily retrieved and manipulated, transmittable, and transportable from a repository to the sites of research, presentation, and teaching. It seems safe to assume that humanities scholars will need the capability to search through and select relevant sources from large bodies of heterogenous materials, to compare sources to each other, and to view specific documents at high levels of granularity. Digital preservation will add little value to the research process if it serves only as an alternative form of storage from which analog replicas are produced for use with conventional analytical methods.

Preserving digital materials in formats that are reliable and usable, however, will require long-term maintenance of structural characteristics, descriptive metadata, and display, computational, and analytical capabilities that are very demanding of both mass storage and software for retrieval and interpretation. Digital preservation requirements may be expressed differently by archives, libraries, and other types of repositories that are struggling to meet escalating user expectations with limited financial and technical resources. Storage systems should be capable of handling digital information in a wide variety of formats, including text, data, graphics, video, and sound. Digital storage is not only an alternative means for storing print formats because many types of digital objects do not have print equivalents and cannot be preserved in non-digital formats.

Ideally, storage media will have a long life expectancy, a high degree of disaster resistance, sufficient durability to withstand regular use, and very large storage capacities. Conversion from analog to digital formats and migration to new generations of technology will be rapid, accurate, and inexpensive enough to permit very large scale transfers of heterogeneous materials. Storage space requirements will be minimal and not demand highly sensitive environmental controls.

Strategy of Digital Preservation

To make digital preservation affordable to the widest possible range of organizations and individuals, equipment, media, and maintenance costs must be modest. Most librarians and archivists have accepted the basic wisdom — for now at least — that digital preservation depends upon copying, not on the survival of the physical media. But copying, also referred to as "refreshing" or "migration" is more complex than simply transferring a stream of bits from old to new media or from one generation of systems to the next.

Complex and expensive transformations of digital objects often are necessary to preserve digital materials so that they remain authentic representations of the original versions and useful sources for analysis and research. Current methods for preserving digital materials do not fully support achieving these objectives. When faced with the responsibility for preserving digital materials, archives and libraries face a series of complex and difficult choices based on the format of the original materials, the anticipated uses for it, and the technical and financial resources available to invest in preservation initiatives. Probably the most commonly used preservation strategy is to transfer digital information from less stable magnetic and optical media by printing page images on paper or microfilm.

It seems ironic that just as libraries and archives are discovering digital conversion as a cost-effective preservation method for certain deteriorating materials, much information that begins its life in electronic form is printed on paper or microfilm for safe, secure long-term storage. Yet, high-quality acid neutral paper can last a century or longer while archival quality microfilm is projected to last 300 years or more. Paper and microfilm have the additional advantage of requiring no special hardware or software for retrieval or viewing.

Perhaps this explains why in many digital conversion projects, the digital images serve as a complement to rather than a replacement for the original hard copy materials. Another strategy for digital preservation is to preserve digital information in the simplest possible digital formats in order to minimize the requirements for sophisticated retrieval software. As new media and storage formats were introduced, the data were migrated without any significant change in their logical structure. This approach has the distinct advantage of being universal and easy to implement. It is a cost-effective strategy for preserving digital information in those cases where retaining the content is paramount, but display, indexing, and computational characteristics are not critical.

As long as the preservation community lacks more robust and cost-effective migration strategies, printing to paper or film and preserving flat files will remain the methods of last resort for many institutions and for certain formats of digital information. Libraries and archives with large, complex, and diverse collections of digital materials are only beginning to test strategies that normalize various types of holdings by converting digital records from the great multiplicity of formats into a smaller, more manageable number of standard formats.

A repository might accept textual documents only in one or a few commonly available commercial word processing formats or require that documents conform to standards like SGML. Databases might be stored in one or a few common formats or converted to a SQL (Structured Query Language) compliant format, while image files might conform to the tagged image file format (TIFF) with standard compression algorithms. This approach has the advantage of preserving more of the display, dissemination, and computational characteristics of the original materials, while reducing the large variety of customized transformations that would otherwise be necessary to migrate material to future generations of technology.

The strategy rests on the assumption that software products which are either compliant with widely adopted standards or are widely dispersed in the marketplace are less volatile than the software market as a whole. Most common commercial products today provide utilities for backward compatibility and for swapping documents, databases, and more complex objects between software systems. Although this strategy simplifies migration and may lower digital preservation costs by reducing the amount of customized reformatting needed as technology changes, it does not eliminate the need for regular migration of digital materials.

Software and standards both continue to evolve and even repositories with structurally homogeneous holdings can expect to be required to migrate their digital materials periodically. Current methods fall far short of what is required to preserve digital materials. All current preservation methods involve trade-offs between what is desirable from the standpoint of functionality, dependability, and cost and what is possible and affordable with current technologies and methods.

Consequently, most repositories are coping by employing interim and less than desirable strategies, if they are addressing digital preservation issues at all. For example, the simplicity and universality of printing to paper or microfilm come at the expense of great losses in the functionality of digital information. Migration strategies that involve reformatting of digital materials to a simple standard format usually eliminate the structure of documents and relationships imbedded in databases.

Computation capabilities, graphic display, indexing, and other features often are lost, thus limiting future analytical potential. Normalization to standard formats is not always technically feasible and it usually is quite costly. Archives and libraries must also contend with entirely new forms of electronically-enabled discourse and new forms of artistic and cultural expression that do not have predecessors in the analog world. No current preservation method is adequate for preserving dynamic data objects from complex systems. There are no established conceptual models or technical processes for preserving multi-media works, interactive hyper-media, on-line dialogues, or many of the new electronic forms being created today.

The archival requirements to preserve content, context, and structure and to maintain the capability to display, link, and manipulate digital objects only heighten their software dependency. The preservation community is only beginning to explore possible alternatives to storing digital information in "software-independent" form. Rothenberg proposed an approach for maintaining the content of digital materials intact without losing the ability to retrieve meaning-rich sources. He recommended retaining the original document in its original format encapsulated in a virtual "envelope" that contains software instructions for retrieval, display, and processing of the message in the envelope.

The envelopes would contain contextual information and the transformational history of each object. Execution of the instructions would rely on an archive of hardware and software emulators or on instructions in the envelope with specifications to construct emulators. Important research is underway to define standards for data interchange that can support electronic commerce and satisfy business requirements in a variety of environments. Archives, libraries, and other institutions with preservation responsibilities will benefit if systems are built to implement such metadata standards.

Wide scale adoption of data and communication standards by the originators of digital information to support current business needs will also facilitate long-term preservation. Standards initiatives that address business needs for the secure and reliable exchange of digital information among the current generation of systems will impose standardization and normalization of data that ultimately will facilitate migrations to new generations of technology.

Only a few libraries, archives, and other institutions have established digital preservation programs, while most research and innovation comes from pilot projects and prototypes. Tested methods that have proven effective on a small scale in a limited number of repositories are not feasible for preservation of many of the types of digital materials that archives and libraries will confront in their preservation endeavors. The current state of digital preservation suggests several fruitful areas for research and development. The major areas are:

— storage media,

— migration,

— conversion, and

— management tools.

These four domains are often mutually dependent and ultimately must to be integrated into an infrastructure for digital preservation. Yet better solutions are necessary in all four areas before such integration can occur.

Storage Media: Recent research on the longevity of magnetic media indicate a useful life span of 10 to 30 years if they are handled and stored properly. Some optical disk technologies promise life spans of up to 100 years. Most authorities argue that enhanced media longevity is of little value because current media outlast the software and devices needed to retrieve recorded information. Nevertheless, improvements in the stability, capacity, and longevity of the base storage media are needed to drastically reduce the vulnerability of digital materials to loss and alteration and to lower storage costs. Ample research and experience provide evidence of what can go wrong with magnetic media as a result of binder degradation, magnetic particle instabilities, and substrate deformation.

Optical media are susceptible to damage from high humidity, rapid and extreme temperature fluctuations, and contamination from airborne particulate matter. To prevent these problems, it is imperative to store magnetic and optical media under strict environmental controls that are not always available, affordable, or convenient. Even modest improvements which produce storage media with larger per unit storage capacities and greater tolerance to variations in temperature and humidity will lower preservation costs by lessening the need for strict environmental controls, reducing the frequency with which digital media must be "refreshed" through recopying, and decreasing the number of storage units that must be handled.

Migration: Better methods for migration of digital materials to new generations of hardware and software are much needed for digital preservation regardless of breakthroughs in mass storage technologies. Planning for migration is difficult because there is limited experience with the types of migrations needed to maintain access to complex digital objects over extended periods of time. When a custodian assumes responsibility for preserving a digital object it may be difficult to predict when migration will be necessary, how much reformatting will be needed, and how much migration will cost.

There are no reliable or comprehensive data on costs associated with migrations, either for specific technologies and formats or for particular collections, and little research underway on methodologies that would reduce the costs and burdens of migration. The preservation community as a whole would benefit tremendously from the development of backward compatibility paths that would be included as a standard feature of all software. Backward compatibility or migration paths would enable a new generation of software to "read" data from older systems without substantial reformatting and without loss of retrieval, display and computational capabilities.

Although backward compatibility is increasingly common within software product lines, migration paths are not commonly provided between competing software products or for products that fail in the marketplace. Stewards of digital material have a range of options for preserving digital information. One might preserve an exact replica of a digital record with complete display, retrieval, and computational functionality, or a representation of the record with only partial computation capabilities, or a surrogate for the record such as an abstract, summary, or aggregation.

Enhancements are technologically possible through clean-up, mark-up, and linkage, or by adding indexing and other features. These technological possibilities in turn impose serious new responsibilities to present digital materials to users in a way that allows them to determine the authenticity of the information and its relationship to the original record. Methods to document changes in digital objects during their life span need to be incorporated as an integral part of improved migration methods. There are few well developed methods for preserving and migrating software so that it might be used to recreate digital documents that have the "look and feel" of the original sources.

Maintaining repositories of obsolete hardware and software has been discussed periodically, but usually dismissed out of hand as too expensive and not demonstrably feasible. This approach deserves more serious consideration as a strategy for maintaining continuing access to certain types of digital materials. Feasibility studies and cost/benefit analyses should be conducted to determine the technological, economic, and commercial feasibility of maintaining selected legacy software systems and performing specialized migrations or, alternatively, of building and maintaining software emulators. Such an approach would support replay of original sources and contribute to the preservation of software as a significant cultural and intellectual resource in its own right.

Conversion: Faster, cheaper, and higher resolution conversion technologies are another critical element needed to make digital preservation feasible on a large scale. Most archivists and librarians accept the fact that we live in a hybrid environment where paper, microfilm, video, and magnetic and optical media need to interoperate in a more integrated and transparent manner. The vast majority of primary sources today still reside on paper and/or microfilm with little chance that we will see the mass conversion of existing archival and library holdings to digital formats.

Research and planning for digital preservation must recognize that we will be dealing with conversion for a long time and that investments in improving capture rates, accuracy, resolution, and verification will have long-term benefits. Moreover, improvements in conversion technologies may support hybrid solutions to preservation and access problems by permitting repositories to store certain formats of digital material on stable media, such as microfilm, with on demand conversion to digital form for analysis and reuse.

Management Tools: A fourth area for research is in the development of management tools for digital libraries and archives that integrate descriptive control and maintenance with storage technologies. Dynamic digital objects, such as those found in hypertext systems, pose special management problems for both current and future retrieval and reuse. The boundaries of hypertext sources, like those found on the World Wide Web today, are difficult to ascertain because no single party or institution controls changes in the nodes and links that make hypertext objects live and highly responsive information resources.

A high degree of volatility accompanies these objects because the contents of nodes change, the sites where information resources are stored change, and the links between nodes change, move, and vanish. While tools such as these are useful for current maintenance, they do not address long-term preservation concerns. If further developed to address preservation problems, tools such as these have the potential to serve as filters, identify similar or identical objects, and monitor for maintenance problems. Research and development of tools that would imbed more intelligence about the preservation status of digital material into the objects themselves would make monitoring and maintenance of large digital collections more automatic.

Current methods for monitoring the physical status of digital materials are labor intensive, unreliable, and potentially damaging to the materials themselves. Recommended procedures for monitoring physical deterioration of magnetic tape, for example, involve reading a small sample of tapes periodically to determine whether any data losses have occurred. The potential exists to build monitoring and reporting mechanisms into digital objects, storage systems, and network architectures that could support self- reporting of physical status and initiate automatic maintenance procedures. Despite differences, some lessons from traditional preservation are transferable to the digital environment

In order to avoid commitments that far exceed available resources and costly rescue and restoration efforts, preservation must become an integral part of the planning, design, and resource allocation for digital libraries and archives. Integration of preservation requirements and methods with access and maintenance systems is essential to fully and efficiently support the processes of migration, regeneration, and documentation of the life of digital objects.

Planning for preservation must become an integral part of the design and management of digital libraries and archives. If left as an afterthought, there is little reason to believe that long-term preservation of digital information will be any more affordable than preservation of conventional formats has been. Preservation is a response to the threat of destruction. Some individual ultimately must initiate the response when the threat has been recognised, and the scale of the reaction may be in proportion to the value that is placed on the object under threat.

Their reaction incurs a cost which will continue to be incurred, while the threat appears to remain. Funds will be drawn upon, and resources will be mobilised, that have been held in reserve explicitly for the purpose of preservation. Other stakeholders are drawn into the preservation activity as time passes. In the world of digital material, the old rules do not apply so clearly. The cost and effort required to preserve candidate digital material may not be proportionate to the value of the material, nor are they related directly to the urgency created by the threat.

Whereas before benign neglect of printed paper-based material was a viable course of action, and a delayed reaction could in itself be an act of preservation. With digital material, decisions are required, supported by authorised expenditure, to enable resources to be deployed quickly in order to counter the threat of irreversible loss. The resources may involve substantial capital investment as well as specialist labour, both available in the near term only at a premium. Because so much of a digital item is connected to its immediate technical regime, the preservation specialist is concerned not to leave out any information that will later prove to be valuable. Only what is sufficient and necessary should be carried forward.

The preserved material, held as though in a sealed capsule, must be accompanied by material that moves forward technologically in step with the changing world, changing its format and style, while still being able to fulfil its purpose. Otherwise when the capsule is opened the instructions on how to use the material may be in a perfect state of repair, but all the same incomprehensible. In other words in order to preserve the integrity of digital material, the surrounding medium may need to be changed frequently, losing data in the process. The straightforward process of managing the archive is complicated by the possibility that opportunities exist for archive managers to avoid using the procedures rigorously.

Unlike the existing national archives of printed material, the value of the digital material may not be directly proportionate to its age or cost of production. Digital material may need to be treated exactly the same, whatever its provenance. All technology consists mainly of electronic storage used for different purposes, having different orders of size, security, and cost. The first major factor affecting the approach to the preservation of digital items is the type of material. For example, textual documents are possibly the simplest items to preserve, they are well-scoped, containing all the information relating to document within the file, when it is presented for preservation. Complexity remains low if they use a standard mark-up language.

The complexity rating rises when a document links to other objects, outside itself, or when essential extra functionality for document formatting is introduced, or the document contains a macro, or the document is intended to work in a networked environment and contains HTML linkages. The risk is that some of these features may not be reproducible, or inaccurately, in the future. Either way the evidential nature of the record is diminished, potentially catastrophically. At present, when such documents are retrieved, these functions are usually lost, and the unformatted text is displayed or "default" templates are used. The loss is restricted to formatting and presentation. Therefore, by proliferation, the facilities will become embedded and supported in more and more products, irrespective of vendor.

The material and the format become bound together, similar to a book. From the perspective of preservation and future access, the resources that maintain the usefulness of the material have been "donated" by the software vendors, although from self-interest. Technology Watch will monitor their continued willingness to donate the resources without change and without major change. The second major factor affecting the approach to the preservation of digital items is the type of file format. Most software developers aim to make their products able to import and export objects into many different formats. The translation from one into the other is not fool-proof but it serves the purpose of exchangeability.

With preservation of evidence in mind, the future decoding of these formats will be critical. Exchangeability between current software products is not a sufficient mechanism to provide permanence. Documents in a non-current, non-standard formats cannot be stored in their native format, unless a "launch" or "view" mechanism can be stored in a capsule with them. With text-based documents, the rules of evidence do not require the archive to retain the original data with its full format characteristics.

It is necessary instead to provide supporting evidence that the text could not have been amended during the time the item was in the archive. The most complex to guarantee preservation at present are the graphics formats. They are continuously evolving, and the evolution has still some time to run. Each software company adapts standards to suit their product, to limit the problems of upward compatibility, and to enforce customer loyalty. It is too soon to predict that formats, promoted as open and potentially non-proprietary, even valuable contributions to inter-changeability such as

PDF, are here to stay as a long term standard. A "launch" or "view" facility will have to be stored with them, or the graphic objects will have to be stored in a non-proprietary format, TIFF or BMP.

The original tape storage mechanisms have changed size, recording density, encoding, capacity, speed and reliability, so that they are no longer recognisable. After tape, the disk is the most durable, but the disk has changed more radically than the tape. Optical, magneto-optical, magnetic and solid state devices now compete to hold commercial data. Many other variants and hybrids of these two dominant technologies and others have missed becoming museum pieces, but their legacy in terms of data storage remains. The two technologies combine portability, reliability, speed of access and a greater capacity.

Preservation of Electronic Information Sources

Electronic information sources are often more expensive than print and may be appropriate candidates for central funding or split funding. The Library's responsibility to preserve electronic information is equal to its responsibilities for collections of printed materials and other formats. Priority should be given to locally-produced and unique resources that are irreplaceable via standard commercial means. Attention should be given to electronic information in the development of a preservation plan for the Library.

The term "electronic resource" is defined as any work encoded and made available for access through the use of a computer. It includes both online data and electronic data in physical formats (e.g., CD-ROM). To avoid confusion with these terms as used in the copyright process, online will refer to intangible works; physical to a tangible work. The term "acquire" refers to any electronic resource, online or physical, which the Library receives though its various, typical acquisitions processes, or which the Library provides access to through official contractual, licensed, or other agreements; any of these electronic resources may or may not be owned by or housed at the Library. "Collect" refers to electronic resources owned by the Library and selected for the permanent collection, including works created by the Library.

It may also include works stored elsewhere for which the Library has permanent ownership rights. "Link" refers to pointers from the Library's internet resources or bibliographic records to the Library and non-Library elèctronic resources, created and maintained by Library staff for a variety of purposes; "link" is not an act of acquiring, and electronic resources linked do not necessarily constitute an acquisition by the Library. The Library collects materials in many formats to support its universal collections. This policy is intentionally general in order not to restrict the collecting of needed materials and to allow the Library to make these resources available as technology changes. It is the Library's policy with electronic works, as with all others, to obtain them through copyright unless they are not subject to deposit under sections 407 or 408 of the copyright law.

Electronic editions of audio-visual materials, prints, photographs, maps, or related items are also covered by the Collections Policy Statements for their appropriate formats. The criteria used to evaluate electronic resources do not greatly differ from those used for books or materials in other formats. As with more traditional formats (e.g., motion pictures and recorded sound materials), the cost of the work and the requirements of serving, cataloging, storing, and preserving must be considered in the decision. The Library selects electronic works for its permanent collections which rank high on the following list of criteria: usefulness in serving the current or future informational needs of Congress and researchers, reputation of the information provider, amount of unique information provided, scholarly content, currency of the information, frequency of updating, and ease of access.

The Library will not consider these resources part of its permanent collections and will not archive them. In the case of digital works for which the Library has permanent ownership rights but which are stored in off-site repositories not under the jurisdiction of the Library, the Library will legally contract with the repository to make the works available electronically to the Library, ensuring permanent access or future transfer to the Library for archival storage, as in the agreement between the Library and the UMI Company concerning U.S. dissertations. The Library is committed to preserving its electronic resources just as it is to ensuring enduring access to its collections in print and other formats.

When the Library collects both electronic and print (or microform) versions of an item, the Library will retain for its permanent collections the print (or microform) edition of an item, as well as the electronic edition. The Library will select a representative sample of general purpose and application specific software and computer games for its permanent collection to document the history and development of this genre. Custodial divisions and others using the electronic resources are, to the best of their ability, responsible for ensuring compliance with all license and deposit agreements.

The traditional library evolved to provide services to make its contents more accessible to its users, the effective digital library develops a range of services to assist its users in finding, understanding, and using its contents. In its digital form the library has the potential to not just emulate traditional libraries in the services it provides but to improve and extend them by capitalizing on advantages inherent in the medium. One important area where the digital library can extend the services it provides beyond that of the traditional library is in integrating and highlighting user contributions. With the exception of especially unique or noteworthy contributions, the traditional library is rarely eager to receive resource contributions outside of its usual channels, as the effort needed to catalog and integrate outside contributions into a physical library is substantial.

Digital libraries, on the other hand, are more often willing to receive contributions. It has been demonstrated that a combination of minimal submission data and basic verification procedures can result in high-quality digital library contributions with low rejection rates. Such contributions enhance the value of the digital library by increasing its size and diversity and the process of cataloging and integrating contributed resources into a digital library often requires less effort. However, the aspects that make digital libraries built from user contributions valuable-diversity of content, potential for large growth-also create potential drawbacks.

For example, search and browse facilities enable users to find resources based on features such as author, subject, and keywords, but as a digital library grows, finding specific resources of interest among the entire collection can become more difficult. At the same time, the prominence of a given contributor's contributions becomes diminished as the library grows. One way to help users find resources of interest in a digital library while ensuring that contributors receive recognition is to borrow a concept that has long been part of traditional libraries: the special collection.

By defining and making available virtual collections believe the digital library can extend the special collection model and-at a modest cost-provide benefits to both its users and contributors that will encourage its own growth and viability. Traditional libraries often contain, in addition to their main holdings, special collections. In these settings a special collection is generally defined as a group of related materials that is given some form of special treatment.

The special treatment might be due to the rare or delicate nature of the materials, or because the library wants to highlight the materials in some way. In contrast to traditional libraries, the special or sub-collections of digital libraries can be much more fluid. Where the holdings of a traditional library are physically constrained to a single space and a single ordering, resources in a digital library can be distributed across many servers, can be owned by different organizations, and can be displayed in many different orderings and arrangements. This fluid nature makes defining collections and sub-collections in the digital environment less straightforward.

Adhering closely to the traditional library definition, one could consider a digital library collection to be all those resources that reside on a single server, or alternatively, all those that can be accessed though a given library's interface, even if they are physically distributed. As suggested in, however, even a broad definition of a collection in the context of digital libraries can be ambiguous. It can, for example, be influenced by the point of view of those making the definition. The people responsible for managing resources stored in separate databases might think of each as a distinct collection, while an end user with access to them all is more likely to consider them a single collection.

Defining sub-collections can be even more flexible as there are many possible factors that can suggest how sub-collections can be formed. A sub-collection can be defined by including all those resources that share a topic or other significant attribute, those contributed by a specific organization, or those used for a specific purpose. These sub-collection examples are instances of collections that cannot be easily replicated in traditional libraries.. They are made possible by exploiting advantages the digital environment inherently provides: objects can exist in multiple collections, collections with the same objects grouped in different ways can co-exist, collections can be created dynamically and exist for varying amounts of time.

They become virtual collections and as such-in contrast to the traditional library-enable a digital library to provide a limitless number of sub-collections based on a wide range of features. Most digital libraries do create the most basic of virtual collections—the result set dynamically created from a search request or category browsing—but rarely do they explicitly create and promote the sort of virtual collections described above. A digital library that contains virtual collections helps its users in several ways. A new user who may be intimidated by a digital library's search interface or the number of results returned by a query might be better introduced to the digital library through the more easily exploreable partitioned set of resources in a virtual collection

A directory of the virtual collections contained by a digital library, can provide a good introduction and overview of the library's contents to new or casual users. Associating resources with virtual collections enables those resources to be found more easily, either by browsing the contents of a highlighted virtual collection or through standard search and browse interfaces. Looking at the use of the digital library from a "work-oriented perspective", other benefits to the user stem from a more productive use of time. In it is suggested that sub-collections can facilitate work by isolating a group of related content and enabling a user to focus on those resources.

Defining virtual collections makes it easier for users to find and work with such groupings of related content, or by a "related resources" link based on virtual collection associations and tied to specific resources. Additionally, the virtual collection description might include links to related information outside the digital library, thus guiding users to more materials for their work.

Virtual collections can benefit contributors in several ways. First, they provide an alternative distribution outlet. Contributors often have collections in which they have invested effort in creating and would like to see used more widely. Because a digital library will generally have a much larger base of regular users than the contributor, contributing the collection gives the contributor's resources more exposure. By grouping a contributor's resources through a virtual collection the digital library helps maintain the resources' association with the contributor and in effect provides publicity and recognition to contributors.

By explicitly highlighting virtual collections and the people and organizations that contributed them, a digital library can increase the visibility of contributors. As a result, contributors are likely to benefit from more traffic to their own web sites, and can point people to their contributions at hosting digital library. Virtual collections can not only help improve the "brand" of a set of resources and support their distribution, but can also offer basic infrastructure services. In some cases, contributing resources enables the contributor to share resources without the overhead of storing and managing them, while retaining an association with them. The benefits of virtual collections do not come without a price, of course.

For a digital library to be able to easily create and remove virtual collections, to associate resources with different virtual collections in a flexible way, and to help users find and use the virtual collections, the library must have a structured approach to representing these collections. Moreover, to make creating such collections practical, this approach should also strive to minimize the costs associated with creating virtual collections. In the remainder of this matter describe an approach to implementing virtual collections based on work in creating collections for two different digital libraries.

Metadata can be automatically-generated or human-created with the latter clearly imposing more significant costs in terms of human effort and time. In the context of collections, describes two types of roughly corresponding metadata: inherent metadata, or information that can be extracted from the resource objects themselves, such as total number of objects or total file-size of the collection; and contextual metadata, or metadata which involves human judgment to create, such as a textual description of a collection of resources. There are significant advantages to utilizing inherent metadata as much as possible. Because it can be generated automatically, inherent metadata has minimal costs associated with its creation and maintenance and can be updated on a regular, automated schedule.

In contrast, human-created metadata is time-consuming, error-prone, costly to create, and more likely to be inconsistent. A person assigned to create metadata may only perform this task on an occasional, as-needed basis, and it may be a lower priority task than others for which that person is also responsible. Inconsistencies in metadata assigned to resources can arise due to variations in a given cataloger's judgment over time and because different catalogers may make varied judgements in cataloging resources.

There are drawbacks to relying solely on inherent metadata to define virtual collections, however. A risk in complete automation is the loss of many of the benefits of creating a virtual collection. Contextual metadata is important because it enables us to give some character and cohesiveness to the virtual collection. A collection is likely to be more than an accretion of all it contains; it has been gathered for a purpose. Humancreated metadata is thus vital for articulating the scope, intent, and function of a particular collection-attributes that are likely to make the collection easier to locate, and easier to use.

The use of contextual metadata and human judgment in selecting resources to be included in a virtual collection has other benefits. Virtual collections can be described "in terms of expected use in addition to being characterized by the terms they actually contain". Resources can be more carefully chosen for inclusion in a virtual collection, with consideration of expected use, resulting in a more concise collection of high-quality resources that is easier to for the user to search or browse.

It is important to recognise, however, that a collection-level schema that relies heavily on contextual metadata is relatively costly to implement and thus less likely to be maintained in the long term. A more viable approach is to define a schema for virtual collections that balances the costs and benefits of each type of metadata. In short, a cost-effective schema should include useful inherent metadata, supplemented by contextual metadata that captures human judgments of a collection's nature and the selection of criteria for inclusion in the collection.

Intellectual Property and Electronic Library

The private institutions participate in the full spectrum of activities regulated by the laws governing copyright and must be sensitive to the balance of interests embodied in them. While a degree of consensus has been reached concerning the rights of creators, copyright holders, and users of information in the print environment, new proposals for the copy rights of digital works are threatening to disrupt the balance between the rights of owners and public access in the electronic world. As they revolutionize the means by which information is recorded, disseminated, accessed, and stored digital technologies are eliminating the technical limits that have supplemented the legal framework of balance between ownership and public dissemination: Unlimited technological capacity to disseminate transmission in ways that can violate the rights of copyright holders confronts equally unlimited technological capacity to prevent works from being used in ways contemplated by law.

Carried to its logical extreme, either trend would destroy the balance, with results that would likely undermine core educational functions as well as radically transform the information marketplace. The educational community is heavily invested in scholarly communication. This process includes such functions as exchange of cutting-edge discoveries and works-in-progress among scholars, scientists, curators; publication of new and synthetic works for the broad scholarly community; dissemination of new and existing knowledge to students through teaching; establishment of repositories to enable handing knowledge down from generation to generation; and transmission of knowledge beyond the educational community to the public. It requires the ability to cite and quote the work of others, regardless of format. Whereas quotations from text can be manually transcribed, quotations from digital objects may require machine mediation.

Scholarly communication involves individuals, academic departments and research units, libraries, archives, university presses, museums, commercial publishers, external research sponsors, academic and industrial software developers, and others. Because it carries information that ranges from complex graphical and sound data to plain text, and must reach an audience that ranges from Nobel scientists to freshmen in remedial courses to citizens visiting a local museum, scholarly communication must include the full range of content and take place in all media.

It must flow back and forth between all of its participants and be capable of moving rapidly enough to contribute to the evolution of understanding and knowledge. It must be disseminated through an economically viable system, and it must not be overwhelmed by a permissions system so burdensome that it makes rapid movement impossible. Scholarly communication is based on an ethic of authorship that both compels publication and condemns plagiarism. It demands accurate attribution and respect for the integrity of works while asserting the importance of evaluating and interrogating sources for cumulative advance of knowledge.

By promoting trust between authors, owners, and users, adherence to this ethic facilitates the rapid and broad dissemination of information. Educational institutions have developed organizational structures that insulate faculty, curators, and students — the core, but not the only participants in scholarly communication — from direct dependence on economic returns from specific intellectual properties. Instead, they rely first on institutional rewards for their cumulative success in creation and dissemination. The institutions, however, function as both owners and consumers of the intellectual properties that circulate in the process of scholarly communication.

As such, some of these institutions, such as museums, university presses, and scholarly societies, depend on the revenue from copyright ownership to support their educational, dissemination, and preservation missions. New knowledge cannot be created without extensive reference to work already done by others and to the accumulated records of human and natural phenomena. or can the accumulated collective knowledge of a society be transmitted intact to succeeding generations without its preservation and organization. Libraries, museums, and archives play crucial roles as custodians of knowledge and must continue to do so in order to carry out core educational missions.

Faced with an exponential increase in the rate at which documentation is growing, libraries, museums, and archives increasingly seek to exploit the unprecedented storage capacities and facility for more effective access strategies of digital media. Moreover, the increased data creation and storage capacities generate new pressures on systems for preservation, organization, and access. Although the functionalities of digital technologies will continue to give rise to practices and relationships that bear little resemblance to those surrounding print, neither novel arrangements nor enhanced capabilities should obscure the fundamental continuity of purpose underlying preservation and organization.

The requirements of the academic mission and the accumulation of a cultural heritage do not cease when information and documentation cease to have commercial value and pass out of the marketplace. Hence, relations among copyright holders, educational institutions, and the law must reflect the needs of the future as well as the present and should acknowledge the added value to society of preservation and of well-ordered systems for navigating information. During 1995 and 1996, the U.S. Congress and the World Intellectual Property Organization (WIPO) have l attempted to revise intellectual property law to address issues raised by the still evolving digital environment.

Internationally, the WIPO treaties proved more supportive of the principle of balance between the rights of owners and the need for public use. But the treaties must now return to the U.S. for ratification and the possible development of implementing and related legislation. The educational community urges that changes in the law be carefully crafted to enhance rather than impede the rich and timely circulation of information as well as its preservation and organization.

In preparation for the ongoing legislative debates on intellectual property in the digital environment. the educational community believes it necessary to develop its own consensus on a common set of broad principles which would provide standards against which coalitions and individual institutions can evaluate legislative proposals. Faced with the strong interests of the infotainment industry to maintain tight control of intellectual property in a global marketplace, the educational community may strengthen its more balanced position by speaking as one voice guided by the principles.

Copyright law provisions for digital works should maintain a balance between the interests of creators and copyright owners and the public that is equivalent to that embodied in current statute. The existing legal balance is consonant with the educational ethic of responsible use of intellectual properties, promotes the free exchange of ideas, and protects the economic interests of copyright holders. Intellectual property is a significant form of social capital, whose growth depends on its circulation, exploitation, and use.

Copyright law recognizes the tension between the needs of society and the rights of creators by permitting a defense against charges of infringement for certain uses of copyrighted works as specified in sections 107 -110 of the U.S. Copyright

Act of 1976. Among these uses are: the fair use of copyrighted works for teaching, scholarship, or research, among other activities; the reproduction of copyrighted works by libraries and archives under certain conditions for specific purposes; and the performance or display of a work by instructors or pupils in the course of face-to-face instruction.

3

Electronic Library Environment

The archival community is one of the smallest and, arguably, the least well understood of the professional communities working in the digital information environment and in knowledge management in general. The archival community comprises practicing archivists, manuscript curators, archival academics, and policy makers who work to define and promote the social utility of records and to identify, preserve, and provide access to documentary heritage regardless of format. Archival holdings are noncurrent organizational records of enduring value that are preserved by the archives of the creating organization.

Manuscript collections, however, are also often collocated with archival holdings. Manuscript collections are unpublished materials that are created or gathered by an organization or individual but are transferred from the original custodian to an archives, a historical society, or university library. The archival perspective brings an evidence-based approach to the management of recorded knowledge. It is fundamentally concerned with the organizational and personal processes and contexts through which records and knowledge are created as well as the ways in which records individually and collectively reflect those processes.

This perspective distinguishes the archival community from other communities of information professionals that manage decontextualized information and tend to be focused more on users, systems, or institutions. Exhortations for archivists to move beyond customary custodial roles and become advocates for information that must be preserved because of its enduring legal, fiscal, administrative, research or other societal value reflect a growing awareness among archivists that along with their concern for the nature of the materials, there is a critical need to promote the materials' long-term requirements and enduring value to society.

Maintaining massive quantities of digital materials of continuing value over time, especially the evidential qualities of those materials, is essential but complex. The challenge of identifying and maintaining such materials has led archivists to work with information creators to design systems capable of keeping records that will endure with their evidential integrity intact and with the preservation community to provide testbeds and evaluation for new preservation technologies and processes. The archivist exists in order to make other people's work possible, unknown people for the most part and working very possibly on lines equally unknown to him: some of them perhaps in the quite distant future and upon lines as yet unpredictable. The perspectives of different information professions tend to be understood in terms of their manifestation in the practices of physical institutions.

Over the past two centuries, a range of information institutions have evolved that play distinct roles within society. These roles reflect the many ways in which information is created, used, valued, preserved, and disposed of by individuals, organizations, and communities in the conduct of business, scholarship, learning, and personal affairs. Libraries are engaged in the tangible activities of identifying, acquiring, preserving, and providing access to published information. They are also engaged in less tangible, value-laden activities such as promoting intellectual freedom and serving as focal points for various communities.

It is assumed that seamless integration of information resources is a prerequisite for moving beyond the walls of individual physical institutions into virtual information space and knowledge construction practices. Transparency (i.e., rendering differences between diverse information resources invisible to end users) achieved through homogeneity in information retrieval methods and display of retrieved materials also seems to be important. Asserting individua institutional or professional differences always carries with i the potential to confuse the user and impede interoperability

It is important, however, to recognize that varian practices have arisen for sound intellectual and pragmati reasons as institutions have fulfilled their various societal role and managed their collections from diverse but equall legitimate perspectives. A new paradigm needs to be create that will facilitate the right blend of commonality an distinctiveness. The Society of American Archivists define archives as "(1) The 'non-current records' of an organizatio or institution preserved because of their continuing value; th term 'archival records' or 'archival materials' signifies ar physical medium which is employed to transmit information, such as paper, photographs, audio or video tape, computer tapes or disks, etc. (2) The 'agency or program' responsible for selecting, preserving, and making available archival materials; also referred to as an 'archival agency.' (3) The 'building' or part of a building where such materials are located." Additional definition is required to help us understand more fully the roles that archives can and should play in the digital environment. First, archival institutions serve an important legal function in society. Archival institutions are generally legally constituted entities responsible for identifying, managing, and preserving the integrity of an institution's official records of long-term value.

These activities prove the actions of the institution and provide essential protection for the institution's legal rights and those of its constituents or the general citizenry. Archival institutions enable legally constituted access to records, access that must also constantly address a range of legal concerns that become more pressing in the digital environment. These concerns include intellectual property, the privacy of individuals mentioned in materials, the conditions under which certain types of materials can be accessed and made available, and the protection of the integrity of digital materials from accidental or deliberate tampering.

Concern for retaining the evidential value of records has placed the archival community at the vanguard of research and development in digital preservation and authentication. Second, because archives focus on records, archivists have an awareness of the societal, institutional, and individual construction of memory and an understanding of the implications of how that memory is represented and transmitted over time. This awareness becomes increasingly important as more of the world's collections are reformatted and represented online. It is also important for retaining evidence in time and over time, especially through digital preservation processes. Third, libraries have focused predominantly on the organization, dissemination, and use of existing information, archives focus on these activities too, but are also intimately engaged in the creation of information and its ultimate disposition.

Since the 1960s, the archival community has worked closely with the creators of records and record-keeping systems to develop means to identify and preserve digital records that have no paper counterpart. The problem of what to do about records that are born digital has forced archivists to reexamine and reinvent their principles and practices in light of a digital challenge that emerged before the advent of digital libraries. Archival theory, methodology, and practice together constitute archival science. Because archival science is scholarly as well as practical and uses a distinct methodology to gain knowledge, it can be considered both a discipline and a profession.

The disciplinary and professional aspects of archival science together compose the archival paradigm—a set of assumptions, principles, and practices that are common to the archival community and are a model for its activities and outlook. Although archives have existed for thousands of years, much of the archival paradigm—not unlike that of library science—coalesced between the mid-nineteenth and twentieth centuries. The archival paradigm has been extensively influenced by the so-called auxiliary and ancillary disciplines—diplomatics, history, law, textual criticism, management and organizational theory, and library science.

Perhaps most influential have been the research methods of modern scientific history and legal theories of evidence that developed during the nineteenth century largely from diplomatics. Diplomatics was developed to help establish the authenticity of medieval ecclesiastical records. It is the study of the genesis, forms, and transmission of archival documents; their relation to the facts represented in them; and their relation to their creator, in order to identify, evaluate, and communicate their true nature. As a result of these influences, most of the archival community working with public records focused on developing principles for archival arrangement and description that emphasized the organic nature of records and the circumstances of their creation. The manuscript community and some national archives, however, adopted bibliographic practices of subject control.

In the United States, where the archival profession was only just beginning to coalesce, historian and later archivist Waldo Gifford Leland presented a paper at the First Conference of Archivists in 1909 calling for the reorganization of archives according to the principle of provenance rather than library methods. The bifurcation of public archives and historical manuscript descriptive practices in the United States can most easily be explained in terms of prospective use and archival setting. For archivists administering records programs within their own institutions, the primary uses of records were legal proof and administrative research, often conducted by the records creators.

For those engaged in manuscript administration, the focus was on secondary use by historical scholars, often in a research library, where there was more pressure to apply bibliographic models of description. Arguably, therefore, library science has influenced archival science less through the contribution of specific practices than through the encouragement of greater emphasis on access and user orientation. Archivists and the bibliographic community worked together to increase use and facilitate access to archival and manuscript holdings.

In 1983, they developed the machine-readable cataloging (MARC) archival and manuscripts control (AMC) format to describe their holdings. Their goal was to integrate standardized information about archival holdings into bibliographic utilities and online public access catalogs and encourage wider use of the holdings. Although MARC AMC was widely adopted by university archivists as well as many state and local historical repositories, many archivists were not comfortable with what they perceived to be the forcing of archival descriptive practices into a data structure that was still essentially bibliographic. In 1993, work began on encoded archival description (EAD), which took the core archival descriptive tool—the finding aid—and used it to develop a standard generalized mark-up language (SGML) document type definition.

This definition could be used to disseminate archival descriptive information on the World Wide Web and could be mapped onto other kinds of descriptive metadata in digital information resources. In the United States, where archival practice developed later than in Europe, a whole new focus on the management of current records emerged between the 1930s and 1960s. Faced with vast quantities of modern records generated by two world wars and a huge federal bureaucracy and with early adoption of new record-keeping and reproduction technologies, archivists at the National Archives realized that they could not possibly keep everything.

Thus, they developed revolutionary approaches that engaged archivists at the point of record creation in identifying active records of long-term value and arranging for the orderly retiring of inactive records. This development had two important consequences: the addition to the archival paradigm of a new set of theories relating to life cycle management of records and appraisal and the establishment of the records management profession with the founding in 1956 of the American Records Management Association. From the 1970s until the early 1990s, the archival community in the United States hotly debated the extent to which archival principles and practices were based in theory versus expediency.

In 1981, F. Gerald Ham said that technology and a changing social role for archives would lead to more active management of archival records and a reexamination of many basic assumptions about archival theory and practice. The debate gave way to the reexamination, as Ham predicted. Archivists needed to cope with emerging electronic record-keeping technologies, new modes of scholarly research and increasing user expectations that archivists should provide automated information access. The archival community has argued that archival needs exist in wider information systems design and in the processes of document creation and preservation. It has also considered what its approaches have to offer in the wider realm of information management.

Many of the information professions interact closely with other disciplines and derive much of their outlook from those relationships. For example, the practices and perspectives of information scientists have been strongly influenced by science and computer science. Archivists are closely aligned with professions such as law, history, journalism, anthropology, and archaeology. Evidence in the archival sense can be defined as the passive ability of documents and objects and their associated contexts to provide insight into the processes, activities, and events that led to their creation for legal, historical, archaeological, and other purposes. The concern for evidence permeates all archival activities and demands complex approaches to the management of information; it also sets high benchmarks for information systems and services, particularly with respect to archival description and preservation.

Recently, the paramount importance of identifying and maintaining the evidential value of archival materials has been reemphasized, partly as a result of the challenges posed by electronic records but partly also to differentiate the information and preservation practices of the archival community from those of the library community. The integrity of the evidential value of materials is ensured by demonstrating an unbroken chain of custody, precisely documenting the aggregation of archival materials as received from their creator and integrated with the rest of the archives' holdings of the same provenance, and tracking all preservation activities associated with the materials.

Jenkinson described this process as the physical and moral defense of the record. Schellenberg expanded archival notions about evidence when he discussed the values that archivists should use to help them decide which materials to retain. The primary values of archival records are related to the legal, fiscal, and administrative purposes of the records creators; the secondary values are related to subsequent researchers. Schellenberg argued that the secondary values of public records can be ascertained most easily if they are considered in relation to "(1) the evidence they contain of the organization and functioning of the Government body that produced them, and (2) the information they contain on persons, corporate bodies, things [e.g., places, buildings, physical objects], problems, conditions, and the like, with which the Government dealt." His argument acknowledges both the strict legal requirements of records that must be satisfied by archival processes and the wider concept of historical and cultural evidence that is contained in the materials and can be interpreted by secondary users.

The archival concern for the description and preservation of evidence involves a rich understanding of the implicit and explicit values of materials at creation and over time. It also involves an acute awareness of how such values can be diminished or lost when the integrity of materials is compromised. Evidential value in the widest sense is reflected to some extent in any information artifact, but only a subset of all information is subject to legal or regulatory requirements concerning creation and maintenance.

Primary sources particularly lend themselves to such kinds of analysis and interpretation, and such materials are increasingly being incorporated into digital information resources. Maintaining the evidential value of information is important not only to creators of materials that are subject to legal or regulatory requirements but also to many researchers. In particular, reformatting, description, and preservation need to be considered. Reformatting has been discussed extensively in the professional literature in relation to the digitization of library and archival collections. Information professionals involved in digitally reformatting their collections must understand when a user may need to work with the original information object to appreciate some intrinsic characteristic, such as the weight of the paper; when a digital copy will do; and whether a copy needs to be high or low resolution, color or black and white.

Information professionals must also decide how much of a collection needs to be digitized and what kind of metadata will enable a user to place information objects in context. Archival practice places a premium on both collective and contextual description. The key is to explain the physical aspects and intellectual structure of the collection that may not be apparent and to provide enough contextual information for the user to understand the historical circumstances and organizational processes of the object's creation.

Description should also demonstrate that the physical and the intellectual form of the materials have not been altered in any undocumented way. Counterintuitively, perhaps, it is during the preservation of digital materials that evidential value is often most at risk of being compromised. Digital preservation techniques have moved beyond a concern for the longevity of digital media to a concern for the preservation of the information stored in those media during recurrent migration to new software and hardware.

In the process, many of the intrinsic characteristics of information objects can disappear—data structures can be modified and presentation of the object on a computer screen can be altered. Although the tenets are interpreted differently by different archival traditions, they nevertheless represent the essence of the archival perspective and its blend of intellectual and pragmatic rationales. The principle ofrespect des fonds was first codified in 1839 in regulations issued by the French minister of public instruction. The principle stated that records should be grouped according to the nature of the institution that accumulated them.

Originally conceived of in physical terms, this principle facilitates physical and intellectual access to records generated and received by the same institution or person by gathering and describing them as an intellectual whole, regardless of their form, medium, or volume. The principle of provenance enhanced this approach by ensuring that the records remained as much as possible as they were originally created. From a practical viewpoint, the principle of original order obviated the need for resource-intensive and contentious rearrangement according to subject. From an intellectual viewpoint, it preserved the objectivity of the records and provided insight into the functions, processes, and personal relationships of the records creator as reflected in the arrangement of the records. In recent years, the conceptualization of these basic tenets has become more complex as bureaucratic structures have evolved and digital systems have been increasingly used for record keeping.

Archivists have had difficulty establishing the provenance of records of multi-institutional collaborations or those contained in multifunctional databases and distributed information systems. In archival appraisal, more sophisticated conceptions of provenance, such as functional provenance and multiprovenance, have been developed for electronic records that apply business process analysis and functional decomposition. Functional provenance views the business function through which a record came into being as that record's provenance rather than the office or individual creating the record. This view is based on the rationale that record-keeping functions are likely to remain more or less constant whereas bureaucratic hierarchies and technologies shift over time. Multiprovenance recognizes that a record may be simultaneously created through the interaction of multiple offices or jurisdictions.

In archival description, developments such as EAD and the Australian series system recognize that a one-to-many relationship may exist for groups of records created by changing bureaucratic structures. Taken together, respect des fonds, provenance, and original order ensure that the intellectual integrity of aggregations of records is maintained and that individual records are always contextualized. Adhering to these principles is a less resource-intensive way of providing access to high-volume collections than are classifying by subject and cataloging of individual documents.

Considerable cataloging expertise and the availability of specialized standardized vocabularies are required for correct and consistent assignment of subject access points to heterogeneous unsynthesized and unpublished materials. Because the language used in archival materials is often archaic or technical, assigning a modern subject term that accurately reflects the concepts being expressed in the records can be difficult. On the basis of their insight about how users working with historical and organizational materials might wish to search, archivists have broadened the notion of subject access, suggesting access points such as temporal and geographic coverage and form of material.

Today we can see the application of such approaches in the resource type and coverage elements that have been integrated into the Dublin Core for use in resource discovery of networked electronic resources. A huge volume of digital information has not gone through editorial and publication processes. Subject access and item control practices are not sufficient for effective and efficient organization of such information. The archival approach offers the concepts of collective arrangement and description according to the provenance of the materials; these provide benefits even when information managers or users are not interested in the evidential value of the materials. Applying these concepts makes it possible to unite related digital, nondigital, and predigital materials according to their intellectual rather than their physical characteristics.

These concepts build context, which is a powerful and underused tool for facilitating understanding and ultimately creating knowledge. They prompt the user to consider the degree to which the material's source is authoritative. The archival approach focuses on the context, organic development, and content of the collection, allowing the user to ask the "how," "why," and "so what" questions so integral to research. The U.S. National Archives and Records Administration developed the concept of the records life cycle to model how the functions of, use of, and responsibility for records change as records age and move from the control of their creator to the physical custody of the archives.

Records creators must develop logical systems for classifying or registering records and implement procedures to ensure the integrity of the records. Records managers and archivists also ensure that active records are scheduled for systematic elimination or permanent retention. As records age, they gradually become less heavily referenced and finally become inactive. During the second phase, the archives is a neutral third party responsible for ensuring the long-term integrity of the records. When the records enter the archives, they are physically and intellectually integrated with other archival materials of the same provenance, thus establishing the archival bond. Their physical integrity is ensured through preservation management; their intellectual integrity, through archival description.

Archival records are then available for secondary use. Changes in methods of record creation and in perceptions of their continuing value have recently led archivists to consider how to apply the life cycle model in a digital environment. The principles underlying the life cycle have been refined through projects such as Preservation of the Integrity of Electronic Records, conducted from 1994 to 1996 by archival researchers at the University of British Columbia. An alternate model—the records continuum—has been proposed. This model now undergirds the conceptualization of the role and activities of the record-keeping professions in Australia and is gaining in acceptance in the United States and Europe. The UBC Project sought to develop a generic model to identify and define by-products of electronic information systems and methods for protecting the integrity of the by-products, which constitute evidence of action.

Using a deductive method drawing on the principles of diplomatics and archival science, the project identified the procedures necessary to ensure control over reliable records creation during the first phase of the records life cycle and to maintain the integrity of archival records during the second phase. The project reiterates the need in the digital environment for completed records placed under the jurisdiction of the archives. The records continuum model takes a different approach. Records managers and archivists are involved with records beginning when a record-keeping system is designed.

Physical transfer to the archives is not required; archivists establish requirements for appropriate maintenance of the records and monitor compliance by records creators. The intellectual interrelationships of active and archival records are established by integrating metadata from active records into the archival authority's information system. This postcustodial model expands the role of the archivist to include active participation in the production and use of records.

Archival practice assumes that materials within a fond can be most effectively organized and retrieved collectively. Although collective management and description are pragmatic ways to gain basic levels of control over large quantities of heterogeneous information, for archivists the rationale behind these practices lies in the inherent characteristics of records and other materials that are the by-product of human activities. When materials are generated by the activity of an individual or organization, an interdependent relationship exists between the materials and their creator. A complex web of relationships also exists between the materials and the historical, legal, and procedural contexts of their development as well as among all materials created by the same activity.

The organic nature of records refers to all these interrelationships, and archival practices are designed to collectively document, capture, and exploit them. These practices recognize that the value of an individual record is derived in part from the sequence of records within which it is located. They also recognize that it can be difficult to understand an individual record without understanding its historical, legal, procedural, and documentary context. The perspective gained from working with information collectively can also be applied to the description, preservation, and use of Web resources.

Resources created on the Web are not unlike archival fonds in that they include a complex of hyperlinks to pages related by provenance, topic, or some other feature. An advantage in the Web environment is that hyperlinks are explicit rather than largely implicit, as is the case with paper records. As a result, those who manage and use these resources can more easily identify and exploit organic relationships. A Web page without its hyperlinks may be less valuable to users because of its diminished evidential content.

Recent developments in information organization have exploited the structure of information content and its metadata to provide smarter access to materials, especially those that are hard to locate by subject or keyword. This is particularly evident in efforts to apply extensible mark-up language (XML) to develop structures that are more predictable for Web resources and in the application of the text encoding initiative for the SGML encoding of literary and historical texts. Structure can be both intellectual and physical; it can exist within an information object, collections of information objects, and descriptions of those information objects.

Archival practices explicitly recognize the existence of such structures and exploit those that are hierarchical. Developing and using hierarchies are intuitive ways for humans to model information; as a result, much information and many information systems have hierarchical characteristics. To ascertain authenticity, archivists use principles derived from diplomatics to analyze how the intellectual form of records reflects the functions by which they were created. Diplomatics maintains that the intellectual form of records usually has three components—protocol, text, and eschatocol. Each of these components contains groups of additional elements of form; for example, the protocol contains elements such as the name of the author, the date the record was created, the name of the person to whom the record is directed, and the subject of the record.

The eschatocol contains elements that validate the document, such as the official title of the author and signatures of witnesses and countersigners. When elements are absent or irregular, the records' authenticity may be questioned. Records have an innate hierarchy imposed by the creating agency's filing practices and position in a bureaucratic hierarchy and by the processes through which the records were created. A fond may contain sous-fonds or a record group may contain subgroups, which may in turn contain many series of records, each relating to a different activity. Individual record series may be divided into subseries and even subsubseries, which may be further divided into filing units that contain individual documents. Archival description, through inventories and registers collectively referred to as finding aids, has traditionally reflected these hierarchies.

A high-level summary description provides basic intellectual control and collection management information for a set of records; progressively more granular descriptions are prepared for subordinate levels in the hierarchy. In the digital environment, hierarchical and collective description lend themselves to hierarchical and object-oriented metadata structures such as SGML. The development since 1995 of the SGML document type definition for EAD has turned descriptive practices that may have seemed cumbersome into a powerful infrastructure for online information systems. The archival community is making significant contributions to research and development in the digital information environment by using integrity, metadata, knowledge management, risk management, and knowledge preservation.

Ensuring the integrity of information over time is a prominent concern in the digital environment because physical and intellectual integrity can easily be consciously or unconsciously compromised and variant versions can easily be created and distributed. This concern has two aspects—checking and certifying data integrity (associated with technical processes such as integrity checking, certification, digital watermarking, steganography, and user and authentication protocols) and identifying the intellectual qualities of information that make it authentic (associated with legal, cultural, and philosophical concepts such as trustworthiness and completeness). Functional requirements are particularly well articulated in highly regulated communities such as the pharmaceutical and bioengineering industries. Less well explored is how to identify and preserve the intellectual integrity of information.

The intellectual mechanisms by which we come to trust traditional forms of published information include a consideration of provenance, citation practices, peer review, editorial practices, and an assessment of the intellectual form of the information. In the digital environment, information may not conform to predictable forms or may not have been through traditional publication processes; a more complex understanding of information characteristics and management procedures is required for the intellectual integrity of information to be understood.

Attempts are often made to implement digital versions of procedures traditionally used in record keeping and archival administration. Such attempts include establishing trusted servers or repositories that can serve as a witness or notary public; distributing information to multiple servers, thus making it harder to damage or eliminate all copies; developing certified digital archives as trusted third-party repositories; and identifying canonical versions of information resources. The International Project on Permanent Records in Electronic Systems (InterPARES) is a three-year project using archival and diplomatics principles to examine the characteristics inherent in digital information objects created by electronic record-keeping technologies in order to establish their authenticity and how that authenticity might be maintained over time. The project is funded by several agencies, including the U.S. National Historical Records and Publications Commission and Canada's Social Sciences and Humanities research Consortium.

An interdisciplinary team of researchers drawn from archival science, preservation management, library and information science, computer science, and electrical engineering is working with an industry group and major archival repositories, including the national archives of several countries. The project builds on previous research conducted at the University of British Columbia that examined the preservation of the integrity of electronic records and theoretically defined the concepts of reliability and authenticity in relation to electronic records. It also identified the procedural requirements and responsibilities for ensuring the reliability of active records and the authenticity of preserved records.

The philosophy underlying InterPARES is that the theories and methodologies necessary to ensure the long-term preservation of authentic electronic records must be centered on the nature and meaning of the records themselves. Despite the new media and formats of electronic records, from the perspective of archival science the integral components that identify and authenticate a record have not changed. By combining principles of diplomatics and archival principles, the project is developing a template that can be used to identify requirements for authenticity for different kinds of electronic records and systems that generate records. To use this template and to understand the extent to which electronic records resemble traditional records, the project is analyzing a variety of electronic information and record-keeping systems, including large-scale object-oriented databases, geographic information systems, dynamic Web resources, and digital music systems in many national legal and organizational contexts.

These analyses will be translated into recommended systems-design requirements and authentication processes, record-keeping policies and procedures, and preservation strategies for different types of records. Different preservation processes will also be evaluated to ascertain their ability to maintain the elements of different types of records identified as essential to preserving the records' authenticity. Although this project is focused on the authenticity requirement of records rather than on more generic forms of information, its findings will likely be relevant to digital information or information systems that need to retain the integrity of physical and intellectual characteristics over time.

The library community frequently uses metadata to refer to cataloging and other forms of descriptive information, but it is also used to refer to information about the administration, preservation, use, and technical functionality of digital information resources. With the increasing diversity of distributed and interactive digital information systems comes a need for a metadata infrastructure that can implement the functional requirements of each information community and promote interoperability. The challenge is not just to identify the areas where it is possible to map between different types of metadata.

It is also necessary to identify the tensions between the rich and complex metadata sets that individual communities have developed and the need for simpler metadata sets that are easier for nonspecialists to use and systems designers to maintain. For information communities that work with cultural information there are several important elements in ensuring authenticity and facilitating the use of an information object. They include metadata such as contextual description, indications of relationships between collections of materials, annotations that have accrued around information objects, documentation of intellectual property rights, and documentation of processes that the information objects have undergone, such as reformatting and migration. Rich metadata sets that incorporate aspects such as these are essential if the object is to be used to its fullest potential.

However, considerable demand exists for leaner metadata that will enable users to move between information systems that might contain different types of materials on the same subject. Encoded Archival Description (EAD) is a new archival descriptive standard adopted in the United States and being developed as a potential international standard. A hierarchical, object-oriented way of describing the context and content of archival collections, EAD can be a flexible metadata infrastructure for integrating descriptions with actual digital and digitized archival materials within an archival information system. It can also be mapped into other metadata structures such as MARC. Perhaps EAD's greatest potential lies in its ability to be manipulated for information retrieval and display without compromising how it documents the provenance, original order, and organic nature of archival collections.

As a result, it moves beyond the static concept of the paper finding aid and can facilitate appropriate access for diverse users at the collection and item levels. A measure of the utility and sophistication of EAD is the interest it has created in other professional communities. The Online Archive of California (OAC), now part of the California Digital Library, is an example of a multi-institutional database containing encoded finding aids and digitized content drawn from archives and special collections of the University of California, California State University, and numerous other universities and repositories throughout the state.

The size and scope of OAC have enabled it to develop best practices for encoding and model evaluation processes and to examine its own usability not only as a scholarly resource but also as a resource for K-12 education. A constituent OAC project, Museums in the Online Archive of California (MOAC), which is being conducted by several museums across California, is applying EAD to the description of museum collections. This development has the potential not only to map between the descriptive practices of two professional communities but to integrate access to intellectually related two- and three-dimensional historical and cultural resources that have often been located in different institutions.

Over the past five years, several metadata projects conducted in Australia have built on the records continuum model by specifying, standardizing, and integrating into active electronic record-keeping systems the kinds of metadata necessary for effective record keeping and for ensuring the long-term management and archival use of essential evidence. These projects include the Victoria Electronic Records Strategy metadata set and the Australian Government Locator System. The most recent of these projects is the SPIRT (Strategic Partnership with Industry—Research and Training) Recordkeeping Metadata Standards Project for Managing and Accessing Information Resources in Networked Environments Over Time for Government, Commerce, Social and Cultural Purposes, directed by Monash University in association with the National Archives of Australia. This project builds on the work of previous projects and provides a framework for standardizing sets of interoperable record-keeping metadata that can be associated with records from creation through processes such as embedding, encapsulation, or linking to metadata stores.

Metadata elements are classified by purpose and are being mapped against related generic and sector-specific metadata sets such as Dublin Core. In this way, archivists build a business case for including archival considerations in the workflow because of the need to manage risk and the role of records in supporting organizational decision making. Like the term metadata, the term knowledge management is being widely used, although its meaning and how it differs from information management are less than clear.

Knowledge management refers to the practices, skills, and technologies associated with creating, organizing, storing, presenting, retrieving, using, preserving, disposing of, and re-using information resources to help identify, capture, and produce knowledge. Knowledge management is often used to create entrepreneurial opportunities by identifying and exploiting an organization's knowledge capital. Knowledge management activities can include data and metadata mining as well as digital asset management. In many respects, such activities are a logical extension of records management and archival activities such as those under way in Australia.

The rationales for building and sustaining electronic records and other digital information resources are derived not only from abstract concepts of information and research needs but from administrative and legal necessity, the corporate bottom line, and institutional or repository enterprise. Knowledge management systems are often hybrids of born-digital, digitized, and traditional media in the form of organizational records, nonrecord information, and digital products. Such systems include digital images and texts as well as sound, moving images, graphics, and animation.

They also contain procedural and administrative information such as rights management for digital assets. Whereas digital libraries are built around assumptions about current and potential uses but with few hard data, digital asset management systems are created organically out of organizational activities and the need for agility sufficient to respond to emerging institutional priorities. This way of looking at information resources—regarding their content and metadata as assets with dynamic values and market demand—is a different mindset for many information professionals.

It involves adopting a holistic rather than a piecemeal approach to information systems and shifting from a linear to an organic perspective. The digital asset management approach has been extensively developed by the media industries, particularly publishing and entertainment, where both the product and the information and records associated with its production are primarily digital. In the entertainment industry, studios are hiring archivists with experience in electronic records management to build digital asset management or metadata management systems for the assets created during production.

In some cases, a two-phase approach is adopted whereby digital production is handled in a production management system and its contents are created, described, and organized by the primary users. After production is completed, all associated materials are transferred to the asset management system, where the digital asset manager or digital archivist organizes and describes them for secondary use.

Metadata are developed to track levels and types of use and allow maximum flexibility in retrieving and interrelating assets. This approach has tremendous potential for supporting the vision, relevance, utility, and sustainability of digital library and archives resources. It incorporates the interests of the information creator and makes preservation management integral to creation and retention. It offers a new economic and use-based framework to help institutions prioritize selection of information content and decide what and how much metadata to create; which resources to keep online; and which assets to preserve, purge, or allow to decay gradually. Evaluation practices of library and information retrieval systems have traditionally been based on four factors—effectiveness, benefits, cost-effectiveness, and cost benefits.

Research on electronic archival records has postulated another form of evaluation—risk management—borrowed from professions such as auditing, quality control, insurance, and law. Although this concept has not been applied directly to other information environments, it has implications for assessing risk in terms of ensuring the reliability and authenticity, appropriate elimination, and preservation of digital information. Archivists seeking to develop blueprints for the management of electronic records have undertaken several important projects in recent years. This research showed that electronic records are likely to endure with their evidential value intact beyond their active life only if functional requirements for record-keeping systems design and policies and procedures for record keeping are addressed during the design and implementation of the system. This increases the likelihood that appropriate software and hardware standards will be used, making the records easier to preserve.

Records will also be created in such a way that they can be identified, audited, rendered immutable on completion, physically or intellectually removed, and brought under archival control. Missing from this approach is the motivation for organizations to invest the resources required to implement expensive archival requirements in their active record-keeping systems. With the digital asset management approach discussed previously, the motivation to preserve usable digital information comes from the organization itself and is intimately tied to enterprise management.

The Australian metadata projects apply two other strategies. The first is demonstrating that well-designed record-keeping systems and metadata will enhance organizational decision making. The second is risk management: persuading the organization that the resources invested in electronic record keeping will reduce the organizational risk incurred by not complying with archival and record-keeping requirements. Organizations such as public bodies and regulated industries are generally aware of the penalties for noncompliance.

Noncompliance by a public body could result in a costly lawsuit. Noncompliance by a regulated industry could result in not getting regulatory approval to market a new product. The cost of noncompliance with record-keeping requirements may be significantly higher than that of compliance. In other environments the risk analysis may be less straightforward because the risks may be less evident or the costs of noncompliance less tangible.

Knowledge Preservation is arguably the single biggest challenge facing everyone who creates, maintains, or relies on digital information. Awareness of the immense scope of the potential preservation crisis has brought many groups together to experiment with new preservation strategies and technologies. Preserving knowledge is more complex than preserving only media or content. It is about preserving the intellectual integrity of information objects, including capturing information about the various contexts within which information is created, organized, and used; organic relationships with other information objects; and characteristics that provide meaning and evidential value.

Preservation of knowledge also requires appreciating the continuing relationships between digital and nondigital information. The archival mission of preserving evidence over time has resulted in demanding criteria for measuring the efficacy of the range of strategies now being discussed for digital preservation, including migration, emulation, bundling, and persistent object preservation. Projects using archival testbeds are under way in several countries with the aim of understanding the extent to which different strategies work with a range of materials and what limitations need to be addressed procedurally, through the development of new technological approaches, or both.

The Digital Repository Project of the National Archives of the Netherlands is concerned with the authenticity, accessibility, and longevity of archival records created by Dutch government agencies. The project brings together two important concepts—the emulation technique devised by Jeff Rothenberg and the reference model for an open archival information system (OAIS) developed by the U.S. National Aeronautics and Space Administration, which is being adopted as an ISO standard. The emulation technique involves creating emulators for future computers to enable them to run the software on which archived material was created and maintained, thus recreating the functionality, look, and feel of the material.

The OAIS reference model is a high-level record-keeping model developed to assist in the archiving of high-volume information. It delineates the processes involved in the ingestion, storage, administrative and logistical maintenance, intellectual metadata management, and access and delivery of electronic records. The Digital Repository Project is most concerned with determining the functionality of the repository, scope of the metadata, standards to be applied, and differentiation of the intellectual and the physical and technical form of the records.

Persistent object preservation is a highly generic technological approach that has been developed jointly by the U.S. National Archives and Records Administration and the San Diego Supercomputer Center. This project is addressing the need of the National Archives to find efficient and fast methods for acquiring and preserving, in context, millions of files that can be applied to many types of records and that comply with archival principles. The approach focuses on storing the information objects that make up a collection and identifying their metadata attributes and behaviors that can be used to recreate the collection. Like the Digital Repository Project, persistent object preservation is built around the OAIS reference model. It supports archival processes from accessioning through preservation and use, and it recognizes the importance of collection-based management.

Persistent object preservation also exploits inherent hierarchical structures within records, predictable record forms, and dependencies between them. It is designed to be consistent, comprehensive, and independent of infrastructure.

Role of Digital Libraries in Education

In recent years, many professional associations have published curricula guidelines about information technology; these include the American Library Association (ALA), Association for Information Systems (AIS), International Federation of Library Associations and Institutions (IFLA), Association for

Information Science and Technology (ASIS&T), Association for Computing Machinery (ACM), and Computer Society (IEEE). The Computer Curricula report acknowledges early on that designing an undergraduate curriculum for Computing is an interdisciplinary task. It names four disciplines that are related: Computer Engineering, Software Engineering, Information Systems (IS), and Computer Science [COM01].

The IFLA Guidelines don't explicitly mention interdisciplinarity or specify the level of professional education for LIS graduates beyond noting that it is university level (includeing both undergraduate and graduate levels); they call for a broad general education (topics from other disciplines) and highlight the importance of a variety of information contexts in LIS educational preparation [IFL00]. Additionally, the Computing Curricula outlines DL as an elective area with topics such as digitization, storage and interchange, digital objects, composites and packages, metadata, cataloguing, author submission, etc. [COM01]. Tennant, a professional librarian, discusses the shortage of digital librarians and explains why public service LIS professionals must become tech-savvy [Ten02].

Anecdotal evidence suggests that both approaches leave novice LIS graduates with overwhelming feelings of information overload, the impression that the library profession is in chaos, and a sense that there is no real core LIS disciplinary knowledge beyond the service ethic, descriptive and procedural knowledge of information resources and their use. Since the impact of IT on all disciplines will only continue to increase, the time is ripe for different approaches—approaches that view curriculum development intellectually at the unit level (what topics and learning objectives/competencies are common across related disciplines) and how best to facilitate this development for professional graduates.

At the very least, such approaches use research findings about interdisciplinary learning to improve the problem solving and competencies of graduates. They also coalesce education for the information professions. At the undergraduate level, interdisciplinary courses have been shown to provide students with many cognitive, as well as affective, benefits.

Disciplinary cultures produce objects and methods of study, the credentialed practitioners of the discipline, values and ways of knowing, and identities. "The impact of knowledge on action—whether in the field of social or natural phenomena—forces interaction between the disciplines and even generates new disciplines. The 'inter-discipline' of today is the 'discipline' of tomorrow." Therefore, proposing and structuring Digital Libraries as an academic inter-discipline is in one sense knowledge fragmentation but it also has the potential for unification. Since interdisciplinarity can be defined as the integration of concepts and epistemologies from different disciplines, digital libraries constitute a problem domain to which both LIS and Computing (among others) contribute. Explicating the nature of the disciplines and professions involved may move us closer to the goal of interdisciplinary DL education.

Many theories exist about human information seeking behaviours. There are also classification theories, codes, and concepts about the representation and organization of human produced, recorded information. More advanced than LIS, but still does not have—and may never have—a single theory that is widely accepted for all phenomena in its subject matter.

The concept of the algorithm at the heart of every computer program, stored programs, computer as an image of the human brain, all come close to providing an overarching theory.

LIS and Computing are also professional programs of study; they train people for specific professions and occupations. LIS trains librarians and information professionals, and the study is generally at the graduate level. On campuses, computing areas are spread across diverse disciplinary departments such as Electrical and Computer Engineering, Computer Science, Industrial Engineering, and Management Information Systems. Depending on the focus, these programs train for technical and semi-technical positions.

Technical positions include computer software engineers, computer hardware engineers, programmers, computer and information systems managers, database administrators, and systems analysts; professional study for these jobs, while often terminal at the undergraduate level, increases to include graduate school for complex positions. Computer support specialists and systems administrators comprise the semi-technical group and are projected to be among the fastest growing occupations over the 2000-2010 period.

While most jobs in this category require a bachelor's degree in some computing area, many will accept less formal education. Certification in the specific technology is fast becoming essential. Occupational projections indicate that the number of computing graduates trained or needed is much larger than the number of LIS graduates trained or needed. The levels of study, number and types of occupations and professions, and numbers of students in these programs are all potentially powerful barriers for interdisciplinary program development involving these disciplines. However, while LIS and Computing are grounded in different academic disciplines, they are increasingly related professional and occupational categories with potential for interdisciplinary curriculum development.

Preserving Electronic Heritage

The "digital library" is not merely equivalent to a digitized collection with information management tools. It is also a series of activities that brings together collections, services, and people in support of the full life cycle of creation, dissemination, use, and preservation of data, information, and knowledge.

Libraries now license so many databases and collections of online content that they increasingly offer a way for users to search for a resource based on their topic. For example, some libraries are involved with the Open Archives Initiative (OAI), which aims to share metadata among working paper archives. Therefore, an OAI-compliant archive will likely "dumb down" its metadata (in some cases making granular metadata more homogenous) to meet this minimum specification. Internal compliance means storing the metadata in a particular standard even when it makes little sense to do so. Some standards are meant to provide interoperability among systems, while others are designed to provide a base level of standardization upon which software systems can be built. Therefore, not all metadata standards are created equal. They are sometimes inadequate for your internal needs or would prevent you from complying with a different standard.

In the case of the OAI-compliant archive above, for example, being internally compliant with the Dublin Core would make no sense in and of itself. So long as it could "speak" Dublin Core when required, a richer set of internal metadata may allow many other additional uses of the same information. Good granularity doesn't necessarily mean that any single metadata standard or container must chop up every field into the smallest reduceable part.

Therefore, a digital object described using the METS schema may, in fact, refer to a MARC record for descriptive metadata. Granularity of metadata is hard-won and easily lost. Identifying and appropriately encoding metadata elements usually requires a person-and one with training. Once granularity has been achieved, it should not be permanently surrendered through internal compliance with an external standard, unless the benefits clearly outweigh the drawbacks and no alternatives are possible. The time of cataloguing staff is valuable, and once granularity is lost it may not be practical to recover it.

Libraries depend on metadata. They are becoming even more dependent as we move into the realm of creating, managing, and preserving collections in digital form. The Dublin Core is a metadata element set intended to facilitate discovery of electronic resources. Originally conceived for author-generated description of Web resources, it has attracted the attention of formal resource description communities such as museums, libraries, government agencies, and commercial organizations so they, too, can find the electronic resources they need. Dublin Core is building of an interdisciplinary, international consensus around a core element set. This progress represents the emergent wisdom and collective experience of many stakeholders in the resource description arena. An open mailing list supports ongoing work.

The Dublin Core promotes a commonly understood set of descriptors that increases the possibility of finding what you are looking for across disciplines. The Dublin Core benefits from active participation and promotion in over 20 countries in North America, Europe, Australia, and Asia. The Dublin Core provides an economical alternative to more elaborate description models. It is also flexible and extensible enough to encode structures and elaborate semantics usually only found in richer description standards. The World Wide Web Consortium (W3C) has begun implementing an architecture for metadata on the Web.

The Dublin Core's Resource Description Framework (RDF) is designed to support the different metadata needs of vendors and information providers. Representatives of the Dublin Core are actively involved in developing this architecture. The standards are coming and many are almost complete. Those participating in the email groups and meetings feel the progress and see the opportunities. That's an understandable excuse for now, but won't work much longer. If you do not begin thinking and planning now, you will be unprepared when these new tools arrive.

Specifications like Dublin Core, IEEE Learning Object Metadata (LOM), or IMS have been developed for tagging metadata in a standard xml format [IMS Specification]. Frameworks are being developed to provide interoperability for digital libraries with many using the protocol for metadata harvesting developed by the Open Archives Initiative (OAI).

iLumina is a digital library of undergraduate teaching materials for science, mathematics, technology and engineering (SMETE) education, now being developed by Eduprise, the University of North Carolina at Wilmington

(UNCW), Georgia State University, Grand Valley State, and Virginia Tech. That faculty across the country have created a wealth of digital resources for teaching, often small or granular in size, and are willing to share them. However, faculty lack a repository where they can submit their materials, find related ones, create new content, and collectively improve both the quantity and quality of digital teaching resources. iLumina will provide such a repository, and related community and user services.

To promote such sharing, iLumina not only provides services to facilitate the creation and acquisition of resources, but also offers tools to end-users that will enable them to find and make use of digital objects. One related theme is that IMS metadata can underpin tools that enable resource sharing. iLumina uses IMS metadata tools to create rich and standardized descriptions of the learning objects that it manages. However, for this to work effectively, the costs of creating such rich metadata must be (relatively) low in comparison to its benefits. Many have argued that minimalist metadata (such as DC Core), is not only easier to create than IMS/IEEE descriptions, but also more cost-effective. One question the iLumina project is addressing is whether this is true. Architecturally, iLumina is both distributed (content) and centralized (metadata).

That is, we encourage content providers to maintain their own materials, but we gather and manage their metadata so end-users can come to a single site - the iLumina portal - to find these distributed collections. iLumina implements the full IMS metadata information model (including recent updates) and maintains the data through relational mappings into an SQL Server. Building on this model, we have developed a set of tools to create, manage, search and view IMS metadata and the iLumina resources they describe. This has enabled us to catalogue numerous library resources. Many of these resources are actually collections embedded in the larger iLumina collection, and we provide tools to describe and view not only individual resources, but the special collections themselves.

IMS metadata provides a foundation for a number of core library services already in place, including basic (and advanced) search, browsing, and a contribution form allowing new content providers to catalogue their materials for iLumina (although materials are reviewed before being finally admitted to the library). Maintaining profile or identity data for users is one of the services iLumina provides to simplify contributions. A registered user of the iLumina site can create and edit a profile of personal information.

When the user logs on and chooses to make a contribution, this profile information is used to automatically populate the contributor's fields in the metadata specification. Thus, users do not have to re-enter their personal information for each contribution. iLumina acquires metadata both by cataloguing metadata from individuals and by importing metadata in batches. While importing yields high amounts of metadata, those processes do not invite users to participate in the library environment.

Therefore, a web-based Contribution Form was designed for registered users to play an active role in contributing a resource and its metadata into iLumina. To minimize cataloguing errors, we collect metadata using a combination of drop-down lists containing controlled vocabularies and fill-in-the-blank fields. Only resources that have been accepted will be publicly available through the iLumina portal and services. Undergraduate math and science students are hired and trained as cataloguers for iLumina. After a minimal amount of training, these students have proven to be effective cataloguers.

In some cases, student cataloguers fill out the iLumina contribution form for the resource author. In other cases, authors fill in a minimal amount of metadata and student cataloguers complete the remaining metadata. Student cataloguers also clean up metadata by using the iLumina browse tools to pinpoint anomalies in the data. Under the Open Archives Initiative (OAI), numerous repositories provide a standard protocol for harvesting their metadata. Metadata can be harvested in a variety of standard formats like Dublin Core (the required OAI format) or IMS. After importing metadata from an OAI data provider and working with the metadata for integrations with iLumina services, we realized that opportunities exist to enrich, or add value to the metadata.

One of the services provided by iLumina is a browse facility that provides a profile of the learning resources. Thus, some of the functionality of the iLumina site is built on the expectation that data will be present in certain fields to drive the browse functionality. For example, the browse page provides views of the metadata based on media type and learning resource type. The media type is developed from mapping the data type (essentially a mime type) in /lom/technical/format. In the data we imported into iLumina, however, neither the /lom/technical/format or /lom/educational/learningresourcetype are populated, so the imported data is not visible in these browser views of the metadata. This is not an error (since learning resource type is not a required IMS metadata element), but it highlights differences in the cataloguing of metadata and the risks of building site (browse) functionality based on the expectation that specific (non-mandatory) elements would have value in imported metadata records.

To some extent, the problems that arise from missing elements in imported metadata - or from elements in imported metadata whose values are from different vocabularies used in the importing digital library environment - might be solved if cataloguers were free to modify or enrich imported metadata by adding values for unpopulated elements. The problem is the lack of clarity about the conventions and/or courtesies surrounding the use of, and freedom to change, the shared metadata. Another import problem occurred when the field size of an imported element exceeded the field size in the database.

As a starting point, iLumina can make individual agreements with other repositories that specify under what circumstances iLumina can make changes to the metadata and whether or not iLumina can export the revised metadata. iLumina should be able to roundtrip the original metadata and provide it for export on request. For enriched metadata, iLumina's modification of the metadata could be reflected only in a vague way, via the IMS specification, by adding a meta-metadata entry for validation with a 'known' iLumina entity. There is no mechanism that would track specific modifications. For example, if iLumina fleshed out the metadata by adding previously unpopulated tags or correcting errors after validating values, the meta-metadata entry would only indicate iLumina as the metadata contributor as well as provide a date.

On the browse page, the imported data is revealed under the discipline element. The problem here is not that the imported data omits the discipline element, but rather that it often uses a discipline classification scheme different from that used by iLumina. More generally, the imported metadata had several elements that used different vocabularies from iLumina. Therefore, even though the other repository also uses a controlled vocabulary, since it is a different vocabulary, the metadata does not fully exploit the services provided by iLumina. This is not a problem unique to iLumina and the libraries from which we have imported materials. Currently, although many OAI data providers use controlled vocabularies, there is little standardization on which controlled vocabulary is used [Liu].

This situation complicates the ability of the service provider to develop generic services for data generated by a variety of providers. In light of diverse controlled vocabularies, in the next stage of iLumina development more care will be taken to develop a flexible architecture. The digital library is not equivalent to a digitized collection with information management tools. It is also a series of activities that brings together collections, services, and people in support of the full life cycle of creation, dissemination, use, and preservation of information. A digital library should be a seamless extension of the library that provides faculty and students with access to information in any format that has been evaluated, organized, archived, and preserved.

Access to evolving digital information is provided through global as well as personalized systems and through the services of information professionals. Digital libraries and traditional libraries should not be separate, but should coalesce to accomplish more than either can do independently to serve the user community on the highest order. While their goals are lofty-to improve access to information-they concentrate solely on computer processing of information and ignore those aspects of libraries that can not be preprogrammed or digitized.

The computer scientists who discuss and conduct research and write about DLs are on a noble mission, but because they often isolate themselves from librarians and libraries, the broad range of services and the human environmental factors of the building structure, eludes them. Librarians and information professionals do not try to meet the needs of library users and other information seekers with just one format, even one that is becoming as pervasive as digital. Similarly, few libraries limit their collections to just works available in paper, but also include magnetic tapes with audio and video recordings as well as bits and bytes, and vinyl, and microforms. When a diverse group of teaching, research, and library faculty came together because of our interest in applying for grant funds to support DL research, it quickly became evident that we lacked a common understanding of "library."

Computer Science faculty focused on programming access to digital resources, ignoring the role of subject bibliographers who evaluate and develop collections that meet the needs of the breadth of a research university as well as the needs of degree programs and the specific research needs of the faculty, i.e., collection development and collection management. The classroom, like the library, needs to be thought of as having a component that is independent of time and place. However, they would not eliminate the instructor from the course, but they would consider eliminating the librarian from the library. In both cases the one that resides wholly on a computer or a network of computers is not a complete replacement of the other, but is more effective as a component.

The challenges and opportunities that motivate an advanced DL research initiative should be associated with this broad view of the DL environment. A DL should be a seamless extension of the library that provides scholars with access to information in any format that has been evaluated, organized, archived, and preserved. Access to this evolving collection of digital information is provided through personalized systems as well as through the services of information professionals. The DL adds value and saves time while extending the hours of access. It reduces the need for proximity to information resources, but still emphasizes the quality of those resources. It is a library that can be individually customized and, ultimately, will be easy to use.

Libraries are more than their information resources, their collections, the buildings that house them, the systems that they run on, or the services they provide. Libraries have information professionals that make judgments and interpret user needs; they provide services and resources to people (students, faculty, and others, and organizations). Some traditional library services can be replicated in the DL, partially or wholly, but some cannot be replicated.

4

Archival Collections

The reach of the Internet is increasing a sense of simultaneity as ideas emerging on one side of the world can almost instantaneously be picked up through the Internet and absorbed into the local context by communities on the other. Creative use of new documents no longer involves direct challenges to old ones, with on-line forms replacing hard-copy predecessors. Rather, these new forms appear to reinvigorate the old, extending their useful social life not ending it. Thus, as another example, on-line library catalogues providing abstracts, indexing, and in some cases full texts for print journals have reinforced these journals rather than undermined them.

The journals still remain the best social filter for the flood of writing available on any topic as well as the best repositories of the development of ideas and attitudes. In these realms, digital media, as yet, do not compete. The electronic resources, however, have made using print journals much easier than during the Gutenberg era. There are differences between internal communication — where the stripped down zine, often uninterpretable to outsiders, has proved uniquely powerful — and external communication — which requires more explicit documents like contracts and business letters.

Intercommunal and intracommunal documents are not, however, necessarily two quite different sorts of document. More usually, they involve two different practices built around the same documents. Within communities, documents face the challenge of gaining attention of community members. Between communities they face that challenge and the difficulty of coordinating practice despite different interpretive strategies. The French sociologist Bruno Latour points out that a primary characteristic of documents is their mobility. Documents quickly pass beyond the reach and protection of their maker and have to fend for themselves.

A central challenge, then, is to engage the interests of the community they are intended for. As the number of documents multiplies dramatically and their reach is extended by information technology, the challenge of engaging an intended audience grows too. The central issue here is for the intended audience to be able to recognize documents intended for them. Faced with similar problems, and realizing that books were not universal documents but addressed different audiences, book designers long ago developed numerous strategies that help readers distinguish different kinds of books.

Consequently, books use far more than their title to engage certain audiences and tell others to pass by. In an increasingly crowded attention economy, the challenge of reaching an intended audience accounts for the demand for sophisticated Web-page designers and the importance of autonomous agents on the net that can plant links in strategic sites. Despite this work, with most links and pages, it's still very hard even to make even a reasonable guess at the intended audience. This difficulty may reflect an implicit assumption by many that documents have universal appeal or that content alone will marshal an audience.

Yet if the overall form appears unclear, few will linger over the content, especially given the ease with which links allow people to pass by. Documents that pass successfully between communities need to be able to engage two interpretive strategies and to survive where the recipients can no longer be assumed to share the interpretive assumptions of the members of the originating community. Within a community highly condensed forms of communication, which rely on the shared assumptions of the community, work well. Between communities these must be elaborated, often to the exasperation of the original community, whose members can see the elaboration as redundant. Anyone who has used the Internet much has probably come across the different approaches.

Most ftp sites, which are usually constructed primarily for use within a known community, are almost completely inscrutable — a collection of files with semiliterate names. Successful web sites designed to engage people from different communities have, by contrast, a much more public face. In passing between communities, documents play an important role, bringing people from different groups together to negotiate and coordinate common practices. Such negotiations are particularly significant in institutions, such as bureaucracies and corporations, that comprise many different communities. Here the direction of the institution as a whole depends on the successful outcome of negotiations among its constituent groups, all of whom have particular interests at stake.

Both the means and a willingness to come to a shared understanding are vital to the effectiveness of such institutions. Because documents passing between communities face different interpretive strategies in each one, the challenge of coordinating practice around them is always theoretically and often practically problematic. One result of frequent intercommunal communication may be cross-border communities, groups of people who are, collectively, capable of dealing with the codes of both worlds and of talking a common language among themselves. These groups are essentially bilingual in terms of the two dominant communities their members come from. Institutions can strive to create such groups, but the more effective ones tend to emerge. But intercommunal communication isn't only a matter of comprehension and coordination. Documents are also used to patrol and control. In the first case, documents can patrol community boundaries rather than cross them.

Strange formats, unexplained generic conventions, jargon, abbreviations, allusions, as well as private languages are all examples of ways in which documents keep people out as much as bring them in. More simple than obfuscation, of course, is simple secrecy. Documents are kept from certain eyes. Encryption, blind "carbon" copies, restricted access and so forth, make secrecy quite as prevalent on the Internet as it has been in the world of paper documents. Many Internet sites simply restrict access to registered users. Intercommunal documents can both promote and retard institutional development, depending on whether boundary objects lead to collaboration or control.

Understanding the potential for both is thus particularly important for large institutions. The issue of documents as instruments of power and control is an important one. Much debate around this issue, however, tends to argue that document technologies determine certain social processes — either for good or for ill. While document technology is undoubtedly linked to both, neither of these accounts gives the whole picture. And neither result is inevitable. As Oswyn Murray has suggested, it's more reasonable to think of technology as an enabler with the potential to support various scenarios. Which scenarios will play out, will be the result of a great deal of social work, conflict, coordination, and creativity, conducted around but not determined by the technology. This argument surely holds for the Internet, too.

Some argue it will fulfill social democratic ideals, others that it will undermine civil, political, and economic institutions. Each outcome is no doubt feasible, but the technology alone guarantees neither. The outcome of contemporary social-technological pressures for change, whether for good or for ill, will be the result of social struggle and negotiation. Consequently, the means of negotiation are particularly important. Here, the Internet and related technologies are intriguingly both the forum and the topic of debate. Changes in documentary forms have lead some to foresee a shift from "objects" to "performance."

The journalist John Perry Barlow, for instance, points out that recordings of rock bands are rapidly losing value because they can so easily be pirated. Cheap analog recording devices like the conventional tape recorder produced such poor copies of originals that for most fans it was worth paying to buy a professionally cut disc. Similarly, with print documents it has usually been easier to buy than to copy. But now digital technology makes the production of copies indistinguishable in all essentials from the original, making copying often the cheaper and easier choice. Simultaneously, some claim that written documents are moving from the permanence of old forms to the performance of new ones.

Certainly, notions of "real-time response," "collaborative work," "multi-authored hypertexts," "shared documents," "relational databases," "on-line editing," "continuous up-dates," "interlinked data," "live video links," and other properties suggest that their malleability makes new documents significantly different from old ones. Those who struggled for years with stencils and White Out undoubtedly appreciate the shift from fixed to a different sense of fluid. Nevertheless, it's important not to ignore some counterpressures developing within the new technologies themselves.

While many technologies strive to achieve the immediacy of the conversation, the phone call, and other live links, people occasionally use new technologies to achieve the opposite: to escape that very immediacy. For instance, e-mail and faxes may be used to overcome the delay of "snail mail." But people also use them for messages that could be delivered by the more conversational phone call. While voice mail allows us to leave messages for people we cannot reach, occasionally people use it to avoid reaching someone they would prefer not to talk to. Similarly, people allow an answering machine to pick up and announce "I'm not here, now," even though "I" is indeed "here" and listening in, just to add a little delay between message and response. Practices like these are not simply desperate responses to the burdensome pressures of modern life or information overload.

They are as much innovative ways to reintroduce time and physical traces into what would otherwise be immediate and ephemeral exchanges. At the very least, they suggest that delay and fixity may be just as important to all of us as immediacy, mutability, and indivisibility. While everyone can benefit from technology capable of overcoming separations of space and time and the convergence of producer and consumer, it seems people are beginning to appreciate how important these distinctions can be.

New technologies help us to transcend burdensome barriers of space and time. But, in part through the improvisations of users, the same technologies are also valued for their ability to reinject both space and time into communication. Written forms have long done this. In general, new technologies have minimized the technological separation of producer and consumer. It is a shift of some significance that the computer we read on is also the one we write on, whereas the book we read is very different from the manuscript we write.

This single medium makes the intertextual relationship of reading and writing more than an abstruse intellectual concept. Changes in technology make it clear that we can no longer take for granted a correspondence between social purpose and technological resources. Now a trace may appear where it wasn't expected, or disappear when it was taken for granted. This change doesn't insist we simply leap from product to performance, renounce fixity and embrace transience, become digital where once we were material. Rather, it suggests that we should consider a symbiosis between the two.

As the social roles of continuity and change, of areas of stasis and areas open to dynamic revision, are better understood, social institutions may develop around this joint capacity in intriguing ways, much as libraries developed their usefulness out of the juxtaposition of fixed individual texts combined to an ever expanding collection and a continually revised set of interlinked catalogues. This interplay between fixity and fluidity, formerly possible only on the scale of collections may now become a central feature of individual documents. Since the Web explosion of the 1990s, a wide variety of digital collections have emerged on the Internet.

While digital collections may differ in content or structure, they all share one commonality—the need for metadata. Frequently described as "data about data," metadata is a critical component of all digital collections. Metadata facilitates the discovery and retrieval of information, it provides for resource presentation and navigation, and it contains the information needed to preserve digital data files. While several digital collections of books have been created for the Internet, it is only recently that libraries and archives have begun to digitize archival collections for Web delivery.

A search of the Internet for similar archival projects revealed that online archival collections were most often presented in one of two ways: as an online exhibition or as a simple database of independent archival documents. Following the "exhibition" method, institutions presented archival collections online in much the same way as they would present an exhibition of physical materials; narrative descriptions or transcriptions of items were presented with links to digital representations of those items.

These Web sites tended to be small in size and highlighted materials that were considered important. The second approach followed by many institutions was to create a database-driven Web site with basic search and browse techniques. In these digital repositories, each archival document was treated as a separate entity and basic descriptive metadata elements such as title, author, and date were given for each item. Although the Barren Lands project team found aspects of both methods of delivery appealing, they decided that neither approach was fully compatible with their vision of the project. While the "exhibition" approach provided an abundance of narrative contextual information, this method was deemed impracticable for the size of the digital collection. Similarly, a strict database approach was also not favoured, as it did not retain the contextual linkages between the documents.

In most digital collections, each book, article, map, etc. is considered to be an independent digital object. The Barren Lands project was different in that the archival collection consisted of many documents that were inter-related with each other. For example, in the case of J.B. Tyrrell's correspondence, the meaning and significance of an individual letter can only be understood if it is read within the context of a series of letters. It was essential that these natural connections be retained within the digital environment. At the same time, it was necessary that each document remain an independent digital object for the purpose of resource discovery and retrieval.

Problems with the pre-existing descriptive metadata were three-fold: first, the metadata was not in electronic format; second, the metadata did not contain all of the necessary descriptive information; and third, the archival materials were not described consistently according to archival descriptive standards. Because of these problems, the project team decided to re-describe both collections according to the Canadian descriptive standard, the Rules for Archival Description (RAD). Once the descriptive metadata was complete, it was necessary to encode this information in a standard data structure.

In order to retain the relationships between archival materials, the project team adopted the Encoded Archival Description (EAD) data structure standard, which is jointly administered by the Society of American Archivists and the Library of Congress. EAD is a non-proprietary standard in the form of a Standard Generalized Markup Language (SGML) and Extensible Markup Language (XML) Document Type Definition (DTD). Developed specifically for archival finding aids, the EAD standard has the ability to accurately represent the multilevel nature of archives in a machine-readable format.

Consequently, the EAD standard facilitates access by allowing users to "drill down" into an archival finding aid, beginning at the fonds or collection level description down to the descriptions of individual items. In the Barren Lands project, the descriptions of the J.B. Tyrrell and James W. Tyrrell fonds were encoded using the XML version of the EAD DTD. In these multi-level records, users are provided with descriptions of the entire fonds, the various series of documents that make up the fonds, and file level descriptions (e.g. descriptions of photo albums and letterbooks) if they exist.

Within the description of each series or file containing digitized objects, a link is made from the title of the object to a separate item level description. While EAD does provide the capability to describe archival materials down to the item level of description, the project team decided that within the context of the project, the standard was unsuitable for that purpose. Item level descriptions could not be included in the EAD description for three reasons. First, the EAD standard did not provide for the inclusion of all the required descriptive metadata elements for item level records. Second, EAD did not have the capability to embed the OCR or rekeyed text within the item level description. And third, the standard did not allow for the incorporation of the structural metadata needed for the project.

The Barren Lands project consists of a variety of documentary forms, all of which needed to be handled in a slightly different manner. For example, published reports required OCR, manuscript letters and newspaper clippings needed to be manually re-keyed, and no additional work was required for maps and photographs. To simplify the development of the digital collection, it was necessary to create a method for quickly identifying the document type for each digital object. As a form of structural metadata, the file naming structure was used to distinguish between documentary forms. Directories were created for each type of document, such as letters, diaries, published text, maps, photographs, and so on.

Then, as each archival document was scanned, a unique identifier, containing a letter to identify the documentary form followed by a five-digit number, was recorded in a relational database. The project team felt strongly that no semantic information be included in the file naming system as this type of information would likely become confusing rather than helpful in the long run. This file-naming system not only ensured that we had a simple, well-organized repository for the images, it also allowed the team to quickly identify which image files required OCR and which files needed rekeying.

Collecting an adequate amount of structural metadata is critical to this linking process. In the Barren Lands project, structural information such as unique identifiers, page sequence numbers, page numbers as stated on the document, special features such as tables of contents and indexes, and other relevant information was collected in a relational database at the point of scanning. Some descriptive metadata relating to individual pages of the digital object, such as titles of maps or illustrations and content dates were also recorded in the database. In addition to descriptive and structural metadata, the Barren Lands project team also captured administrative or technical metadata during the scanning process.

As each image was scanned, information relating to the source type, file format, scanning date, and scanner was captured in a relational database. Other types of administrative metadata, such as file compression format, image resolution, and image height and width were captured in the TIFF tags associated with each image. Although this administrative information was not used in the construction of the digital collection, it was important to capture this technical information just in case it was needed in the future. Adobe Portable Document Format (PDF) is a widely used standard for electronic document distribution worldwide in many institutional settings. Much of its popularity comes from its ability to faithfully encode both the text and the visual appearance of source documents, preserving their fonts, formatting, colors, and graphics.

PDF files can be viewed, navigated, and printed with a free Adobe Acrobat Reader, available on all major computing platforms. PDF has many applications and is commonly used to publish government, public, and academic documents. Many of the electronic journals and other digital resources acquired by libraries are published in PDF format. As libraries grow more dependent on electronic resources, they need to consider how they can preserve these resources for the long term. Many libraries retain back runs of print journals that are over 100 years old, and which are still consulted by researchers.

No digital technology has lasted nearly that long, and many data formats have already become obsolete and not easily readable in a much shorter time period. PDF is a platform-independent document format developed by Adobe as a follow-up to its Postscript language. Although Postscript was designed specifically for printing, PDF is meant to support on-line, secure, interactive use, as well as printing. PDF combines attributes of structured text formats and traditional image formats, so that a document can be used both in terms of its text and in terms of its "look" on-screen or on the page.

This allows PDF readers not only to display and print documents, but also to carry out text-oriented operations such as searching for text strings, or cutting-and-pasting. Like Postscript, PDF is, at its heart, a page description language. However, unlike Postscript, it is more of a declarative than a procedural language. This makes PDF easier to manipulate and analyze than Postscript. As with Postscript, the specification of PDF is openly and freely published, but Adobe controls its development. Three revisions of PDF have been published to date, with PDF 1.3 the latest version for which specifications are published. So far, all of the revisions for which specifications have been published are backward-compatible. Because the basic standard is public, Adobe does not have a monopoly on PDF tools, and third parties have developed tools that also work with PDF.

However, because the standard is complex, and changes from time to time, much of the support for the format, as well as the tools that are considered to set the standard for PDF use, comes from Adobe. A typical PDF document consists of a sequence of pages, each of which includes data that indicates what should be "drawn" on a particular page. This data includes text, font specifications, margins, layout, graphical elements, and background and text colors. A PDF file does not always contain the full glyph specification of characters in the document, but at least includes the name of the fonts used and specifies the space all characters will occupy.

PDF includes metadata on the document, specifying things such as page size, page numbering, and a structured table of contents. Add-ons, such as hyperlinks, forms, and even pieces of scripting code in Java or Postscript that control dynamic displays or the user interface, can also be included. Not all PDF documents encode the text of a document directly. It is possible to embed images of a page in PDF, so that a picture of text is encoded but not the text itself. Some scanners, for instance, can output this "uninterpreted" form of PDF.

Such uninterpreted PDF files tend to be much larger than PDF files that encode text directly as characters, and text-oriented operations such as searching and textual copying and pasting are not supported by these files. Still, some libraries have produced these large, uninterpreted PDF files for their users as a way of quickly and inexpensively distributing scans of print materials. For applications such as electronic reserves, where scanned copies are typically not kept beyond a semester or two, this form of PDF can be acceptable.

Some programs also exist that will attempt to recognize whatever text they can in a scanned PDF document, and replace the images of this text with a briefer encoding of the characters and fonts. Such programs tend to produce "hybrid" PDF files where encoded text strings in appropriate fonts are positioned inside page images, and any unrecognized characters are kept on the page in the form of images. Although such PDF files can be smaller than those that consist only of uninterpreted page images, they also often have only partial, and choppy, encoding of their underlying text, because recognition programs typically cannot recognize 100% of the text in a typical page scan.

Moreover, misrecognized characters may even introduce errors into the "hybrid" document. PDF was originally designed for 8-bit character sets (which can support at most 256 characters). Some limited support for Unicode also exists, but the format has not yet taken full advantage of Unicode's capabilities. One consequence of this design is that some multilingual documents may be represented by switching between different, sometimes customized, 256-character sets. Alternatively, some "exotic" characters may be represented as small images, rather than as text. Unlike XML, PDF was not originally designed for arbitrary structural annotations, although the last revision of PDF includes some facilities for user-defined structural markup.

PDF is a less efficient format for text analysis than purely text-based formats such as XML or HTML, and readers have noted that searching for words within a PDF viewer can be noticeably slower than searching for words in an HTML viewer. The central role that appearance plays in PDF is both a strength and a weakness; it allows publishers to specify exactly how they want a document to look, but it also makes it difficult for users to reformat or repaginate the document if that would be better for them. PDF includes facilities for encrypting content, or directing that a document not be printable. It is possible to use encryption so that a document cannot be decrypted without a password.

However, once the document is decrypted, it is possible, in theory, to make an unlocked copy that can be freely copied, read, or printed. Even if it is technically possible to do so, though, legal and practical restrictions to doing so may still exist. As data formats go, PDF is particularly likely to be supported for a long time, and to spawn migration paths. This has been the case with Adobe's Postscript, which is now an industry standard, and for which PDF itself can be seen as the next step in migration. Adobe is highly invested in the success of PDF, but even if Adobe fails or abruptly changes course, a community of third-party tools for handling PDF has started to emerge.

PDF is used widely by many well-funded bodies so there should be widespread support for using and migrating PDF, should Adobe fail to provide adequate support for the format.

Even so, it is likely that PDF will one day be superseded by another format. It may be a successor format, or it may be a completely different format that users prefer over PDF. Hence, it is necessary to have migration strategies planned for PDF. Currently, there is no other format that can encompass all of the features of PDF in a form that standard tools can interpret.

However, it is possible to easily migrate two important aspects of PDF documents: the page images and the text. These aspects may be sufficient for the types of preservation that libraries require. Any program that displays or prints PDF files in effect converts PDF pages into static page images. Most page image formats are pixel-oriented, where pictures are encoded using a grid with each grid cell (known as a pixel) associated with a particular color (or with no added color).

Some image formats, including PDF and Postscript, are stroke-oriented, encoded with instructions about lines to plot, regions to color, and text to place. They can also include instructions to embed pixel-oriented images at specified locations. Pixel-oriented formats have a well-understood mathematical representation, making them easy to migrate. Stroke-oriented image formats are not so standardized. They can encode information about the structure of a picture, such as the lines that are drawn in it, that can only be approximated to a certain resolution in purely pixel-oriented formats.

On the other hand, since pixel-oriented formats can typically accommodate very fine resolutions, an image converted from a stroke-oriented format to a pixel-oriented format at fine enough resolution can be visually indistinguishable from its original. Third-party software exists to turn PDF both into Postscript, and into pixel-oriented image formats. Converting from PDF to most image formats loses direct encoding of the text. Structural information and other PDF extras would also be lost in such a conversion.PDF can also be converted into text, at least when the text (rather than pictures of the text) has been directly encoded in PDF files. Formatting and layout information would be lost in a straight text conversion, and the text conversion of certain pages with complex layout may not always be read in "logical" reading order, without human intervention.

For example, if a PDF encoding of a two-column page first renders the left column and then the right, a simple text extraction from the PDF will yield a readable text transcription. On the other hand, if the PDF encoding goes back and forth between the two columns, or renders the right column before the left column, programs may have a much more difficult time reconstructing the text in the order it was meant to be read. Different PDF-generating programs may be more or less accommodating about rendering PDF text in a logical reading order. A straight text conversion would also lose structural information and other PDF extras, as well non-textual items such as pictures, diagrams, and possibly equations.

However, it is possible to write conversions to HTML or XML that would include a "table of contents" header that incorporated the structure of the PDF document, and that would preserve certain types of PDF hyperlinks. Text in non-European languages may also be difficult to migrate correctly, because of the previously-described limitations of PDF's support for Unicode, unless a standard set of well-defined fonts, with widely available specifications, is used to represent non-European characters. Although it is possible to migrate the appearance of PDF files, or the text, migrating both of them into a single document would be more difficult.

The only other formats commonly used to specify both the text and the appearance of documents are word-processor formats, and those tend to be proprietary, system-dependent, and more ephemeral than PDF itself is likely to be. Converting to these formats may also lead to subtly different appearances, depending on the implementation of the word processing program. RTF (Rich Text Format) may be the best target for word-processor-oriented conversions at this time, though it is far from a perfect choice. Even if it is infeasible to migrate both the text and the look of PDF into a single document, it may still be possible to migrate PDF documents into a presentation that allows one to switch between text-oriented and image-oriented views of the same document. In theory, it is possible to convert all of the information in a PDF file into an XML format with appropriate tags and attributes.

However, at present there is no standard XML format used for representing PDF-like documents. Unless such a format were standardized, and then supported with software, converting to XML might be largely an academic exercise, since no software currently exists to interpret such a format, and software developed especially to interpret the new XML format could probably just as easily interpret the information in its original PDF form. On the other hand, an XML-based form of PDF might be easier for existing XML-based search and analysis software to process. Interactive features of PDF would be harder to migrate, and Postscript, JavaScript, or other scripting snippets may be impractical to migrate on a large scale, because it is much harder to migrate program code than data.

Libraries may want to avoid committing to preserving these "extra" features of PDF files, except in carefully limited cases. Certain preservation techniques, such as integrity checks and backups, are necessary to preserve any type of digital information. In addition to establishing standards for acquired PDF files, institutions may also find it useful to have tools to automatically check incoming PDF files and warn of any unexpected PDF constructs appearing in them. Such automated checks could be used to automatically flag malformed PDF files, or files that failed to meet institutional encoding standards, while avoiding expensive manual checks on all incoming files.

However, writing such tools, or buying suitable tools developed by third parties, may also be nontrivial. Institutions with a common interest in preserving PDF may wish to collaborate on the development of such tools. Some software tools exist for extracting text and images from PDF files, and can be used for migration. Especially useful are tools that can be invoked automatically without human interaction.

Some commercial conversion tools exist as well. Further research and development may be necessary to ensure that these conversion tools will correctly migrate all of the PDF files of interest to institutions. At present, image-based conversion does not appear difficult to complete and verify, but automatic extraction of text, due to the nature of text layout, may not always be perfect. One possible technique for increasing the reliability of automatically extracted text would be similar to the "double-keying" principle for data entry: run two independently developed text extractors against the same PDF file, and flag points where the extractors yield different text in a different order.

It remains to be seen how useful this technique would be in practice. It may be useful to run migration routines on new PDF files as soon as they are acquired, even if migrated files are not yet required. After the migration is attempted, checks could be run to see if any problems were detected in the process. Institutions do not necessarily have to keep migrated copies of the files, as long as they have verified that migration works, and they preserve the original PDF files and the programs that will perform the migration. If one were being especially careful, though, it may be advisable to save alternative forms immediately, not just in digital form, but also in print form. Although such practices would further decrease the probability of total loss of PDF documents, they also may substantially increase the per-volume cost of preserving these documents. It is probably sufficient to have trusted methods of backup, integrity checking, mirroring, and migrating.

Dynamic electronic journals are often defined as e-journals in which the content changes frequently. In reality, this is not yet happening much. E-journals may publish articles as they are ready, without waiting for a whole issue's worth of articles, but this change is sequential addition. Dynamic e-journals can be defined as those that contain moving elements or make elements move. Moving elements include, for example, audio and video clips as well as animations. Because moving elements are not printable, libraries can no longer rely on printing the e-journals as a primary preservation strategy.

Microfilm and microform are likewise static and cannot accommodate moving elements either. We will refer to these as "dynamic elements." E-journals that can make elements move typically include embedded software that enables movement, or scripts and programs that render content on the fly. We will refer to this sort of dynamism as functionality. Because one cannot print dynamic e-journals to preserve them, the task at hand is to define new ways of preserving content that makes no sense without these constituent, dynamic aspects.

Cataloging, indexing, and retrieving the kind of content that cannot be rendered without interactive functionality are particularly vexing hurdles, especially if the content changes with every user's instantiation of that content. Dynamic electronic journals are a natural outgrowth of Internet and Web technologies. The electronic journals were born in Web environments and are meant to be rendered and displayed in current Web environments. However we preserve them, for the time being they must also be Web accessible.

In the future, it is likely that electronic material will be rendered in other digital (and perhaps even non-digital) environments. Of course, besides dynamic elements and functionalities, dynamic e-journals contain text and other intellectually significant elements. The long-term preservation of e-journals will require a large repository, replete with ingest functions, search engine, and display mechanisms. In order for a digital store of this magnitude and complexity to be accessed many years from now, it would have to be exercised, that is, put to use to verify the data's integrity, to insure the functioning of all mechanisms and the usefulness of the metadata, etc.

The Open Archival Information System (OAIS) Reference Model developed by the ISO Consultative Committee for Space Data Systems addresses this issue by encapsulating specific metadata as needed for each object type in a consistent data model. The Long Term Environmental Research (LTER) Network has developed mechanisms for "fitting" its network-specific metadata information into the broader scheme of the Federal Geographic Data Committee content standard for geographic data and other standards related to ecology. For those archives that do not copy the digital material immediately into the archive, the movement of material from server to server or from directory to directory on the network, resulting in a change in the URL, is problematic.

The use of the server as the location identifier can result in a lack of persistence over time both for the source object and any linked objects. Despite possible problems, most archives continue to use the URL when referencing the location for the digital object. However, there are some projects that are changing this practice. The OCLC archive uses PURLs, persistent identifiers to which the changeable URL is mapped.

The American Chemical Society uses the Digital Object Identifier for its journal articles and also maintains the original Manuscript Number assigned to the item at the beginning of the publication process. A multifaceted identification system is used by the American Astronomical Society (AAS). Name resolution is used instead of URLs. In addition, the AAS uses astronomy's standard identifier, called a "Bibcode", which has been in use for fifteen years. In the spring of 1999, AAS added PubRef numbers; other identifiers can be added as needed to maintain links.

The reference model addresses a full range of archival information preservation functions including ingest, archival storage, data management, access, and dissemination. It also addresses the migration of digital information to new media and forms, the data models used to represent the information, the role of software in information preservation, and the exchange of digital information among archives. It identifies both internal and external interfaces to the archive functions, and it identifies a number of high-level services at these interfaces. It provides various illustrative examples and some ,best practice' recommendations.

It defines a minimal set of responsibilities for an archive to be called an OAIS, and it also defines a maximal archive to provide a broad set of useful terms and concepts. A tremendous growth in computational power, and in networking bandwidth and connectivity, has resulted in an explosion in the number of organizations making digital information available.

Transactions among all types of organizations are being conducted using digital forms that are taking the place of more traditional media such as paper. Preserving information in digital forms is much more difficult than preserving information in forms such as paper and film. This is not only a problem for traditional archives, but also for many organizations that have never thought of themselves as performing an archival function. It is expected that this reference model, by establishing minimum requirements for an OAIS archive along with a set of archival concepts, will provide a common framework from which to view archival challenges, particularly as they relate to digital information. This should enable more organizations to understand the issues and take the proper steps to ensure Long Term information preservation.

It should also provide a basis for more standardization and, therefore, a larger market that vendors can support in meeting archival requirements. The term, archive' has come to be used to refer to a wide variety of storage and preservation functions and systems. Traditional archives are understood as facilities or organizations which preserve records, originally generated by or for a government organization, institution, or corporation, for access by public or private communities.

The archive accomplishes this task by taking ownership of the records, ensuring that they are understandable to the accessing community, and managing them so as to preserve their information content and authenticity. Historically, these records have been in such forms as books, papers, maps, photographs, and film, which can be read directly by humans, or read with the aid of simple optical magnification and scanning aids. The major focus for preserving this information has been to ensure that they are on media with long-term stability and that access to this media is carefully controlled. The explosive growth of information in digital forms has posed a severe challenge not only for traditional archives and their information providers, but also for many other organizations in the government, commercial and non-profit sectors.

These organizations are finding, or will find, that they need to take on the information preservation functions typically associated with traditional archives because digital information is easily lost or corrupted. The pace of technology evolution is causing some hardware and software systems to become obsolete in a matter of a few years, and these changes can put severe pressure on the ability of the related data structures or formats to continue effective representation of the full information desired.

Because much of the supporting information necessary to preserve this information is more easily available or only available at the time when the original information is produced, these organizations need to be active participants in the long-term preservation effort, and they need to follow the principles espoused in this OAIS reference model to ensure that the information can be preserved for the Long Term. Participation in these efforts will minimize the lifecycle costs and enable effective long-term preservation of the information. The explosion of computer processing power and digital media has resulted in many systems where the Producer role and the archive role are the responsibility of the same entity.

These systems, which are sometimes known as Active Archives, should subscribe to the goals of Long Term Preservation discussed in this document. The design process must realize that some of the Long Term Preservation activities may conflict with the goals of rapid production and dissemination of products to Consumers. The designers and architects of such systems should document the solutions that have been reached. A major purpose of this reference model is to facilitate a much wider understanding of what is required to preserve and access information for the Long Term.

To avoid confusion with simple ,bit storage' functions, the reference model defines an Open Archival Information System (OAIS) which performs a long-term information preservation and access function. An OAIS archive is one that intends to preserve information for access and use by a

Designated Community. It includes archives that have to keep up with steady input streams of information as well as those that experience primarily aperiodic inputs. It includes archives that provide a wide variety of sophisticated access services as well as those that support only the simplest types of requests. The OAIS model recognizes the already highly distributed nature of digital information holdings and the need for local implementations of effective policies and procedures supporting information preservation.

This allows, in principle, a wide variety of organizational arrangements, including various roles for traditional archives, in achieving this preservation. It is expected that organizations attempting to preserve information will find that using OAIS terms and concepts will assist them in achieving their information preservation goals. Management is the role played by those who set overall OAIS policy as one component in a broader policy domain. In other words, Management control of the OAIS is only one of Management's responsibilities.

Management is not involved in day-to-day archive operations. OAIS archives are not shown explicitly. Such archives may establish particular agreements among themselves consistent with Management and OAIS needs. Some archives may interact with a particular archive for a variety of reasons and with varying degrees of formalism for any pre-arranged agreements. One OAIS may take the role of Producer to another OAIS; an example is when the responsibility for preserving a type of information is to be moved to this other archive. One OAIS may take the role of Consumer to another OAIS; an example is when the first OAIS decides to rely on the other OAIS for a type of information it seldom needs and chooses not to preserve locally. Such reliance should have some formal basis that includes the requirement for communication between the archives of any policy changes that might affect this reliance.

A person, or system, can be said to have a Knowledge Base, which allows them to understand received information. For example, a person who has a Knowledge Base that includes an understanding of English will be able to read, and understand, an English text. Information is defined as any type of knowledge that can be exchanged, and this information is always expressed (i.e., represented) by some type of data. For example, the information in a hardcopy book is typically expressed by the observable characters (the data) which, when they are combined with a knowledge of the language used (the Knowledge Base), are converted to more meaningful information. If the recipient does not already include English in its Knowledge Base, then the English text (the data) needs to be accompanied by English dictionary and grammar information (i.e., Representation Information) in a form that is understandable using the recipient's Knowledge Base.

Similarly, the information stored within a CD-ROM file is expressed by the bits (the data) it contains which, when they are combined with the Representation Information for those bits, are converted to more meaningful information as long as the Representation Information is understandable using the recipient's Knowledge Base. For example, assume the bits represent an ASCII table of numbers giving the coordinates of a location on the Earth measured in degrees latitude and East longitude. The Representation Information will typically include the definition of ASCII together with descriptions of the format of the numbers and their locations in the file, their definitions as latitude and longitude, and the definition of their units as degrees. For digital information, this means the OAIS must clearly identify the bits and the Representation Information that applies to those bits.

This required transparency to the bit level is a distinguishing feature of digital information preservation, and it runs counter to object-oriented concepts which try to hide these implementation issues. This presents a significant challenge to the preservation of digital information. As a further complication, the recursive nature of Representation Information, which typically is composed of its own data and other Representation Information, typically leads to a network of Representation Information objects. Since a key purpose of an OAIS is to preserve information for a Designated Community, the OAIS must understand the Knowledge Base of its Designated Community to understand the minimum Representation Information that must be maintained. The OAIS should then make a decision between maintaining the minimum Representation Information needed for its Designated Community, or maintaining a larger amount of Representation Information that may allow understanding by a larger Consumer community with a less specialized Knowledge Base.

Over time, evolution of the Designated Community's Knowledge Base may require updates to the Representation Information to ensure continued understanding. As a practical matter, software is used to access the Information Object, and it will incorporate some understanding of the network of Representation Information objects involved. However, this software should not be used as rationale for avoiding identifying and gathering readily understandable

Representation Information that defines the Information Object, because it is harder to preserve working software than to preserve information in digital or hardcopy forms. The OAIS reference model emphasizes the preservation of information content.

As digital technology evolves, multimedia technology and the dependency on complex interplay between the data and presentation technologies will lead some organizations to require that the look and feel of the original presentation of the information be preserved. This type of preservation requirement may necessitate that the software programs and interfaces used to access the data be preserved. This problem may be further complicated by the proprietary nature of some of the software. Various techniques for preserving the look and feel of information access are currently the subject of research and prototyping.

These techniques, which include hardware level emulation, emulation of various common service APIs, and the development of a virtual machine, investigate the preservation of the original bit steam and software across technology. Though the OAIS reference model does not focus on these emerging techniques, it should provide architectural basis for the prototyping and comparison of these techniques. An Information Package is a conceptual container of two types of information called Content Information and Preservation Description Information (PDI).

The Content Information and PDI are viewed as being encapsulated and identifiable by the Packaging Information. The resulting package is viewed as being discoverable by virtue of the Descriptive Information. The Content Information is that information which is the original target of preservation.

It consists of the Content Data Object (Physical Object or Digital Object, i.e., bits) and its associated Representation Information needed to make the Content Data Object understandable to the Designated Community. For example, the CDO may be an image that is provided as the bit content of one CD-ROM file together with other files, on the same CD-ROM, that contain Representation Information.

Only after the Content Information has been clearly defined can an assessment of the Preservation Description Information be made. The Preservation Description Information applies to the Content Information and is needed to preserve the Content Information, to ensure it is clearly identified, and to understand the environment in which the Content Information was created. The Preservation Description Information is divided into four types of preserving information called

— Provenance,

— Context,

— Reference, and

— Fixity.

Provenance describes the source of the Content Information, who has had custody of it since its origination, and its history.

Context describes how the Content Information relates to other information outside the Information Package. For example, it would describe why the Content Information was produced, and it may include a description of how it relates to another Content Information object that is available.

Reference provides one or more identifiers, or systems of identifiers, by which the Content Information may be uniquely identified. Examples include an ISBN number for a book, or a set of attributes that distinguish one instance of Content Information from another.

Fixity provides a wrapper, or protective shield, that protects the Content Information from undocumented alteration. For example, it may involve a check sum over the Content Information of a digital Information Package.

OAIS may provide information to Consumers that does not include all the Representation Information or all the PDI with the associated Content Information being disseminated. These variants are referred to as the Submission Information Package (SIP), the Archival Information Package (AIP), and the Dissemination Information Package (DIP). The Submission Information Package (SIP) is that package that is sent to an OAIS by a Producer. Its form and detailed content are typically negotiated between the Producer and the OAIS.

Most SIPs will have some Content Information and some PDI, but it may require several SIPs to provide a complete set of Content Information and associated PDI to form an AIP. A single SIP may contain information that is to be included in several AIPs. The Packaging Information will always be present in some form. Within the OAIS one or more SIPs are transformed into one or more Archival Information Packages (AIP) for preservation. The AIP has a complete set of PDI for the associated Content Information.

The Packaging Information of the AIP will conform to OAIS internal standards, and it may vary as it is managed by the OAIS. In response to a request, the OAIS provides all or a part of an AIP to a Consumer in the form of a Dissemination Information Package (DIP). The DIP may also include collections of AIPs, and it may or may not have complete PDI. The Packaging Information will necessarily be present in some form so that the Consumer can clearly distinguish the information that was requested. Depending on the dissemination media and Consumer requirements, the Packaging Information may take various forms.

The first contact between the OAIS and the Producer is a request that the OAIS preserve the data products created by the Producer. This contact may be initiated by the OAIS, the Producer or Management. The Producer establishes a Submission Agreement with the OAIS, which identifies the SIPs to be submitted and may span any length of time for this submission. Some Submission Agreements will reflect a mandatory requirement to provide information to the OAIS, while others will reflect a voluntary offering of information.

Even in the case where no formal Submission Agreement exists, such as a World Wide Web (WWW) site, a virtual Submission Agreement may exist specifying the file formats and the general subject matter the site will accept. Within the Submission Agreement, one or more Data Submission Sessions are specified. There may be significant time gaps between the Data Submission Sessions. A Data Submission Session will contain one or more SIPs anu may be a delivered set of media or a single telecommunications session. The Data Submission Session content is based on a data model negotiated between the OAIS and the Producer in the Submission Agreement.

This data model identifies the logical components of the SIP (e.g., the Content Information, PDI, Packaging Information, and Descriptive Information) that are to be provided and how (and whether) they are represented in each

Data Submission Session. All data deliveries within a Submission Agreement are recognized as belonging to that Submission Agreement and will generally have a consistent data model, which is specified in the Submission Agreement. For example, a Data Submission Session may consist of a set of Content Information corresponding to a set of observations, which are carried by a set of files on a CD-ROM.

The Preservation Description Information is split between two other files. All of these files need Representation Information which must be provided in some way. The CD-ROM and its directory/file structure are the Packaging Information, which provides encapsulation and identification of the Content Information and PDI in the Data Submission Session.

The Submission Agreement indicates how the Representation Information for each file is to be provided, how the CD-ROM is to be recognized, how the Packaging Information will be used to identify and encapsulate the SIP Content Information and PDI, and how frequently Data Submission Sessions (e.g., one per month for two years) will occur. It also gives other needed information such as access restrictions to the data. Each SIP in a Data Submission Session is expected to meet minimum OAIS requirements for completeness. However, in some cases multiple SIPs may need to be received before an acceptable AIP can be formed and fully ingested within the OAIS.

In other cases, a single SIP may contain data to be included in many AIPs. A Submission Agreement also includes, or references, the procedures and protocols by which an OAIS will either verify the arrival and completeness of a

Data Submission Session with the Producer or question the Producer on the contents of the Data Submission Session. There are many types of interactions between the Consumer and the OAIS. These interactions include questions to a help desk, requests for literature, catalog searches, orders and order status requests.

The ordering process is of special interest to the OAIS Reference Model, since it deals with the flow of archive holdings between the OAIS and the Consumer. The Consumer establishes an Order Agreement with the OAIS for information. This information may currently exist in the archive or be expected to be ingested in the future. The Order Agreement may span any length of time, and under it one or more Data Dissemination Sessions may take place. A Data Dissemination Session may involve the transfer of a set of media or a single telecommunications session.

The Order Agreement identifies one or more AIPs of interest, how those AIPs are to be transformed and mapped into Dissemination Information Packages (DIPs) and how those DIPs will be packaged in a Data Dissemination Session. The Order Agreement will also specify other needed information such as delivery information (e.g., name or mailing address), and any pricing agreements as applicable.

Mandatory responsibilities that an organization must discharge in order to operate an OAIS archive. The OAIS must: i) Negotiate for and accept appropriate information from information Producers. ii) Obtain sufficient control of the information provided to the level needed to ensure Long-Term Preservation. iii) Determine, either by itself or in conjunction with other parties, which communities should become the Designated Community and, therefore, should be able to understand the information provided. iv) Ensure that the information to be preserved is Independently Understandable to the Designated Community.

In other words, the community should be able to understand the information without needing the assistance of the experts who produced the information. An organization operating an OAIS will have established some criteria that aids in determining the types of information that it is willing to, or it is required to, accept. These criteria may include, among others, subject matter, information source, degree of uniqueness or originality, and the nature of the techniques used to represent the information (e.g., physical media, digital media, format). The information may, in general, be submitted using a wide variety of common and not-so-common forms, such as books, documents, maps, data sets, and moon rocks using a variety of communication paths including networks, mail, and special delivery.

The OAIS negotiates with the Producer to ensure it acquires appropriate Content Information and associated PDI for its mission and the Designated Community. Considerable iteration may be required to agree on the right information to be submitted, and to get it into forms acceptable to the OAIS. For example, this may include digitizing audio or video material, or scanning text.

The OAIS should extract, or otherwise obtain, sufficient Descriptive Information to assist the Designated Community in finding the Content Information of interest. It also should ensure that the information meets all OAIS internal standards. It is important for the OAIS to recognize the separation that can exist between physical ownership or possession of Content Information and ownership of intellectual property rights in this information. If it has created the information and is the legal owner of the Content Information, the OAIS already has the independence to do what is required to preserve the information and make it available. When acquiring the Content Information from any other producer or entity, the OAIS must ensure that there is a legally valid transfer agreement that either transfers intellectual property rights to the OAIS, or clearly specifies the rights granted to the OAIS and any limitations imposed by the rightsholder(s).

The OAIS must ensure that its subsequent actions to preserve the information and make it available conform with these rights and limitations. When the OAIS does not acquire the intellectual property rights, the agreement should specify what involvement the rightsholder(s) will have in preservation, management or release of the information. In most cases, it will be preferable for the OAIS to negotiate an agreement that specifies the rightsholder(s) requirements and authorizes the OAIS to act in accordance with those requirements without active involvement of the rightsholder(s) in individual cases. The OAIS must assume sufficient control over the Content Information and Preservation Description Information so that it is able to preserve it for the Long Term.

These issues occur when the OAIS acts as a custodian. An OAIS should understand the copyright concepts and applicable laws prior to accepting copyright materials into the OAIS. It can establish guidelines for ingestion of information and rules for dissemination and duplication of the information when necessary. It is beyond the scope of this document to provide details of national and international copyright laws. Authority to modify Representation Information: Although the Fixity information within the

Preservation Description Information of an AIP ensures that the Content Information-related bits have not been altered, there will come a time when Content Information bits are not in a form that is convenient for the Consumers from the Designated Community. The Content Information bits may be fully documented in available hardcopy forms, so technically the information has not been lost, but practically the information has become inaccessible.

The OAIS needs the authority to migrate the Content Information to new representation forms. If it is acting as a custodian, it may need to seek additional permission to make such changes. If the information is copyrighted, the OAIS should already have negotiated permission to make the changes needed to meet preservation objectives. It may employ subject matter experts, from outside the OAIS, to help ensure that information is not lost. Ideally, when this situation arises, both the original AIPs and new AIPs will be retained.

An OAIS may establish a variety of agreements with other organizations to assist in its preservation objectives. For example, it may establish an agreement with another OAIS so that it does not have to preserve all the common Representation Information objects related to its Content Information objects. Agreements with other organizations should be monitored to be sure they are being followed and remain useful. The submission, or planned submission, of Content Information and associated PDI requires a determination as to who the expected Consumers, or Designated Community, of this information will be. This is necessary in order to determine if the information, as represented, will be understandable to that community.

For example, an archive may decide that certain Content Information should be understandable to the general public and, therefore, this becomes the Designated Community. For some scientific information, the Designated Community of Consumers might be described as those with a first year graduate level education in a related scientific discipline. This is a more difficult case as it is less clear what degree of specialized scientific terminology might actually be acceptable.

The Producers of such specialized information are often familiar with a narrowly recognized set of terminology, so it is especially critical to clearly define the Designated Community for their information and to make the effort to ensure that this community can understand the information. The possible evolution of the definition of the Designated Community also needs consideration. Information originally intended for a narrowly defined community may need to be made more widely understandable at some future date.

For example, information originally intended to be understandable to a particular scientific community may need to be made understandable to the general public. This is likely to mean adding explanations in support of the Representation Information and the Preservation Description Information, and it can become increasingly difficult to obtain this information over time. Selecting a broader definition of the Designated Community when the information is first proposed for Long-Term Preservation can reduce this concern and also improve the likelihood that the information will be understandable to all in the original community. The degree to which Content Information and its associated PDI conveys information to a Designated Community is, in general, quite subjective.

Nevertheless, it is essential that an archive make this determination in order to maximize information preservation. Digital Content Information and PDI need adequate Representation Information to be Independently Understandable to the Designated Community. For example, consider Content Information from a digital set of observations of rainfall, temperature, pressure, wind velocities, and other parameters measured all over the world for a year. This type of information is very extensive, and is not usually in a form intended for direct human browsing or reading, but it is in a form appropriate to searching and manipulation by application software. Such content may only be understandable to the original Producers, unless there is adequate documentation of the meaning of the various fields and their interrelationships, and how the values relate back to the original instrumentation that made the observations.

In such specialized fields extra effort is needed to ensure that the Content Information and the Preservation Description Information are understandable to a Designated Community. If the archive does not have this level of expertise in-house, it may have outside community representatives review the information for long-term understandability. Otherwise some of the information may be understandable to only a few specialists and be lost when they are no longer available.

Even when a set of information has been determined to be understandable to a particular Designated Community, over time the Knowledge Base of this community may evolve to the point that important aspects of the information may no longer be readily understandable. At this point it may be necessary for the OAIS to enhance the associated Representation Information so that it is again readily understandable to the Designated Community. As another example, a manuscript's Content Information may be written in English and therefore its content may be generally understandable to a wide audience. However, unless the purpose for which it was created is clearly documented, much of its meaning may be lost. Software is needed for efficient access to Digital Content Information.

The danger of information loss is great when such software is relied upon for information preservation and understanding because it may cease to function under only small changes to the hardware and software environment. This may not be recognized unless there is a vigorous, ongoing, testing and validation program.

It is essential for an OAIS to have documented policies and procedures for preserving its AIPs, and it should follow those procedures. The appropriate policies and procedures will depend, at minimum, on the nature of the AIPs and any ,backup' relationships the archive may have with other archives. The Producer and Consumer communities should be provided with submission and dissemination standards, policies, and procedures to support the preservation objectives of the OAIS. The Designated Community should be monitored to be sure the Content Information is still understandable to them.

The Designated Community may lose its familiarity with some terminology, and the definition of the community may be broadened to include other members with different backgrounds. A long-term technology usage plan, updated as technology evolves, is essential to avoid being caught with very costly system maintenance, emergency system replacements, and costly data representation transformations.

By definition, an OAIS makes its AIPs visible and available to its Designated Communities. Multiple views of its holdings, supported by various search aids that may cut across collections of AIPs, may be provided. Some AIPs may only exist as the output of algorithms operating on other AIPs. They appear as DIPs that, upon dissemination, should include documentation on how they were derived from other AIPs. The expectations of OAIS Consumers regarding access services will vary widely among archives and over time as technology evolves.

Pressures for more effective access must be balanced with the requirements for preservation under the available resource constraints. Some AIPs may have restricted access and therefore may only be disseminated to Consumers who meet access restrictions. The OAIS should have published policies on access and restrictions so that the rights of all parties are protected. In general, DIPs may be distributed by all varieties of communication paths, including networks and physical media. Preservation Planning also designs IP templates and provides design assistance and review to specialize these templates into SIPs and AIPs for specific submissions. . Preservation Planning also develops detailed Migration plans, software prototypes and test plans to enable implementation of Administration migration goals.

Access functions include communicating with Consumers to receive requests, applying controls to limit access to specially protected information, coordinating the execution of requests to successful completion, generating responses and delivering the responses to Consumers. In addition to the entities described above, there are various Common Services assumed to be available.

Modern, distributed computing applications assume a number of supporting services such as inter-process communication, name services, temporary storage allocation, exception handling, security, backup and directory services. Much excellent work has already been done in the area of open system environment reference models. Operating system services provide the core services needed to operate and administer the application platform, and provide an interface between application software and the platform.

Operating system security services specify the control of access to system data, functions, hardware, and software resources by users and user processes. Network services provide the capabilities and mechanisms to support distributed applications requiring data access and applications interoperability in heterogeneous, networked environments. Security services capabilities and mechanisms to protect sensitive information and treatments in the information system. The appropriate level of protection is determined based upon the value of the information to the application end-users and the perception of threats to it.

These services include the following: Identification/ authentication service confirms the identities of requesters for use of information system resources. In addition, authentication can apply to providers of data. Access control service prevents the unauthorized use of information system resources. This service also prevents the use of a resource in an unauthorized way. This service may be applied to various aspects of access to a resource or to all accesses to a resource.

Data integrity service ensures that data is not altered or destroyed in an unauthorized manner. This service applies to data in permanent data stores and to data in communications messages. Data confidentiality service ensures that data is not made available or disclosed to unauthorized individuals or computer processes. This service will be applied to devices that permit human interaction with the information system. In addition, this service will ensure that observation of usage patterns of communications resources will not be possible.

Non-repudiation service ensures that entities engaging in an information exchange cannot deny being involved in it. This service may take one or both of two forms. First, the recipient of data is provided with proof of the origin of the data. This protects against any attempt by the sender to falsely deny sending the data or its contents. Second, the sender of data is provided with proof of delivery of data. This protects against any subsequent attempt by the recipient to falsely deny receiving the data or its contents. Digital SIPs may be delivered via electronic transfer (e.g., FTP), loaded from media submitted to the archive, or simply mounted (e.g., CD-ROM) on the archive file system for access.

Non-digital SIPs would likely be delivered by conventional shipping procedures. The Receive Submission function may represent a legal transfer of custody for the Content Information in the SIP, and may require that special access controls be placed on the contents. This function provides a confirmation of receipt of a SIP to the Producer, which may include a request to resubmit a SIP in the case of errors resulting from the SIP submission. The Quality Assurance function validates (QA results) the successful transfer of the SIP to the staging area.

For digital submissions, these mechanisms might include Cyclic Redundancy Checks (CRCs) or checksums associated with each data file, or the use of system log files to record and identify any file transfer or media read/write errors. The Generate AIP function transforms one or more SIPs into one or more AIPs that conform to the archive's data formatting and documentation standards. This may involve file format conversions, data representation conversions or reorganization of the content information in the SIPs.

The Generate AIP function may issue report requests to Data Management to obtain reports of information needed by the Generate AIP function to produce the Descriptive Information that completes the AIP. The Generate Descriptive Information function extracts Descriptive Information from the AIPs and collects Descriptive Information from other sources to provide to Coordinate Updates, and ultimately Data Management. This includes metadata to support searching and retrieving AIPs (e.g., who, what, when, where, why), and could also include special browse products (thumbnails, images) to be used by Finding Aids. The Coordinate Updates function is responsible for transferring the AIPs to Archival Storage and the Descriptive Information to Data Management.

Transfer of the AIP includes a storage request and may represent an electronic, physical, or a virtual (i.e., data stays in place) transfer. After the transfer is completed and verified, Archival Storage returns a storage confirmation indicating (or verifying) the storage identification information for the AIP. The Coordinate Updates function also incorporates the storage identification information into the Descriptive Information for the AIP and transfers it to the Data Management entity along with a database update request. In return, Data Management provides a database update response indicating the status of the update.

The storage facility procedures should provide for random verification of the integrity of data objects using CRCs or some other error checking mechanism. The Disaster Recovery function provides a mechanism for duplicating the digital contents of the archive collection and storing the duplicate in a physically separate facility. This function is normally accomplished by copying the archive contents to some form of removable storage media (e.g., digital linear tape, compact disc), but may also be performed via hardware transport or network data transfers. The Provide Data function provides copies of stored AIPs to Access.

This function receives an AIP request that identifies the requested AIP(s) and provides them on the requested media type or transfers them to a staging area. This function also sends a notice of data transfer to Access upon completion of an order. The Administer Database function is responsible for maintaining the integrity of the Data Management database, which contains both Descriptive Information and system information.

Descriptive Information identifies and describes the archive holdings, and system information is used to support archive operations. The Administer Database function is responsible for creating any schema or table definitions required to support Data Management functions; for providing the capability to create, maintain and access customized user views of the contents of this storage; and for providing internal validation (e.g., referential integrity) of the contents of the database. The Administer Database function is carried out in accordance with policies received from Administration. The Perform Queries function receives a query request from Access and executes the query to generate a result set that is transmitted to the requester.

The Generate Report function receives a report request from Ingest, Access or Administration and executes any queries or other processes necessary to generate the report that it supplies to the requester. Typical reports might include summaries of archive holdings by category, or usage statistics for accesses to archive holdings. It may also receive a report request from Access and provides descriptive information for a specific AIP. The Receive Database Updates function adds, modifies or deletes information in the Data Management persistent storage.

The main sources of updates are Ingest, which provides Descriptive Information for the new AIPs, and Administration, which provides system updates and review updates. Ingest transactions consist of Descriptive Information which identifies new AIPs stored in the archive. System updates include all system-related information (operational statistics, Consumer information, and request status). The Negotiate Submission Agreement function solicits desirable archival information for the OAIS and negotiates Submission Agreements with Producers.

This function also negotiates a data submission schedule with the Producer. It maintains a calendar of expected Data Submission Sessions that will be needed to transfer one or more SIPs to the OAIS and the resource requirements to support their ingestion. This function receives AIP/SIP templates and customization advise from Preservation Planning and sends SIP designs and SIPs to the Audit Submission function as part of the submission approval process.

The data submission formats and procedures must be clearly documented in the archive's data submission policies, and the deliverables must be identified by the Producer in the Submission Agreement. The Manage System Configuration function provides system engineering for the archive system to continuously monitor the functionality of the entire archive system and systematically control changes to the configuration. This function maintains integrity and tractability of the configuration during all phases of the system life cycle. It also audits system operations, system performance, and system usage. It sends report requests for system information to Data Management and receives reports; it receives operational statistics from Archival Storage. It summarizes those reports and periodically provides OAIS performance information and archive holding inventory reports to Preservation Planning.

It sends performance information to Establish Standards and Policies. It receives migration packages from Preservation Planning. It receives system evolution policies from the Establish Standards and Procedures function. Based on these inputs it develops and implements plans for system evolution. It sends change requests, procedures and tools to Archive Information Update. The Archival Information Update function provides a mechanism for updating the contents of the archive. It receives change requests, procedures and tools from Manage System Configuration. It provides updates by sending a dissemination request to Access, updating the contents of the resulting DIPs and resubmitting them as SIPs to Ingest. The Physical Access Control function provides mechanisms to restrict or allow physical access (doors, locks, guards) to elements of the archive, as determined by archive policies.

The Establish Standards and Policies function is responsible for establishing and maintaining the archive system standards and policies. It receives budget information and policies such as the OAIS charter, scope, resource utilization guidelines, and pricing policies from Management. The Develop Preservation Strategies and Standards function is responsible for developing and recommending strategies and standards to enable the archive to better anticipate future changes in the Designated Community service requirements or technology trends that would require migration of some current archive holdings or new submissions.

This function receives reports from the Monitor Designated Communities and Monitor Technology functions, and it receives performance information, inventory reports and summarized consumer comments from Administration. This function sends recommendations on system evolution to Administration. This function also receives external data standards from Monitor Technology and produces profiles of those standards that are sent to Administration as proposals on their potential usage. This function also receives issues from Develop Packaging Designs and Migration Plans in the case of unanticipated submission requirements, and responds with advice to handle the new requirements. The Develop Packaging Designs and Migration Plans function develops new IP designs and detailed migration plans and prototypes, to implement Administration policies and directives.

This activity also provides advice on the application of these IP designs and Migration plans to specific archive holdings and submissions. This function receives archive approved standards and migration goals from Administration. The standards include format standards, metadata standards and documentation standards. It applies these standards to preservation requirements and provides AIP and SIP template designs to Administration. The Coordinate Access Activities function provides a single user interface to the information holdings of the archive.

This interface will normally be via computer network or dial-up link to an on-line service, but might also be implemented in the form of a walk-in facility, printed catalog ordering service, or fax-back type service. Three categories of Consumer requests are distinguished: query requests, which are executed in Data Management and return immediate result sets for presentation to the user; report requests, which may require a number of queries and produce formatted reports for delivery to the Consumer; and orders, which may access either or both Data Management and Archival Storage to prepare a formal Dissemination Information Package (DIP) for on- or off-line delivery. An order may be an Adhoc Order that is executed only once, or an Event Based Order that will be maintained by the Activate Requests function in Administration, and initiated by a dissemination request that may result in periodic deliveries of requested items.

The Archival Information Update function in Administration also submits dissemination requests to obtain DIPs needed to perform its update functions. The Generate DIP function accepts a dissemination request, retrieves the AIP from Archival Storage, and moves a copy of the data to a staging area for further processing. This function also transmits a report request to Data Management to obtain Descriptive Information needed for the DIP. If special processing is required, the Generate DIP function accesses data objects in staging storage and applies the requested processes. The types of operations, which may be carried out, include statistical functions, sub-sampling in temporal or spatial dimensions, conversions between different data types or output formats, and other specialized processing (e.g., image processing).

This function places the completed DIP response in the staging area and notifies the Coordinate Access Activities function that the DIP is ready for delivery. The Deliver Response function handles both on-line and off-line deliveries of responses (DIPs, result sets, reports and assistance) to Consumers. For on-line delivery, it accepts a response from Coordinate Access Activities and prepares it for on-line distribution in real time via communication links. It identifies the intended recipient, determines the transmission procedure requested, places the response in the staging area to be transmitted, and supports the on-line transmission of the response. For off-line delivery it retrieves the response from the Coordinate Access Activities function, prepares packing lists and other shipping records, and then ships the response.

When the response has been shipped, a notice of shipped order is returned to the Coordinate Access Activities function and billing information is submitted to Administration. Representation Information, which is itself an Information Object, may be expressed in physical forms (e.g., a paper document) or in digital forms. When the Representation Information is in digital form, additional Representation Information is needed to understand the bits of the Representation Information. In principle, this recursion continues until physical forms are encountered.

For example, Representation Information expressed in ASCII needs the additional Representation Information for ASCII, which might be a physical document giving the ASCII standard. Each item of Representation Information can have multiple components, including multiple referenced Representation Information components; each with is own Representation Information. To preserve the meaning of an Information Object, its Representation Information must also be preserved. This is most easily accomplished when the Representation Information objects are expressed in forms that are easily understandable, such as text descriptions that use widely supported standards such as ASCII characters for electronic versions.

One problem with the use of only text descriptions is that such descriptions can be ambiguous. This is addressed by the use of standardized, formal description languages containing well-defined constructs with which to describe data structures. These languages may need to be augmented with text descriptions to fully convey the semantics of the Representation Information Two special types of Representation Information are Representation Rendering Software and Access Software. Representation Rendering Software is able to display the Representation Information in understandable forms.

For example, the file and directory structure of many CD-ROMs conforms to ISO 9660. This standard is Representation Information describing how most CD-ROM file structures are to be implemented, and it may be obtained as a paper document. However it may also be obtained as a digital object that needs to be understood as a PDF object. Rather than actually obtaining the documentation of PDF and writing software to understand the ISO 9660 object, an OAIS may use available PDF display software to render the ISO 9660 documentation humanly visible and readable.

If the OAIS does not also obtain the associated description of PDF, it needs to record and track this fact because when PDF objects are no longer cost-effective for access and display, the ISO 9660 documentation expressed as a PDF object will need to be migrated to a new form. Access Software presents some or all of the information content of an Information Object in forms understandable to humans or systems. It may also provide some types of access service, such as displaying, manipulating, processing, or sub-setting, to an Information Object. For some types of Digital Objects, such software may be widely available. It is not necessary for the OAIS to maintain or provide such software. The OAIS may want to maintain and provide this software for more specialized types of Digital Objects.

Since Access software will incorporate some understanding of the Representation Information, some archives may attempt to use Access Software as a substitute for full Representation Information. Access Software source code, which embodies at least a partial understanding of the associated Representation Information, may be used as documentation expressing such Representation Information.

A problem with this approach is that the desired Representation Information may not be clearly identifiable as it may be mixed with various processing and display algorithms, and may be incomplete since the code assumes an underlying operating environment. It may be difficult to tell, from the software code, what Representation Information is missing. The use of Access Software executables, without the source code, such as may occur with proprietary formats, presents a much greater risk for loss of information because it is more difficult to maintain an operating environment for software than to migrate documentation over time.

The practical use of emulation techniques, to preserve working software, has not yet been shown to be cost-effective. This is a significant issue for those desiring to preserve a look and feel to information access. There are many types of information involved in the long-term preservation of information in an OAIS. Each of these types can be viewed as a complete Information Object in that it contains a data object and adequate Representation Information to understand the data. The Content Information is the set of information that is the original target of preservation by the OAIS. Deciding what is the Content Information may not be obvious and may need to be negotiated with the Producer.

The Representation Information for a digital Content Data Object (both semantic and syntactic) is needed to fully transform the bits into the Content Information. In principal, this even extends to the inclusion of definitions (e.g., dictionary and grammar) of any natural language (e.g., English) used in expressing the Content Information. Over long time periods the meaning of natural language expressions can evolve significantly in both general and in specific discipline usage. As a practical matter, the OAIS needs to have enough Representation Information associated with the bits of the Content Data Object in the Content Information that it feels confident that the members of the Designated Community can enter the Representation Network with enough knowledge to begin accurately interpreting the Representation Information.

Digital storage media have shorter life spans, and digital information requires access technologies that are changing at an ever-increasing pace. Some types of information, such as multimedia, are so closely linked to the software and hardware technologies that they cannot be used outside these proprietary environments. Because of the speed of technological advances, the time frame in which we must consider archiving becomes much shorter. The time between manufacture and preservation is shrinking. While there are traditions of stewardship and best practices that have become institutionalized in the print environment, many of these traditions are inadequate, inappropriate or not well known among the stakeholders in the digital environment. Originators are able to bypass the traditional publishing, dissemination and announcement processes that are part of the traditional path from creation to archiving and preservation.

Groups and individuals who did not previously consider themselves to be archivists are now being drawn into the role, either because of the infrastructure and intellectual property issues involved or because user groups are demanding it. Librarians and archivists who traditionally managed the life cycle of print information from creation to long-term preservation and archiving, must now look to information managers from the computer science tradition to support the development of a system of stewardship in the new digital environment.

In Australia, Wales, the fundamental nature of the Library's work was determined by the Royal Charter that established the Library's existence in 1907. The current wording of the Charter gives as the Library's functions: the collection, preservation and maintenance of manuscripts, printed matter, maps, photographs, visual and audiovisual material relating to Wales and the Celtic peoples and similar material which furthers the aims of higher education and literary and scientific research.

The Charter is the basis for several key features of the Library:

a) its emphasis on material of Welsh (and Celtic) interest

b) its wider collecting responsibilities (these are based on legal deposit and purchase)

c) the fact that it collects material in such a wide variety of media

d) its mission to support researchers and those in higher education

Wales' National Library is an Assembly-Sponsored Public Body, and receives Grant-in-Aid annually from the National Assembly for Wales. The relationship between the Library and the National Assembly is defined by a Management statement and financial memorandum. Valuable pointers to the future of the Library were provided in 1999 by the many responses to Choosing the future, the first large-scale public consultation exercise ever conducted by the Library.

Individuals and organisations expressed clearly and at length their strong views on how they think the Library should evolve. The existence and work of the Library depend on certain principles and values, shared by those who govern it, work in it and use it. They are seen as complimentary to the values and principles of the National Assembly in guiding the Library's work. The Library has a vital role as a collector and guardian of the intellectual record of the life of Wales and the Welsh people. This is important in itself, and is also an important element in defining the cultural identities of the country. The new political status of Wales is a product of, and will itself contribute to, a renewed concern with cultural identities.

The Library is likely to have an important part to play in reflecting, recording and even forming those identities. This intellectual record is not confined to any particular medium, format, period or language. From its beginning the Library has been more than what is conventionally recognised as a 'library', that is, a collection of printed works. It stores a wide - and still widening - range of formats capable of carrying intellectual content. Among these are: books and periodicals, manuscripts and archives, pictures, photographs and maps, sound and moving images, and electronic material. This record of the 'matter of Wales' (and of the other Celtic countries) is, however, part of a wider, indeed world-wide, domain of recorded knowledge, produced in many languages and over many centuries, which the Library attempts to represent in its collections for the benefit of its users.

The Library's wider collections, mainly acquired in print form through legal deposit, are essential to its ability to support study and learning, not only in Welsh or Celtic domains, but also in a very wide range of other subjects. The Library's collections and services exist to meet the needs of all those who can benefit from them. The Library is proud of the fact that it is a public library, in the sense that any adult is able and welcome to use its collections for reference with little formality and without charge. Among the groups that make use of the Library at present for consultation and reference are academic and personal researchers, students and other learners, businesses, the media, and visitors from Britain and overseas.

This right of unrestricted access is part of the democratic rights of citizens in pursuit of information, knowledge and enlightenment, and contributes to the promotion of 'social inclusion'. The Library has a duty not merely to 'hold its doors open', but to encourage awareness and use of its collections and services, by all the means at its disposal. The Library has an important function, as by far the largest and most significant institution of its kind in Wales, in leading, co-ordinating and supporting the development of library and archive services in Wales.

This is not an optional part of its mission, but an essential role in a country where library and archive services tend to be small and scattered. In its turn the National Library is part of a wider, interlocking structure of library, information and archive institutions in the United Kingdom and throughout the world. It co-operates with them to make the best use of the resources that are available to all. The National Library seeks to do everything it does - whether providing answers to enquiries, publishing books, mounting exhibitions, or any other relevant activity - to the highest possible standard, with excellence as a constant ideal in mind. In short, as a thriving, relevant and well-regarded cultural and information resource for the people of Wales and the world.

The essence of what the Library does is contained in its five 'core functions'. These set the minimum boundaries of its policies and practice. The core functions are defined below, with in each case an indication of the chief means by which they are performed. To collect materials by legal deposit, purchase, donation, bequest, exchange and deposit, in accordance with agreed collection development policies. This function is carried out through: i) assembling as complete a collection as possible, in all media, of published material relating to Wales, including printed publications and sound and moving image material ii) maintaining (mainly through legal deposit and purchase) the most comprehensive collection in Wales of printed material published in the United Kingdom and Ireland, and of research material from other countries iii) developing collections of unpublished materials relating to or deriving from Wales, including archives and artistic works iv) accessioning, processing, cataloguing and storing material acquired

To preserve and conserve materials in the collections. This function is carried out through: i) ensuring environmental, storage and handling conditions favourable to the continued preservation of materials ii) intervening to conserve materials and hence arrest deterioration or repair damage iii) transferring, in some cases, information to more suitable preservation formats iv) To provide satisfactory access for users of the Library to its building, collections and services, and adequate information about them. This function is carried out through: v) providing access to public spaces, collections and facilities within the Library's building vi) providing document delivery, enquiry and information services to those wishing to use the Library, in person or remotely vii) providing easy access to catalogues and lists of the Library's collections, and surrogates of selections from them viii) To raise awareness and disseminate knowledge of the Library's collections. This function is carried out through: ix) issuing guides, leaflets and other publicity material x) publishing printed monographs and serials xi) mounting material on the Library's website xii) staging exhibitions derived from the collections xiii) arranging lectures and seminars

The *Digital Library Initiative*, begun in 2001-02, seeks to make a substantial contribution to this objective. In particular, it will extend significantly the ability of the Library to cater for teaching and learning in Wales. The fundamental challenge facing the development of the Library is to open its collections and services to more people, for a wider range of purposes - in particular to contribute to education and lifelong learning.

In order to maintain the ability of the Library to fulfil its core functions and to aid new developments and projects the GIA provided is supplemented by the use of private funds. The Capital Grant is intended to cover the costs of capital items including computer hardware, software, equipment and the repair and enhancement of the Library building. The demands on the capital budget far exceed the grant provided. This has resulted in a significant backlog of works on the building and has restricted the Library's ability to invest in equipment to support existing activities or develop new important areas. Providing navigational tools to support effective access to the resources in the growing digital archive will be a challenge.

Some users will have limited time and a very specific task at hand; they will benefit from the ability to search with precision. Others will have plenty of time and want to gain an overview of what is available in the entire archive or on a general topic before searching for anything in particular. They may prefer to read introductory presentations, take guided tours, browse lists of topical headings, or perform a general search and look at large numbers of individual items. The American Memory archive of historical materials is being assembled collection by collection; these collections have different characteristics.

Collections currently available over the World Wide Web consist of a single general type of material (text, image, audio, or movie), but collections in process incorporate several types. Later, two thematic anthologies comprising textual documents and images will be released, one on the American variety stage and one on the history and development of the environmental conservation movement. Another collection in process, covering the presidency of Calvin Coolidge and the transition to a consumer economy in the 1920s, includes all four types of material. Some digital collections will have individual bibliographic information (catalog records) for each item, with individually assigned subject headings. Others will be described primarily in a finding aid, a structured document with links to the items listed.

The intellectual context and depth or breadth of focus for collections also varies. Some comprise a large proportion of the output of an individual creator. Some are personal selections of collectors or scholars. Others are collections of materials in a particular physical format with no single topical theme. Initially, the only way to access American Memory was to start by browsing a list of the collections. Each collection was described by a sentence and a list of broad subject topics. By early 1996, there was a full list, of about eight collections, and a subsidiary list for the four general types of material.

By the time the latest collections were released in March 1996, the ability to search across all the historical collections simultaneously had been added. It is also possible to search across collections containing items of a certain type (text, image, audio, or movie). For a cross-collection search, the list of hits identifies the parent collection and the item type, as well as the item's title. Each collection currently consists of digital reproductions, a group of linked HTML pages providing archival and intellectual context, and one or more access tools for exploring the collection.

Most of the current American Memory collections have a set of item-level bibliographic records which can be searched. The search engine in use is INQUERY, the text search toolkit from the Center for Intelligent Information Retrieval. A ranked list of "hits" is returned. INQUERY's flexible query commands have been used to list the hits for queries of two or more terms in four sublists:

1. items that contain the entered query as an exact phrase;
2. items that have all the search words within 20 words of each other;
3. items containing all the words, but not close to each other;
4. items with one or more of the entered words, but not all.

The challenge of guiding the selection of collections has at least two aspects: determining the characteristics that best describe and distinguish the collections; and finding ways to present those characteristics in a fashion that lets the user select relevant collections easily. As an alternative or supplement to the traditional text-based searching of catalog records, the User Interface Team plans to explore the use of direct manipulation and rapid feedback during the selection of collections through browsing and filtering operations.

To support these operations in a prototype interface, the team will build an independent set of descriptive (but non-MARC) records for the collections using a format that is easily modified and indexed by INQUERY, but not intended for viewing by users. After the experimental stage, during which the choice and format of attributes will be refined, the Library expects to integrate the content of these records into any standard architecture for collection-level metadata that emerges through broader digital library efforts.

Guiding users to relevant collections is not the only navigational challenge for the user interface. When most items in the digital archive have individual bibliographic records, a search across all items is straightforward. The level of description is roughly comparable and catalogers take considerable effort to be consistent (although consistency is more common within collections than across different collections). The granularity of the chunks of text indexed are also comparable. However, the historical collections will soon provide a more complex structure.

Some items will be described only through section headings and very brief descriptions in a structured finding aid. Textual items will be fully indexed by the words they contain. It is easy to pour all this text into an indexing engine. It is more difficult to structure search options and present results in a way that is both efficient and comprehensible to users.

Another dimension of the challenge in building access tools is that a single interface is unlikely to satisfy the entire range of users. Users will be engaged in very different tasks, from the detailed study of a period in the history of photography to picking one photograph to illustrate a high-school paper on the Civil War.

As part of its educational outreach, the Australian National Digital Library Program has already developed materials and tips aimed particularly at teachers. The initial search interface for American Memory's historical collections was made as simple as possible. Experienced searchers have requested the ability to formulate more precise searches. More complex query forms involving Boolean logic and searching for terms in specific fields are under test in other projects using INQUERY at the Library. The ability to specify queries more precisely will address some searching problems, but mismatches in terminology also prevent users finding relevant items.

Researchers making extensive use of the Library's traditional collections soon learn the subject headings that relate to their field of interest. However, casual users do not naturally use the terms from controlled vocabularies. Topical subject headings for bibliographic records are chosen from controlled vocabularies, such as the Library of Congress Subject Headings (LCSH) and the Thesaurus for Graphic Materials (TGM). A search for photographs using the term "state house" retrieves 50 pictures for which the exact phrase occurs in the bibliographic description.

However, the TGM specifies the synonym "capitols" as the appropriate subject index term and a search on "capitols" retrieves 256 photographs. In many contexts for information retrieval (for example, scientists accessing current literature in their field), the primary users can be assumed to be familiar with the terms in the documents themselves.

For historical texts, that is not necessarily the case, especially for occasional users. Usage changes over time. "Teacher training" is unlikely to appear in a nineteenth century document, but teachers were certainly trained and the collections currently mounted have much to say about this topic, particularly for women and Afro-Americans. Finding the right level of specificity for search terms is also a problem for users. Cataloging guidelines usually recommend the application of the most specific terms, with an emphasis on the concrete. One potential approach is to integrate thesauri into the interface, by providing a browsable hierarchy of terms to assist selection, or by mapping commonly used terms into formal subject headings or to synonyms actually found in text documents.

In short, the computer offers rapid access to an array of resources, but its screen is less convenient than a large table for studying images and than a book for skimming through indexes and pages of text to determine its relevance.

5

Cataloguing and Access

Library cataloging is the practice of organizing a collection of bibliographic items to facilitate their identification, location, access, and use. Perhaps the simplest way to do this is to organize the items themselves, creating what Miksa calls an "item file" — e.g. by arranging papers in a filing cabinet or books on a shelf. This method works well for small collections, but for large collections more elaborate means are needed. The principal method for organizing larger collections is to develop a catalog. A catalog consists of a set of entries, each of which stands for an item in the collection and which describes certain characteristics of the item, such as (for a book) its author, title, publisher, subjects, and so on.

Current cataloging practices involve both strategies. Surrogates are created for the items and arranged in a catalog. The items themselves are also arranged —e.g. books are placed "linearly" on the shelves of a library's stacks. A distinction is made between two types of cataloging activity, both of which are practiced to catalog a particular item:

descriptive cataloging and subject cataloging. Descriptive cataloging is concerned with creating catalog records for items, describing their characteristics as just noted — author, title, and so on.

Subject cataloging is concerned with classifying the subject matter, the intellectual content, of an item. It is the subject cataloger who assigns an item to a class within a classification scheme which in turn determines a place on the shelf. A distinction is also made between bibliographies and catalogs. Both of these in practice describe items. The difference is that a bibliography describes works and editions of works, but not actual physical items.

A catalog, by contrast, primarily describes particular, physical items in a particular collection. It does this partly by describing aspects of a work (e.g. title and author), as does a bibliography, and partly by indicating physical properties, including its location. The development of highly sophisticated, systematically organized catalogs and cataloging procedures is a product of the modern library era, which dates from the second half of the last century. Book catalogs (lists of entries bound in book form) were the first kind used in the U.S.; these began to be displaced by the familiar card catalogs around the turn of the century.

Digital catalogs began to appear in the 1970's and are now widespread; they are rapidly displacing card catalogs Entries in OPACs are commonly encoded in MARC (Machine Readable Cataloging) format, a standard which permits them to be shared among institutions. To a great extent, the MARC standard encodes those features previously recorded on cards; it enables a fairly straightforward translation of card contents into digital form. In libraries today, cataloging is considered part of "technical services" — those services generally concerned with the maintenance of the collection, such as acquisition and binding.

Technical services are distinguished from "public services," such as reference services, which involve direct contact with library users. Nearly all libraries have catalogers, although in very small libraries one person may handle other tasks, e.g. reference work and acquisition of new materials, in addition to cataloging. The cataloger's job is to produce catalog records for newly acquired materials. "Original cataloging" is the process of creating catalog records from scratch — creating a record primarily using the item itself, e.g. by inspection of the book, including, but not limited to, its title page. This is distinguished from "copy cataloging," in which the cataloger makes use of a previously existing catalog record for the item to create a new record tailored to the needs of their own library.

Catalog records that can be used as sources for copy cataloging are maintained by several institutions, including the Library of Congress, OCLC, and RLG. While it may take only a few minutes to copy catalog an item, it is not unusual for the original cataloging of an item to take on the order of an hour. Cataloging is a form of order-making; it is a set of practices which quite literally put a library's collections in order and provide access through a set of systematically organized surrogates; and it is therefore a crucial part of the system by which books and other materials are maintained and made available to readers throughout the world.

The work is ever ongoing, not just because new items are constantly being acquired, but because a collection will crumble — like the old barns one sees in the countryside —

unless it is continually maintained: books disappear and need to be reordered, they are damaged and need to be repaired, they are misshelved, and so on; catalogs need to be similarly maintained. This might seem like an obvious enough point, but cataloging shares with many other forms of order-making a certain invisibility.

For the ordinary library patron, the machinery by which the collection is maintained is out-of-sight, ill-understood, and the order it produces taken for granted. The typical library patron might be excused for not knowing how much work is being done behind the scenes to make an item available; indeed the invisibility of this system is largely a measure of its successful functioning. But it is more curious to observe that within the library community itself, in some quarters, at any rate, the work of cataloging is denigrated; it is considered routine, at best semi-skilled, and unnecessarily detail-oriented work.

Cataloging is not simply a matter of reading off self-evident properties of items, but is a highly skilled interpretative activity by which the properties of items are not simply described, but stabilized and even created. Over the last decade, discussion has ranged over many topics, including: how and whether to catalog digital documents, the future of cataloging, the politics of cataloging, the relationship between cataloging and reference services, teaching cataloging in library schools, and cataloging humor.

Bibliographic materials, it appears, do not always wear their bibliographic properties on their sleeve, and the rules for determining and "transcribing" these properties are quite complex and require interpretation to be applied. Anyone who has written a dissertation or a paper requiring a formal bibliography has encountered this problem in a small way: an item that is hard to categorize, that lacks an expected property, or one of whose properties is ambiguous. Cataloging is not just a matter of "reading off" the properties items have but of normalizing or regularizing the material to conform to standard categories of description and thereby making the properties in the act of describing them.

Cataloging appears to be routine work so long as one believes that the materials just have a regular structure which can be trivially read off. But on inspection, it appears that this regular structure is the output of the work of catalogers, not the input. In this century, the development of film, video, microfilm, and photocopying technologies have all required changes and accommodations in the law, in library practices, in publishing and distribution, in patterns of consumption and use. None of these developments, however, has produced the uncertainty, confusion, and anxiety that has been occasioned by the increasing adoption of digital technologies, for none of these earlier developments challenged the order of the book, the order built around one central type of physical artifact and its modes of production, conservation, and consumption.

From a cataloging perspective, the Net is the wrong unit of analysis, for the Net does not constitute a library in any interesting sense. It may be part of the technological infrastructure which could support a library, but it is not a library — not in the sense of an institution which oversees and provides access to a collection. Moreover, the materials on the Net do not constitute a library collection — not in the sense of a selection of items organized to serve a particular clientele. Digital collections will need to be organized and maintained if they are to remain stable and usable. To those within the library community this point may seem too obvious to make, since it is one of the central premises on which the modern library movement has been built. Yet it is not widely understood outside this community, to judge for example from the way the Web is often talked about.

There seems to be a fairly wide-spread presumption, tacitly held, that materials can maintain their identity and their currency without continual intervention, without continual work. Moreover, it seems certain that the work of stabilizing and maintaining digital collections will require a great deal of systematic human activity. Certainly, powerful technologies will be involved as well as human labor, as is the case now. Again, this is obvious enough to librarians; technologists, by contrast, tend to see the technical infrastructure but not the "invisible" social infrastructure by which most things, not just library collections, are maintained. There can be no doubt that people will continue to make lists of digital resources which they will want to make available to others. Some of these will have broad scope and utility, while others will be of limited scope.

As with any new technology-based idea, there has been considerable controversy over the definition and possibilities of the term "digital library." To the computer science community, the new technical possibilities beckon enticingly. However, as traditionalists in the library community might point out, important issues are being ignored. According to Levy and Marshall, there is the "digital library" narrowly-construed and more broadly-construed. They argue for the broadly-construed digital library.

The library community has been very successful in maintaining traditional libraries and has developed many practices and ideals to do so. Among them are the ideas of unified collections and access methods. In fact, one could argue that many core library activities, such as circulation, technical services, and even shelving, were created by the library to maintain access to its collection over time. It is essential to note that this set of practices and ideals maintain the traditional library as institution and as community of practice together over time.

This equilibrium is in the process of being disturbed or destroyed with the intrusion of new technical possibilities. Only some of the practices of the traditional library will carry into the digital world, perhaps only for a narrow conception of the digital library. Furthermore, the hypertext and computer science communities have no such traditions and practices for the broadly-construed library. In the management of most resources, managerial control can play many roles. In the digital library, different control mechanisms over the collection are possible, and these control mechanisms will influence the possibilities and necessities for maintenance.

Libraries have always managed their collections, selecting and removing items from their shelves. This has been viewed as a critical function of library management. According to the collection management literature, the practices of collection management are dependent on the type of library collection. In a traditional, or paper-based, library, there is considerable control over the collection. Versions of publications are stable. More importantly, because the collection is physically contained, there is considerable control over the collection. Library staff can decide what is and what is not in the collection. Maintenance of the collection is within the purview of the institutional members. At one opposite is the World Wide Web.

The Web nodes often change, in content, location, and even existence. On the other hand, the content in a location does not shift rapidly; it tends to remain relatively stable. There is no control by any given individual over the entire Web. An individual has control only over his nodes and the selection of pointers to others' nodes (URLs) that provide the capability for extended collections. At another opposite is Usenet or similar computer-mediated communication (CMC) systems. The locations do not change, but the contents of any given location change constantly. The control over the collection for this type is also very low for any given individual. In the middle of both dimensions is the organizational information repository.

Since the information resides within an organization and since the organization generally provides a sanctioned organizational member to manage the system, there is considerable control over its collection. Nonetheless, organizational memories tend to be more dynamic than traditional library collections; for example, they may include informal information, time-sensitive information, or bulletin board mechanisms. The variation in collection control determines the type of institutional and technical maintenance possible. Collections that are closer to those in traditional libraries can use more traditional control and maintenance mechanisms.

Digital libraries that incorporate more individualistic, dynamic, and informal information may need to find new maintenance mechanisms. Digital libraries, if self-contained in a manner similar to traditional libraries will be able to draw upon traditional methods and practices. Traditional libraries, as noted above, have developed methods for maintaining their core set of institutional ideals, their community of practice, and their collections of materials. Although many maintenance practices will need to be adapted — such as preservation and circulation control as extreme examples — the existing practices can serve as the bases for new norms and practices.

Therefore, if the adaptation of current practices is successful, then the narrowly-construed digital library will stand a much greater chance of success in the long run. These traditional practices, however, have had their limitations. They were based on a constrained collection; i.e., a selection from the bibliographic universe. A traditional library could never cope with much ephemera; it would require too many resources. To adequately index, catalog, and otherwise conform to the institutional ideals for the broad range of ephemera would be overwhelming. In the past, there were strong institutional reasons to constrict the bibliographic universe.

Going digital, however, changes the cost structure, and collection and maintenance costs need to be revisited. It is not necessary, for example, in a digital universe to hand-index all materials; there are other methods of access. There is considerable evidence that this change in the cost structure is affecting organizational memories. However, the dynamism and volatility of organizational memories tend to be close to that of traditional libraries. That is, organizational members can reliably return to the same location in the organization's information repositories to find the same materials.

Collection maintenance tools will be necessary for the digital library. As examples of these tools, several potential mechanisms for reducing the user's maintenance cost in his continued use of the World Wide Web. These examples are limited. Although many of the same issues exist for other informal materials, the mechanisms for dealing with them may not. For example, trying to capture traffic on Usenet groups might require methods of summarizing series of messages. Still, the Web is a valuable testbed for dealing with maintenance issues.

Additionally, since many computer science pre-press materials are available on the Web, the Web serves as a salient and immediately useful example. The Web shares the same maintenance problems as most hypertext systems. MOMspider (Multi-Owner Maintenance spider) can automatically traverse a focused portion of the Web. It is most valuable in checking a portion of the Web as a local collection. MOMspider identifies items that require the owner's attention such as broken links, moved documents, modified documents, and owned objects with expiration dates near to the current date. It can also provide an index document that can itself be traversed as a hypertext document. This automatic maintenance obviates the need for continuous, manual traversal of a Web collection.

Librarians tend to think in terms of periods of centuries rather than having (or wanting) to recopy every few years. Such considerations may either hinder the adoption of digital technologies for preservation or other purposes or eventually cause some rethinking of the underlying economics of librarianship. The incentive for such potential reevaluation, however, is not limited to the preservation of older materials, nor is the influence of technology the only driving factor. The underlying stimulus is a gradual transition over the centuries—perhaps spurred by the exponential growth of recorded knowledge and information—from documents with associated physical or conceptually useful lifetimes, times between new editions, or, more generically, times between "instances", that can be measured in decades or centuries; to documents with associated times between instances measured in much shorter units of time—even, in the case of "active documents", measured in minutes or seconds. The financial and other implications of this could undoubtedly be far-reaching for libraries, introducing into the library milieu unfamiliar (or, at least, largely unused) concepts associated with continuous processes or processes with relatively short lifetimes, such as "depreciation" and "lifecycle costing."

These are concepts that are familiar to the world of digital electronic processing and quite normal outside of universities, but that have been avoided in worlds—such as research libraries—that depend to a greater or lesser extent upon irregular gifts or grants of varying or unpredictable size, donations directed to the purchase and immediate storage of documents, but not to their maintenance. Indeed, one of the most serious questions facing librarians in the future may be how to effect a match between the changing economic demands of "continuous processes" and the traditional nature of many funding sources. Yet the potential of digital technologies and of the flexibility they offer is boundless.

Over the coming decades, these technologies may open up vistas of ever-increasing storage densities to where entire libraries can be electronically stored in the space of a single room; of blinding access and distribution speeds allowing whole documents to be moved almost instantly across the nation's (and indeed the world's) data networks, leading to the concept of the "distributed library;" of ease of replication at very modest cost (another cause for alarm, particularly to those concerned with protection of intellectual property); of "print-on-demand" where paper copies of documents are only printed "just in time" and not inventoried in advance of need; of accessibility at a distance away from where the "digital document" or preservation copy was created or is stored; and of intelligent automated document analysis.

Indeed, the means of creation and production of documents have already been revolutionized by these technologies. These technologies also open up horizons for totally new document formats, such as active documents whose contents may combine different media such as text, sound, video or voice; or whose contents may change dynamically with time, what Harvey Wheeler called "the fungible book." The preservation of these new "active" formats is not of direct interest to the subject of preservation of more traditional formats, but is of indirect interest because digitally preserved traditional documents can be incorporated into such active documents. Some view the introduction of digital technologies into the world of libraries as likely to cause a revolution as far-reaching as that caused by the printing-press: a massive paradigm shift.

Others view the introduction with concern, an intimidating perturbation that disturbs an equilibrium and modalities of scholarship that have served well for many decades or even for centuries. Either way, digital technologies cannot be ignored. The next twenty years are likely to be times of extraordinary change. Our libraries--indeed our universities, colleges, and our scholarly communities--may well be remade by the consequences of this technological revolution. And yet--in spite of technology's impact and of the revolutionary consequences of that impact--it must be recognized that technology itself is not the ultimate driving force. It is the inexorable pressure caused by the exponential growth of recorded knowledge, and the ever-increasing complexity, costs, and other problems associated with the storage and distribution of, and access to, such information.

Technology can provide some solutions: it is not an end in itself. Furthermore—for many reasons too numerous to detail here—the "digital library" is not about to replace the "paper library." Both will need to coexist in a shifting environment, at least for the foreseeable future. This in itself will present librarians with many economic, organizational, social, technical, and other challenges. Between the eager apostles of technology and those who approach change with extreme caution lies the mass of professionals who are trying to understand and grapple with the potential of this shifting environment, many of them implementing prototype activities designed to elucidate greater insight, many working to close the gap between promise and reality. The rash of new information technology has raised major problems for librarians and archivists, faced with a flood of new kinds of media such as audio and video tape or computer disks.

Most of these technologies were designed and manufactured without permanence as a prime consideration. A worse problem is the short life of the reading devices; even the less than permanent tapes or disks often do not deteriorate until long after the machines to read them become unavailable. Digital preservation thus depends upon copying, not on the survival of the physical media. Librarians and archivists must prepare for reformatting as a regular step in information management. In this, they must join with computer center managers, individual computer owners, and all others who need to keep machine-readable data for more than a few years.

For many new media, technological obsolescence is a greater danger than deterioration. Punched cards, for example, were made of relatively strong paper and would last well if kept in proper humidity, but nobody has a reader for them any more. Many of these technologies involve some kind of format, as well as a physical device. Merely the ability to get the bits off the device may not mean they can be easily used. Digital media can be copied without error, in principle; however the equipment required to do so for some kinds of media, e.g., CD-ROMs, is not found in libraries (or even in most service bureaus or other users of CD-ROM).

Digital media can be copied without error. Thus survival of digital information does not depend upon the permanence of a particular object, but upon widespread distribution of he information, and regular refreshing of it onto new technology. In general the lifetime of the technology is limited by commercial concerns: as technology improves, old storage technologies disappear. Reformatting, instead of being a last resort as material physically collapses, will be a common way of life in the digital age. The steady decrease in the cost and size of digital media would make this attractive even if we were not driven to it by technological obsolescence.

As new media become widely used in the computer industry, and old media become ever less available, libraries should expect to transfer their digital holdings, either by transcribing files themselves, or (more likely) by buying copies on new media from somebody else. These new copies should be not only in a newer physical format, but in whatever software format is closest to standard at the later time. Surprisingly to the novice, the software formats are often longer-lived than the physical devices. Unix word processing software from 1975, for example, is still in use; the storage devices of that time are gone. Unfortunately there is also a much wider variety of logical formats, and much more varied expertise is required to deal with the software content than with the physical material. The same is true traditionally, of course: a specialist in paper conservation can work on a book regardless of the language it is written in, while a specialist in cataloging one discipline or reading one language normally works only with books meeting that condition.

Similarly, it takes fewer experts to keep up with tape and disk machines than it does to keep up with the much wider variety of word processing systems. On the good side, the intervention of machinery between the actual object and the reader means that the users are unlikely to become emotionally attached to the particular physical media, and thus reformatting of advanced technology should not produce the objections that accompany reformatting of books. It is not expected that computer media will have any artifactual value, except odd examples in the Smithsonian. Also, the steady progress of technology means that the difficulty of keeping any particular item decreases with time.

Analog media pose even worse problems. In addition to the technological obsolescence shared with digital media, and which is now wiping out the vinyl record and the devices to play it, for example, the analog media cannot be copied without deterioration and are not necessarily very durable. Both audiotape and videotape, for example, are comparatively fragile, especially if used; a book can be read many more times without falling apart than a videotape can be played without major deterioration.

Since analog material degrades with copying, it should be converted to digital at the first practical opportunity, and carried forward in digital form. Digital material is not only copyable without error, but it gets steadily cheaper to store with time. The sooner the librarian converts to digital, thus, the better off we are. Against this is the high cost of conversion, and there is a danger that a low-quality conversion will cause many users to wish to go back to the originals.

Converting to digital is now feasible for sound, but digitizing video is still not a routine process which libraries can use. There are also some who think that even with sound, the digital copy is degraded from the analog version. Digital storage is made of bits. The storage and preservation of these bits is independent of what they represent. The interpretation of them, on the other hand, is independent of the medium on which they are stored.

In some cases, vendors use proprietary software to gain access to data and do not provide details, sometimes as a way to prevent illegal copying. Such techniques further aggravate problems of future access, and require attention to the availability of the software that reads a particular vendor's data, as well as the availability of the device. Standards may help in the future. A great many kinds of information are kept in digital forms. Most of the decisions will be made far outside the library and archives community, and because of the economies and practicalities of sticking with what is decided for general industry, libraries and archives should expect to go along.

There are many pages for which more careful treatment is desirable: (a) pages for which quality reproduction rather than just readability matters, (b) pages containing halftone images, which are likely to be seriously degraded by the typical 300 dpi one-bit-per-pixel scanner, in the same way that an ordinary photocopier would degrade them, or (c pages which are handwritten, faint, or otherwise requiring special attention. For most library and archives purposes this is likely to be the most important immediate issue. What will arrive will be a variety of word processor formats—Word, Wordperfect, Macwrite, Nota Bene, Troff, LATEX, FrameMaker, Interleaf, Multimate, Scribe, and regrettably many others plus variations within them. Typesetting tapes from various proprietary printing systems are also going to show up at archives. Many of the word processing documents will arrive with typographic markup—i.e., commands such as "italic" or "bold" in the document.

There is no general and simple way to deduce the intellectual markup from the typographic markup. For straightforward typographic transcription of most of the word processing formats, commercial products are available today. Librarians used to the arguments about LCMARC, UKMARC, and EuroMARC will understand some of the problems and the frustrations. There are a great many areas in which numerical data interchange is well developed, e.g., protein structures, the gene sequencing data banks, satellite imaging, and so on.

On balance, libraries and archives can focus for the moment on text and audio. These are practical, and there is some understanding of what should be stored. Images are just about ready for the more advanced organizations to try reformatting. For data and video, libraries and archives can probably stage holding actions with current technology until progress is made by outside standards committees. Technology for doing conversion of older digital formats to newer formats, either physical or logical, is still quite primitive.

The text formatting situation is particularly serious. When faced with a new typesetting tape, for example, it is still sometimes necessary to resort to an octal dump followed by comparison with the printed book. The situation for data is even worse than for text; so far, special documentation is required for each file. The only remotely agreed-upon structure is relational files, i.e., records with fields, and there is no standard way to write relational databases to an interchange format nor is there likely to be any. There is great economy of scale in maintaining new media—not so much the devices, but in sharing the expertise.

Cooperation is essential for libraries to manage. Not only will standard formats help a great deal, but copying digital information is much easier than generating it. Particularly where lots of intellectual effort is required it makes no sense for different groups to work on the same file. It will be much easier for libraries to obtain updated versions from central sources than for each library to manage all its own reformatting. A cooperative program for converting digital information would be appropriate. It should involve both maintaining records of who has what, seeing that conversions are done only once, and seeing to it that important materials are kept in more than one place.

There are a great many existing computer-based archives. Efforts should be made to find funding to put archives of this sort on a firm footing. In the long run, it will be cheaper to have sites of responsibility for particular materials than to attempt to duplicate expertise in specialized records conversion. Furthermore, sites of this form will function in the traditional way to link scholars working in the same area, even if these links are now via electronic mail rather than by physical travel to the site.

Most of the computer-based archives above are textually oriented. Support is needed to extend computer-based archives in the multimedia areas, and also in the areas of numerical data and programs. Some attention is also needed to ways of indexing the material in these archives, as there is no straightforward way to locate information, particularly non-textual information, in machine-readable form. Bibliographic guides will have to be developed, and even the format these should take is not clear. Industrial and government computing groups have often had the problem of maintaining old tape files, and have stimulated much of the work in records management for machine-readable files.

The copyright life of much material greatly exceeds the technological life of the media it is recorded on. A library may well be able to preserve something only by copying it, but may have difficulty obtaining permission to do that. With luck the original issuer will publish the material in a new format, but as the devotees of old records and movies can testify, this does not always happen. Leaving aside the question of how it is accomplished, through either amendment or court interpretation, the concept of "fair use" should be extended to include the copying to new media of a publication which is no longer available for sale, and the distribution of the copy to other libraries.

At the moment, there is an exemption for copying of a publication that a library already owns, but not for distribution to libraries that do not own the original being copied. The law may also pose problems even for information where the copyright law does not bar conversion. A library or archives might wish to store information derived from old, copyright-expired publications; or from public domain sources; or from publications of the university to which it belongs. However, it is doubtful that a copyright can be asserted in a straightforward transcription to machine-readable form of a non-copyrighted document or audiotape.

The rule that a copyright can only be claimed for the result of creative activity is somewhat unclear. It has recently been interpreted to say that (a) collecting and alphabetizing names into a telephone book is not copyrightable but at the very least (b) numbering the pages in a Government-provided text is copyrightable. Although measuring the creativity in these publications is like arguing whether a concrete block is more or less intelligent than a 2x4, the legal uncertainty causes all vendors of electronic information to require specific contracts limiting the use of the purchased data, imposing administrative burdens on everyone. Libraries and archives, depending on the circumstances, might be on either side of this issue.

Presumably, the ability to enforce a copyright in a converted text will encourage someone to do a conversion. On the other hand, if the issuer then disappears, it becomes difficult to get permission to do the next conversion when that becomes necessary. Again, it would be useful to have a rule that the copyright lasts only as long as someone is willing to sell the protected item. The copyright law also affects the question of multiple copies. The United States is developing a very high speed digital network which will soon provide 45 Mbits/second between major sites and should be at 1 Gbit/second before the end of the decade.

Thus, libraries and archives may well feel that there is no need to have their own copy of something, since the delay in getting it remotely may be negligible. But, depending on copyright rules and the developing business practices in the electronic information industry, it may be difficult to arrange access permission. On the other side, it would be unfortunate if the existence of the network meant that important documents were kept in only one copy which was at risk of disappearing. Finally, the insertion of copy-protection into sound recordings acts against the interests of libraries and long-term permanence of the original material.

In this intellectual climate, the development of online information (OI) resources began to take shape. OI resources are curated collections of indexed electronic databases with supporting distribution services. Online service vendors have traditionally provided fee-for-service modem access to mainframes containing these databases of strategic business, scientific, legal and financial information. Initially, the services were entirely text-based. Now, most OI service providers supplement their mainframe offerings with GUI-enhanced CD-ROM products. They have also begun to provide additional access points via consumer utilities like CompuServe and America Online, and the World Wide Web.

Some not-so-successful attempts to commercialize online information were initiated in the early 1980's by joint ventures between cable TV, telecommunications and publishing companies which offered videotext services directly to consumer households. At the time, videotext was considered to be an important vehicle for ushering in the Information Age, but only France's Minitel lived up to the aspirations of its initiators. Jerome Aumente points out that the causes of failure for most videotext services have not been well-researched, but he suggests that technical infeasibilities were to blame and that the services were 'technologically ahead of their time.'

He theorizes that the videotext failures opened a window of opportunity for the slow, steady rise of the plain text online commercial database services, such as DIALOG and NEXIS, and for ERIC--one of the precursors of modern digital libraries. Aumente blames the technology, and few would quarrel that technological feasibility is an essential ingredient in the fabrication of OI resources. But the Minitel success has been largely attributed to an important combination of political and technical factors. These stories, and the social, economic and historical analyses of Bell, Cortada, Porat and Rubin, Yates and others, provide a grounding for the examination of OI resource usability from a variety of perspectives and at several different levels.

New and existing OI resource providers are variously constrained and enabled in their efforts to take advantage of advances in data transfer (like fiber-optics), processing (like massively parallel architectures) and information storage (like terabyte hard drives and CD-ROM.) These technological components define an accessibility baseline of OI resource usability. Digital libraries which contain OI products and services must at least facilitate physical connection to these resources. Non-scholarly users of OI resources in the digital library may be today's consumers of commercial OI services.

The people searching these databases are also called "users", and they are often segmented on the basis of their information usage into two groups: end-users and intermediaries. Intermediaries are usually associated with libraries or corporate information centers. They search the OI resources at their disposal on behalf of others who will use the information retrieved in decision-making or other tasks. There has been a significant amount of research attention paid to the end-user. However, some researchers have found it difficult to segregate the intermediary from the end-user in situated use.

They have concluded that in their studies all individual OI resource users were essentially intermediaries because "the work practices of their settings led them to share their search results with others, either by request or on their own initiative". Who the user is and what the user does has been the quintessentially interesting research question of the OI resource provider and the digital library architect. However, as was demonstrated by the videotext fiasco, the providers and architects are not always willing or able to perform the research and evaluate the results before constructing or marketing the resources. When empirical usability research does not exist or cannot be done because the technologies under construction have no current equivalent, OI resource providers in industry and academia rely on theoretical perspectives that are widely espoused by respected members of their communities to guide them.

One perspective on OI usability is widely and tenaciously held. It can be characterized as optimistically rational, and it is espoused as a complex array of social, political and organizational strategies which emphasize the importance of information, information resources and information technology for economic survival and social progress. These strategies call be called as "informational imperatives." They guide organizations and individuals to adopt more information-intensive practices, and they set expectations for particular socio-technical results. Currently, most empirical studies indicate that the use of online databases in particular, and the use of libraries and information resources in general, has not been integrated into decision-making and strategic planning activities to the degree that informational imperatives might project.

Rationalists believe that when individuals learn about OI resources, they will recognize the potential value of OI contents and use them accordingly. If OI resources are not being used, then it must be because people just don't know enough about them. They believe, as Jon Kaye does, that "to take full advantage of on-line database services, the threshold of awareness of the value of information must be raised. Users are still not understanding the value of information as a strategic tool". However, rationalists working with content usability understand that establishing awareness is only one facet of the problem. Once access and awareness have been established, there are still issues of information retrieval and information overload.

Some researchers, like Ray R. Larson, try to resolve both of these problems simultaneously by developing online systems which use techniques derived from information retrieval research. Recognizing that users sometimes just "give up" when their queries don't return relevant results immediately, Larson attempts to cluster the data into meaningful classifications that, when coupled with statistical ranking mechanisms, can "reduce the cognitive load on the user in selecting relevant documents". It involves the situated use of OI and OI resources. An organization may provide training and support staff to help people use the available resources, or it may not.

The information itself may be used collaboratively among working groups or symbolically as post-decision support. One of the reasons why rationalist managers of an organization may choose not to provide technical support or training on OI resources is because it costs too much. Researchers like Michael Koenig seek to convince them otherwise by extrapolating from economic theory to affirm that organizations systematically underinvest in OI support services and libraries. He then goes on to assert that the existence of these organizational infrastructures enhances the free-flow of information throughout the organization, and leads directly to productivity gains and improved decision-making, but his studies do not identify the mechanism by which they do so. Along with providing OI resource usage support, rational organizations in the Information Age are expected to develop formal organizational strategies to guide the optimized use of both internal and external information available through these resources.

Interorganizational Usability involves use of OI and OI resources within interorganizational networks. This may entail uses of OI to achieve competitive advantage, or to coordinate professionals of the virtual organization. According to

Marchand and Horton, managers must learn to use information strategically, in order to correctly assess environmental changes in their own industries and to spot potential opportunities in heretofore "other" industries. To do this, managers will have to realign the organizational structure with TQM-like methodologies. The profitability and efficiency concerns of corporate information consumers may not be motivating concepts for digital library planners, but an interorganizational usability awareness may allow them to consider that "outsourcing" organizations may take advantage of publicly available digital libraries.

Rational perspectives which encourage efficiency and the attainment of competitive advantage rarely consider the consequences of shifting the productivity burden to public institutions. A preponderant proportion of the OI usability literature reflects a rational point of view. But, within the HCI community, there is a large contingent of researchers who are interested not only in enhancing productivity but also in designing OI resources which enhance the work experience. While rationalists assume that OI resource access naturally leads to use, human relations (HR) theorists seek to broaden the definition of accessibility. HR theorists do not approach OI resource content usability from a perspective which assumes that mere awareness of the potential usefulness of a resource is enough to ensure use.

In fact, Nicholas and Erbach conclude their examination of end-user searching in four commercially available OI resources with an important observation. They find that the services are dissimilar, the pricing structures are divergent, downloading speeds are highly variable independent of baud rates, and in-depth knowledge about even a small set of OI services is difficult for any one person to obtain and maintain. Their findings are based on end-user observations and are motivated by a concern for lowering the frustration level of the end-user by identifying user behaviors which are not well-accommodated by the OI resources in the study.

Nicholas and Erbach make numerous suggestions for improving these existing resources, which if followed, would lead to a standard approach to OI resource design. However, they do not explicitly make this recommendation. Pfaffenberger agrees that there are a great many obstacles to end-user searching in OI resources. He points out that equal opportunity of information access was rhetoricized as the inevitable by-product of technologically enhanced information networks. But he identifies inequity of expertise as the most serious threat to equity of access. Pfaffenberger suggests that online databases will only attract end-users who are highly educated and are able to judge the significance of the material they encounter online.

HR guided researchers are nearly unanimous in their advocacy of training and support infrastructures for OI resource usage. They may suggest that an organization provide basic skills training and technical support for its OI workforce, or they may suggest a kind of self-help system which blends humans and technology into a single package. Mintzberg takes a different tack. Rather than suggesting a technological solution to information access, he concentrates his attention on intermediaries and collaboration. While trying to answer the question: "Why do managers not use information as they apparently should?", he focuses on identifying how managers work. He suggests that organizational impediments to OI resource usage arise from dysfunctional goal setting and the nature of managerial work and advancement.

Mintzberg also encourages the reorganization of work to alleviate the problem, but he states that "[m]anagers need broad-based formal information systems, in large part independent of the computer...There is reason to believe that the best filters and pattern recognizers are intelligent human beings--bright specialists (and alter egos) who can stand between the manager and mass of data out there". The Human Relations perspective usually focuses on issues of job satisfaction and worker productivity, so there is not much HR literature which addresses OI resource usability at an interorganizational level. One notable exception is a report issued in 1982 by the United Nations Centre on Transnational Corporations.

The UN was worried that the "information gap" between developed and developing countries had been widening and lessening the potential for real competition by developing countries in world markets. They commissioned this study which suggested two organizational solutions to level the playing field: build human resource infrastructures in the developing countries, like the Mexican information center, or establish search centers in the information-rich countries. The digital library community has taken many of the guiding principles of the public service library community to heart, and it strongly embraces the concepts of HR theorists.

But concerns for equity of access, fairness in the distribution of work and advocacy for adequate training in distributed, multi-organizational environments should be guided by an awareness of these non-academic contexts of use in addition to traditional academic contexts. A small but significant body of the OI usability literature reflects an institutional perspective. These researchers are interested in how organizational and institutional environments constrain or enable use of OI resources and their contents.

Although, institutionalists may recommend technological fixes to OI resources, they are more likely to recommend policy or procedural modifications that are within an organization's power to change. Institutional discussions of OI resource usage do not assign an active, rational decision-making role to the individual. They are more likely to present OI resource user choices as a complex set of constraints set up by the various organizations and institutions which provide and administer OI services. Aumente presents a historical overview of the videotext and online database industry, with an accent on HCI usability aspects. He finds fault with the usability of videotext formats and the communication exchange capabilities of the medium, but notes that similarly constrained services, like online databases, have been successful.

He looks to see where the technological constraints have been overcome within the videotext arena, for example France's Minitel, and identifies the external political factors as key enablers. Aumente's set of recommendations for the establishment of usable and viable OI resources involves technological enhancements which are tightly coupled with political support for developing a national OI infrastructure. Wanda Orlikowski has examined the introduction of groupware databases which served as digital libraries throughout a large, geographically dispersed organization. Her study found that the groupware had been developed expressly for collaborative use.

For those groups within her organization who shared information in a cooperative mode, the system was usable. But for the consultants, who worked in a competitive, non-information sharing mode, the system was largely unusable. They did not have any established norms for sharing information through digital libraries. Furthermore, they had real economic incentives not to share, but to retain and obtain as much expertise for themselves as possible. Orlikowski does not assume that everyone will want to use the resource, and she does not assume that equal access brings with it any incentives to use. She locates the implementation problem of her study outside the technological infrastructure, within the competitively-focused organizational incentive structures for the consultants, and suggests that modifications will have to be made here before the OI resource usage practices of the consultants can be expected to change.

Institutionalist information retrieval approaches try to acknowledge the taken-for-granted ways of doing things that can be discerned in particular organizations or environments. Oddy et al. have tried to incorporate situational information into OI retrieval systems. They attempt to generate generic research scripts and to match search processes with markers in the script so that the system will "know" where the searcher is in his or her research project. Organizational use of OI resources is often associated with a library or an information center. Research services may be provided to an entire organization by a small group of information specialists who make use of OI resources, and print information resources, on behalf of others. This confounds the issue of who is actually the "user"— someone who performs the OI search, or someone who uses the information retrieved by the searcher.

In cooperative work settings, identifying the end-user of the information as someone separate from the information intermediary becomes even more difficult. O'Day and Jeffries have concluded that, in the organizations they studied, virtually everyone functioned as an intermediary in some fashion; either by updating team members, consulting, broadcasting or putting the information into a shared archive. While informational imperatives may encourage intensive information gathering practices, not all the information gathered is actually used in decision making. In fact, Feldman and March suggest that information gathering is largely a symbolic act of the decision making process. They cite studies which show that little systematic relation can be established between the time of receiving the results of an information search and the time of making a decision.

There are a number of environmental constraints on OI resource use at individual, group and organizational levels. When a resource is constructed expressly for use at the interorganizational level, the reasons for its underutilization may be attributed to these constraints and to additional environmental influences. Francois Libmann's study of European online technology transfer databases shows that reasons for OI resource implementation failure can be linked to cultural concepts. He finds that "[n]o one has sought to create synergies between databases and other elements in the world of technology transfer (interpersonal networks for example)...databases are on the whole little or inefficiently used to optimise innovatory process.

This is a cultural problem and should be dealt with as such, and is one which is not exclusive to technology transfer databases". Libmann suggests that national policy must be modified to address this need. US policy makers have encouraged the construction of digital libraries, and have stressed the importance of their educational support functions. But organizations on the periphery of academia, such as Libmann's who are promoting university/industry technology transfer efforts, are also interested in constructing or using digital library services.

Digital libraries may serve these organizations, or may be embedded within them, depending on how central or supplemental the research function is to their core organizational processes. The philosophical discourse of postmodernists is suffused with an awareness of the power of language and the malleability of 'the text.' They see network technologies, digital libraries and OI resources as important components of the postmodern condition, and variously discuss online databases as new structures of domination and electronic writing as another level of reality—"textuality" or "hyperreality" Postmodern views of OI usability do not fall neatly into the admittedly rationalist framework.

According to Amiran, Unsworth and Chaski, "There is no psycholinguistic evidence that the process of reading suddenly changes when it is conducted in a different medium" But they do find significant differences in the malleability of electronic texts, and suggest that a shift toward electronic scholarly publications may encourage a reinterpretation of the concepts of authorship, ownership and scholarship at individual and institutional levels. Unlike rationalists, Amiran et al. are not preoccupied by providing quick, efficient access to OI resources, and they are less expectant of coordinated consensus as working groups share these resources.

Their expectations for OI resource usability are very like institutionalist views in that they readily identify the legitimating functions of existing ways of using OI resources, but, as postmodernists, they are more likely to attend to signals which indicate that role boundaries, such as those of librarians and other intermediaries, are blurring as a result of OI resource usage.

Although this perspective takes environmental and institutional factors into account, the postmodern view of content usability differs greatly from the institutional view, which is focused on how OI resources are manipulated by users. Postmodernists examine how users' perceptions are modified by the contents of OI resources. With respect to organizational use, the postmodern emphasis is less concerned with training organizational members to use OI resources effectively, and is more focused on understanding how OI resources, as critical components of the technical infrastructure, sustain organizational bureaucracy.

Mark Poster presents an insightful overview of the impacts of Bell's forecasts for the Information Society. He identifies information as the sustaining materiel of bureaucracy, and he acknowledges Foucault's interpretation of online databases as the major structural component of domination in postindustrial society. But he suggests that databases also have a democratic side. In personal communication, he has associated democratic empowerment with database exchanges on the Internet to exemplify the dual potential of OI resources. In either case, the postmodern view of organizational OI resource usability can be seen to resemble the institutional view in some important ways. The end-user of the information is often difficult to identify. She may be the intermediary, the bureaucrat, or some collective identity that is amorpously referred to as 'the organization.'

Interorganizational Usability. In postmodern discussions, the terms 'organizational' and 'interorganizational' may be used interchangeably. Clegg's analysis of modern organizations defines one of the more recent examples, the Benneton firm, "less as an organization per se and rather more as an organized network of market relations premised on complex forms of contracting made possible by advances in microelectronics technology". Clegg does not refer exclusively to OI resources, but to IT generally speaking, when he suggests that the classic Weberian bureaucracy may be replaced by technologically enabled organizational forms such as Benneton's. Unlike Marchand and Horton's rational analysis of interorganizational use of OI resources, Clegg's analysis does not stop at the managerial methodology level.

And unlike institutional analyses which call for governmental intervention to enact cultural change so that existing organizational forms can make more effective use of OI resources and traditional library bureaucracies, Clegg identifies environmental and cultural changes which are redefining the boundaries of the organizations themselves. The postmodern perspective encourages us to recognize that the boundaries which separate digital libraries, academic enclaves and commercial organizations are permeable and changeable. The roles of librarians and information intermediaries may be equally transmutable.

Archiving has become a major problem as more and more information is presented in electronic form. Documents prepared without carefully considering how people access or read information inevitably end up as digital landfill: either inaccessible or, if inadequately networked, forgotten. If electronic data is to survive, it must perpetually "migrate" — that is, transfer from one system to the next before the first system becomes obsolete. For libraries, the costs and challenges of migration are great. While electronic systems have brought inestimable advantages to the library, including the online catalogue and access to remote databases, the tasks of libraries have expanded enormously.

Librarians must now stay on top of technology as well as information, and must maintain archives and provide continuous access when operating platforms and systems change every few years. It is not only libraries and researchers that face the challenges of a rapidly changing information-technology environment. Now, researchers can be their own publishers, the publisher is an archivist of electronic journals, and the librarian is an information speculator, selecting what to purchase and what to save amongst an increasing array of information types. In this shift of roles, fundamental considerations arise, such as who holds copyright, who finances, and who determines when a document is completely "final."

The substantive structure of academic publishing remains largely unchanged. Despite the exponential growth of e-journals — from 417 peer-reviewed electronic journals in 1996 to 1,049 in 1999 — it is not necessarily any easier to be published, nor is the rate of publication necessarily any swifter. Even in the refereed e-journal, the pace of publication remains stoppered by the peer review process. In addition, electronic journals hold limited appeal for some because their legitimacy. Thus, with all the exciting possibilities of online publishing, the researcher may be in the same position as before, waiting for months or years until the article has, first, finished its peer review, and second, secured a berth in an upcoming edition.

In other words, despite the promise of immediacy and currency in the electronic world, academics seeking to publish online, while maintaining the credibility of peer review, may not have their work published any faster. As such, readers may not gain any of the "currency benefit" possible, for instance, in online news reporting. In this collision of needs — that is, the researcher's need to publish, and the publisher's need for profit — the potential benefits of electronic journals are subsumed in a quagmire of financial, reputational and temporal complications. In many ways, little has changed in the staged move to electronic academic journals.

The reality is that Microsoft and others will continue to change operating platforms, hardware, and software every year. Manufacturers operate within a structure of premeditated obsolescence, of staggered improvement and alteration, ensuring that there will be no "end-state" program upon which we can all settle. Because electronic media, software applications, and computer hardware will all continue to change at a rapid rate, and because policies must be developed to address that reality, the archive must change. The very notion of a permanent or fixed archive may have to give way to an ecological preservation system that is in a state of constant change.

To keep pace with technological flux, an ongoing process of selection — of media platforms, of preservation structures, of migratory patterns — is necessary to avoid data extinction. In these various ways, there is an ecological force at work. In fact, there are several ecological themes already in play in electronic archives. These include the encouragement of symbiotic relationships, the use of anti-extinction preservation and migratory schemes, and the deliberate adoption of cloning/breeding campaigns. Successful archiving involves assessing appropriate storage and delivery methods for documents based on cost, usage, appropriateness, and longevity.

The symbiotic, ecological relationship exists in the fact that the paper version needs the electronic version for the sake of its own preservation against constant usage, and the electronic version needs the paper version as a backup in case of technical problems or obsolescence. Symbiotic double conservation contrasts with some previous "preservation" practices such as the effective destruction of books through the removal of bindings to facilitate the microfilming process. A careful consideration of the archival ecosystem allows for effective migration while maximizing conservation in the long term.

Migration is a set of organized tasks designed to achieve the periodic transfer of digital materials from one hardware/ software configuration to another, or from one generation of computer technology to a subsequent generation. The purpose of migration is to preserve the integrity of digital objects and to retain the ability for clients to retrieve, display, and otherwise use them in the face of constantly changing technology. Crucial to that overall process is the independent certification of digital archives and a critical fail-safe mechanism. The primary function of the critical fail-safe mechanism is to enact "an aggressive rescue function to save culturally significant digital information" that may be at risk.

The independent certification is a mechanism through which digital archive standards are reviewed, and whose indicators include the accessibility of stored data and the long-term protection of culturally valuable information. This list of archiving and migration methodologies is by no means exhaustive. Of particular concern are the long-term prospects for the electronic resources and research undertaken in developing countries. While research libraries in the United States and other industrialized nations may have the financial resources and the available workforce to facilitate "perpetual care" activities, in other parts of the world the resources are simply not available.

"Digital aid" to the universities and publishers of the developing world may prove imperative in the coming years. The ecology of the archiving process requires that the whole biosphere of electronic data must be considered in the push for preservation, not just the material of discrete territories. Even where the necessary will and resources are in place, for some electronic data the issue of long-term preservation and/or migration is somewhat more difficult. Central examples are the presentations and publications produced only in multimedia format. As one report put it, there is no "safety net" for purely digital data, "no analogous tangible version you can recapture if you lose the digital version."

If there is a high degree of dependence between a given multimedia presentation and specific hardware or software, the process of "refreshing" — copying digital information from one medium to another — may be insufficiently compatible to maintain the exact interplay of image, sound, and text captured in the original. A two-dimensional replica may still be preserved, but the subtleties of the original may be lost, degraded in the transfer. As has always been the case, decisions will have to be made regarding what will be preserved, either in the symbiotic sense, or in the broader ecological migration to next-generation systems. This process, as always, takes time and resources.

Priorities will be set and value judgments will be made regarding what should be preserved, and how well. Despite the massive technological advances in recent decades, it is a surety that information and data will still be lost in the passage of time. The fate of data will largely depend on the strategies adopted by libraries, publishers, archivists, and individual researchers. The future of the archive depends on how information storage is conceptualized. Rather than making temporary plans in the hopes of a future permanent solution, it is advantageous to visualize all information preservation as an evolving, ever-changing ecosystem.

As technology continues to develop apace, those seeking to preserve and to update are faced with ever-expanding options of how best to do this. It is an exercise in futility to try to pick the technological winner, for "the latest" will be hopelessly outdated in ten years' time. What is necessary is a permanent strategy for handling perpetual change. This will involve periodic reassessment, the migration of material from one platform to the next, and the allocation of resources. The vision of creating digital libraries that will be able to preserve our heritage currently rests on technological quicksand.

There is as yet no viable long-term strategy to ensure that digital information will be readable in the future. Not only are digital documents vulnerable to loss via media decay and obsolescence, but they become equally inaccessible and unreadable if the software needed to interpret them—or the hardware on which that software runs—is lost or becomes obsolete. Documents, data, records, and informational and cultural artifacts of all kinds are rapidly being converted to digital form, if they were not created digitally to begin with.

This rush to digitize is being driven by powerful incentives, including the ability to make perfect copies of digital artifacts, to publish them on a wide range of media, to distribute and disseminate them over networks, to reformat and convert them into alternate forms, to locate them, search their contents, and retrieve them, and to process them with automated and semi-automated tools. Yet the longevity of digital content is problematic for a number of complex and interrelated reasons. It is now generally recognized that the physical lifetimes of digital storage media are often surprisingly short, requiring information to be "refreshed" by copying it onto new media with disturbing frequency.

The technological obsolescence of these media poses a different and equally urgent threat. Moreover, most digital documents and artifacts exist only in encoded form, requiring specific software to bring their bit streams to life and make them truly usable; as these programs become obsolete, the digital documents that depend on them become unreadable—held hostage to their own encoding.

This problem is paradoxical, given the fact that digital documents can be copied perfectly, which is often naively taken to mean that they are eternal. In addition to the technical aspects of this problem, there are administrative, procedural, organizational, and policy issues surrounding the management of digital material. Digital documents are different from traditional paper documents in ways that have significant implications for the means by which they are generated, captured, transmitted, stored, maintained, accessed, and managed. Paramount among these differences is the greatly reduced lifetime of digital information without some form of active preservation. This mandates new approaches to accessioning and saving digital documents to avoid their loss.

These approaches raise nontechnical issues concerning jurisdiction, funding, responsibility for successive phases of the digital document life cycle, and the development of policies requiring adherence to standard techniques and practices to prevent the loss of digital information. However, few of these nontechnical issues can be meaningfully addressed in the absence of a sound, accepted technical solution to the digital longevity problem. Preservation constitutes one leg of a tripod that supports informational institutions such as libraries, the other legs being access and the development and management of collections.

Without preservation, access becomes impossible, and collections decay and disintegrate. Informational artifacts include documents, data, and records of all kinds, in all media, which can be refered to as "documents" for simplicity. The essence of preserving informational artifacts is the retention of their meaning. This requires the ability to recreate the original form and function of a document when it is accessed, for example, to establish its authenticity, validity, and evidential value and to allow the document's users to understand how its creator and original viewers saw it, what they were able to infer from it, what insights it may have conveyed to them, and what aesthetic value it may have had for them.

The term "digital" in this context denotes any means of representing sequences of discrete symbolic values—each value having two or more unambiguously distinguishable states—so that they can, at least in principle, be accessed, manipulated, copied, stored, and transmitted entirely by mechanical means, with high reliability. The preservation of digital documents involves a number of distinctive requirements. In particular, all such documents possess a unique collection of core digital attributes that must be retained. These attributes include their ability to be copied perfectly, to be accessed without geographic constraint, to be disseminated at virtually no incremental cost, and to be machine-readable so that they can be accessed, searched, and processed by automated mechanisms that can modify them, reformat them, and perform arbitrary computations on their contents in all phases of their creation and distribution.

Furthermore, new inherently digital document forms, such as dynamic, distributed, interactive hypertext and hypermedia, must retain their unique functionality, including their ability to integrate information from disparate traditional sources, such as books, periodicals, newspapers, mail, phone messages, data, imagery, and video. In response to the difficulty of saving digital documents it is sometimes suggested that they be printed and saved in hard-copy form. This is a rear-guard action and not a true solution.

Printing any but the simplest, traditional documents results in the loss of their unique functionality, and printing any document makes it no longer truly machine-readable, which in turn destroys its core digital attributes. Beyond this loss of functionality, printing digital documents sacrifices their original form, which may be of unique historical, contextual, or evidential interest. Proposed alternatives to printing digital documents include translating digital documents into standard forms or extracting their contents without regard to their original nature. Though these approaches have traditional analogues, they are fraught with danger.

The meaning of a document may be quite fragile, since meaning is in the eye of the beholder: what may be a trivial transformation to a casual reader may be a disastrous loss to a scholar, historian, or lawyer. Examples of loss of meaning abound in our daily experience of converting digital documents from their native form into that of some other software application in order to read them. At its best, such conversion often sacrifices subtleties; at its worst, it leaves out entire segments or produces meaningless garbage. While it is often useful to create contemporary vernacular transcriptions of historical documents, society places a high value on retaining the originals so that we may verify that content has not been lost in transcription, as well as for scholarly and aesthetic purposes.

For digital documents, retaining an original may not mean retaining the original medium, but it should mean retaining the functionality, look, and feel of the original document. The preservation of digital documents is a matter of more than purely academic concern. The scope of this problem extends beyond the traditional library domain, affecting government records, environmental and scientific baseline data, documentation of toxic waste disposal, medical records, corporate data (such as the documentation of drug trials for pharmaceutical companies or of geologic survey data for petrochemical companies), electronic-commerce transactions, and electronic records needed to support forthcoming digital government initiatives.

The library and archives communities have identified at least some critical aspects of this problem and have recognized that preserving digital documents may require substantial new investments and commitments by institutions and government agencies. Showing admirable foresight, these communities have begun to discuss alternative economic and administrative policies for funding and managing digital preservation and have begun to develop conceptual frameworks for metadata that are not restricted to the print medium.

6

Multimedia Digital Library

The multilingual aspects of the digital library were implemented following a set of functionality specifications that were intended to make the system: comfortable to the user, flexible in terms of number and languages to support, wide and accurate in terms of the information to store and serve, and easy to operate in terms of feeding information. Digital libraries are created in countries and, in general, may be somehow specialized. It is expected that the users in the country where the library operates will want to use it in their native language.

At the same time, users with other native languages than that of the country under consideration may need more international languages, as for example, English or Spanish. Digital libraries in different countries and aiming at different sets of users may operate with distinct sets of languages. As an example, in Brazil a good set of languages is Portuguese, Spanish and English. In Italy or Taiwan the sets of languages would be different. For the same system to be used in many countries, the number of languages must be any as well as the set of languages. Another feature in this area is that all the languages do not have to be included at the same time. In order to fulfill its functions, the digital library must be accurate in terms of information.

This requires that the languages be kept track at any moment of operation by the user; he/she must know the language(s) of the catalog entry and of the content, regardless the navigation language in use. For the search to be effective, no matter the navigation language, the user may submit search arguments in any language and all points of access must be possible to be searched in all languages, regardless of the navigation language of the session. In order to identify contents in original languages and corresponding translations into other languages, a strict translation control must exist. The digital librarian must control all cataloging (original languages and translations) and all the contents (original languages and translations).

For data integrity to be achieved, translation interfaces for the cataloging and translation control applications must be available. In order to make sure that the cataloging be kept under control, the translator must be able to translate but not to include items that have not been technically processed by the librarian. The specifications yielded characteristics to both the database model and to the programs structures since both are language dependent. In terms of the programs and of the database, it does not make any difference which language is used first, since only the navigation language will determine how the interfaces are built in terms of texts. The only control of original and translation is related to contents, as it is in traditional libraries.

There is no restriction on the languages of contents, that is, a content can be in a language that is not a navigation language as it happens in a traditional library. Digital libraries hold items that are of the same nature of traditional libraries as for example digitized books, maps, manuscripts, etc. Besides that, digital libraries are natural bases to distance learning as traditional libraries have been to face-to-face learning. In this model the digital library contains all the learning objects (LO's), besides links to other libraries, references, etc.

Other metadata schemes are used, as for example the metadata specification of the Library of Congress that has almost 80 pieces from which, approximately, 20 are required 13. The LC metadata specification, obviously, contains the 15 elements of DC set. Information technology has played an important role in education for the last 10 years specially when distance learning is considered. The Internet has become an important tool to distance learning; WBE is the designation of Web Based Education and it is well known in the distance learning community.

Since the digital contents used for education are items of a collection, they must be identified to be made available. Both organizations are seriously committed to the creation of standards for distance learning with the support of information technology and the identification of the LO's is one of the concerns. The metadata scheme is one of the characteristics that the digital library & distance learning system has. Other characteristics are grouped into two main categories -the functions and the technological environment. Once the compliance to one of the metadata schemes is chosen, the other cataloging attributes must be defined from the specifications of the system functionality.

This is necessary to assure the system operability since many information pieces are necessary to satisfy specifications of the local environment. Digital libraries, WBE and e-commerce/e-business deal with items that must be identified, with sets of systems functions and technology standards. This makes them analogous in terms of problems and solutions. A multilingual digital library is implemented and operating in the Maxwell System of the Department of Electrical Engineering of PUC-Rio. This system is the implementation of a digital library, a distance learning environment and all the administrative infrastructure to support both.

In the case of this system, not only the digital library is multilingual, the whole system is multilingual. It is also multi-institution and multi-system. Although the Maxwell System can have as many languages as desired, the choice was to use Portuguese, Spanish (the language of our Latin American neighbors) and English. The implemented metadata scheme considered the specifications of both communities since the Maxwell System Digital Library holds LO's besides articles, manuals, ETD's, administrative documents, etc. Many LO's are not electronic versions of originally paper supported contents; they are born digital objects - animations, simulators, interactive exercises, etc. that were developed for educational purposes and stored in the system digital library. Because of the LO's, other attributes were added to the metadata set in the system - the ones of interest to the operation of the system and to the information that the university requires.

For example, the ETD functionality of the digital library added new attributes to the cataloging such as examining committee, date of presentation, date of acceptance, funding agency, etc. Some attributes are specific of some types of library items. Nevertheless, there is a minimum set that all items must comply with, both in terms of contents and of instances. Language control parameters is one of the metadata in all metadata schemes. It is also used in traditional libraries since it is necessary to inform the library user when the record is retrieved to make sure he/she can understand its contents. In the Maxwell System Digital Library, contents and instances are cataloged in 3 languages. Therefore, all information on contents and instances that is language dependent exists in the 3 languages and has a language code associated to it. The Dublin Core Metadata Specification requires 'subject' as one of the cataloging attributes.

The contents of this field can come from traditional library sources as subject headings, like the Library of Congress Subject Headings that is used all over the world in many languages. They can also come from a controlled set of keywords. This was the choice in this implementation. A multilingual controlled set of keywords was created. Each entry is identified by a number and a language code. English is mandatory with any other language. The number is used in the record and related to the vocabulary in the different languages by the use of a relational database. In the process of inputting elements to the controlled set, all words are transformed to uppercase characters and accents are eliminated.

The transformation is performed by the program and requires no actions from the cataloger. The database of the Maxwell System holds all the information that allow the management of contents, instances, users, courses, access control, etc. In many, if not most, of these tables there is data that is written in a language, as for example types of users, functions of the users, titles of the contents, abstracts. Other examples of information that are language dependent are keyword set, names of courses, syllabus of courses, etc.

All the messages the system uses to communicate with users are, obviously, language dependent. Data that is not language dependent are the names of authors, names of students, electronic formats of objects, dates, etc. Since the system is multilingual, the functionality of using the data in the right language, that is the language of the interface in use, must be implemented. For this reason, the database was designed to be neutral in terms language. Another characteristic of the multilingual digital library is the choice of the interface language. For this to be possible, the programs must be developed in a manner that all language dependent information be grouped in an area divided into sections, each one associated to one language.

When the language control parameter specifying the navigation language is identified, the proper language section is displayed. The messages that are displayed (after some processing is performed) are stored in a database table whose primary key is a composite key containing the message number and the language code. The metadata of all contents and instances are captured through programs that store them in the database. Titles, subtitles, abstracts, etc are language dependent while authors' names, cataloging dates, etc. are not. The fields that are language dependent must be associated with language codes too.

The Maxwell System Digital Library contains many different types of digital objects. They differ in the nature of their contents from administrative information about registration to interactive exercises to teach Portuguese. In terms of electronic format there are .html, .doc, .ppt, .pdf, .exe, .xls, .swf, etc. objects. A digital repository is an organization that has responsibility for the long-term maintenance of digital resources, as well as for making them available to communities agreed on by the depositor and the repository. This repository may operate as part of a legal deposit environment, and the producer/creator community may include almost anyone: large commercial publishers that already supply printbased resources to the library; new commercial publishers; individuals engaged in vanity publishing; research networks establishing scholarly journals; digitization contractors; the institution's own staff; writers depositing papers, including computer files; etc. The national library may be also establishing collaborative distributed archiving of some classes of digital collections, such as online publications, with regional and higher education libraries and other memory institutions, as well as publishers, with different partners exercising different levels of archiving function and responsibility over varying periods.

The digital repository is being built in-house using Artesia software and implemented both selectively and incrementally. The library also recognizes a need to take more comprehensive views of digital resources at specified points in their lifecycle. A large university library with a growing collection of digital materials to support teaching and research, including online databases, electronic journals, digitized materials, digital output of university staff and students, digital course materials, and institutional records in electronic form. This repository serves primarily the university's faculty, staff, and students, but secondary users include the wider academic community and local community members who purchase library privileges.

The university assumes that users will gain access to digital collections on campus via the LAN or via the Internet using the high-speed academic network and a personal computer. The producer/creator community for the university library, like the national library, may include almost anyone, from an individual scholar to a large commercial publisher. Locally, the university will have some control over the creation of digital materials, but most of it comes from producers over whom the library exercises little or no influence. The digital repository is hosted through the university computer service, which is contracted to provide this service to the library. A museum with a growing collection of digital materials, including surrogates of museum objects, surrogates created for online exhibitions, and original digital art.

The community the museum serves is very diverse and comprises students, researchers, artists, the general public, and organizations seeking digital material for commercial use. The producer/creator community for the museum, unlike that of the national and university libraries, is generally individual artists over whom the museum has little control. The museum does have control in the creation of some digital surrogates, though not all. The responsibility for archiving the digital materials for the long-term-regardless of creator-belongs to the museum alone. Because the museum lacks technical infrastructure and qualified staff, it will contract with a thirdparty archiving service so that its materials will be professionally managed, controlled, and backed up.

The commercial service is based on an Oracle platform and is Open Archival Information System (OAIS) compliant. Access to materials in the repository is possible through seamless links between the museum's access management system and the repository. Users of archived information in electronic form and of archival services relating to that information need to have assurance that a digital archives is what it says it is and that the information stored there is safe for the long term. The archival and computer professions promulgate a host of concepts and terms that lay a foundation for establishing the defining characteristics of dependable digital archiving repositories.

Commonly used terms such as reliable, responsible, trustworthy, and authentic help to define the nature of the archival enterprise and its myriad relationships with those creating, managing, and using digital objects. Computer scientists worldwide have grappled with definitions and performance measures of trusted military systems for nearly 20 years. Likewise, the airlines industry has required trustworthy, responsible, and authentic systems. In the last decade, groundbreaking work by archivists in Australia, North America, and Europe has resulted in fundamentally new approaches and tools that specify the nature and performance of accountable record keeping systems.

And in the past few years, digital library experts have contributed their experience to a growing body of literature and applications pertaining to the construction and maintenance of secure systems accommodating large quantities of digital resources. Archivists, digital library specialists, computer scientists, and others use the concept of reliability to express both expectations about and requirements for the nature of systems that contain and make available digital cultural materials.

Archivists use the term trust to define records, record keeping systems, and archiving organizations while experts in the fields of digital libraries and computer science increasingly use it to distinguish between reliable and unreliable digital repositories. A Guide to Understanding Audit in Trusted Systems was issued by the National Computer Security Center (NCSC) in 1988. This guide was a then-mature effort to identify the ways that trusted systems could be assessed and measured by third parties and focused very specifically on systems that processed classified military information.

The totality of protection mechanisms within a computer system-including hardware, firmware, and software—the combination of which is responsible for enforcing a security policy. A TCB consists of one or more components that together enforce a unified security policy over a product or system. The ability of a TCB to enforce a security policy correctly depends solely on the mechanisms within the TCB and on the correct input by system administrative personnel of parameters related to the security policy. A mechanism by which a person at a terminal can communicate directly with the TCB. This mechanism can only be activated by the person or the TCB and cannot be imitated by untrusted software. These NCSC documents augment a basic interpretation of trust with the concepts of auditability, security and communication. It should be noted that here communication refers to exchanges between a person and a machine. Later uses of the term denote different forms of exchange.

Necessary security requirements vary based on the type of work being protected, but requirements for the most valuable works should include detection and prevention of tampering. One trusted system has to be able to recognize another trusted system. Copying can be permitted if it is strictly controlled in accordance with the creator's and/or distributor's and rights and interests. A "reliability layer" within the distributed archival repository architecture encompasses a series of functions and mechanisms that the authors believe results in a reliable environment for preserved objects.

Communication in this instance involves exchanges between parts of a system and also between federated member systems. The authors also introduce two new concepts: backup policies and avoiding, detecting, and restoring lost/corrupted information. In May 2000, the Digital Library Federation (DLF) proposed a set of Minimum Criteria for an Archival Repository of Digital Scholarly Journals. Focusing on only one class of digital object (digital scholarly journals), their seven criteria include a mix of definitional and functional requirements.

A reliable digital repository is one whose mission is to provide long-term access to managed digital resources; that accepts responsibility for the long-term maintenance of digital resources on behalf of its depositors and for the benefit of current and future users; that designs its system(s) in accordance with commonly accepted conventions and standards to ensure the ongoing management, access, and security of materials deposited within it; that establishes methodologies for system evaluation that meet community expectations of trustworthiness; that can be depended upon to carry out its long-term responsibilities to depositors and users openly and explicitly; and whose policies, practices, and performance can be audited and measured. Even one that can be agreed to by providers and consumers of these services, is not enough to provide guidance to those who wish either to select an archiving agency or to consider setting up and running one themselves.

In order to distinguish reliable digital repositories from unreliable ones, attributes need to be identified which, when all are present, convince the community that a particular repository can be trusted with the long-term management of digital cultural materials. A trusted digital repository will provide evidence that it has a fundamental commitment to implementing the range of community-agreed standards and best practices that affect its operations-particularly those that directly influence its viability and sustainability. Its reputation for reliability will be an indicator of its trustworthiness. Administrative responsibility extends to meeting appropriate national and/or international standards for the physical environment.

The trusted repository will meet or exceed community standards for performance and will collect and share data measurements routinely with depositors. It will involve external community experts in validating and/or certifying its processes and procedures on a regular schedule. Their mission statements will reflect a commitment to the long-term retention and management of and access to digital cultural assets on behalf of depositors and users. Their legal status and standing will be appropriate to the range of responsibilities they are undertaking. Their business practices will be transparent and forthright.

Staffing levels and areas of expertise will be appropriate to the work undertaken; further, staff training and professional development opportunities, including conference attendance and participation, will be given priority to ensure the currency of staff skill sets. The repository will establish management policies that reflect the commitments asserted in the mission statement. Written agreements with depositors will address all appropriate aspects of acquisition, maintenance, access, and withdrawal.

Further, ongoing risk management and contingency planning will play a routine part of the organization's annual strategic planning activities. A trusted digital repository will adhere to all good business practices and should have a solid, auditable business plan in place. Normal business and financial fitness should be reviewed at least annually to ensure the long-term sustainability of the enterprise. Standard accounting procedures should be used. Both shortand long-term financial planning cycles should be in evidence, demonstrating an ongoing commitment to seeking a balance of risk, benefit, investment, and expenditure.

Operating budgets and reserves should be adequate for enterprises engaged in long-term operations serving a public good. Development opportunities for new sources of revenue should be explored routinely. All appropriate fiscal practices and conduct will be in place to ensure the sustainability of the repository. Community experts currently advocate a range of preservation strategies. A trusted digital repository will consider all relevant options and will communicate openly about the suitability of variant strategies. It will ensure that it has in place all appropriate hardware and software to undertake the forms of acquisition, storage, and access it promises to make available.

The repository will also have policies and plans for replacing technology as needed, including cycles of replacement and funding to achieve them. The repository will comply with all relevant standards and best practices, ensuring that staff have adequate expertise to understand and implement them. It will also undergo regular external audits on its system components and performance. All systems used in the operation of trusted digital repository will be designed to assure the security of the digital assets managed there. Policies and practices will meet community requirements, particularly those pertaining to copying processes, authentication systems, firewalls, and backup systems.

The repository will have written policies and plans for disaster preparedness, response, and recovery, and staff will be trained in carrying out appropriate responsibilities. Special attention will be given to processes that serve to avoid loss of data, detect changes in data, and restore lost or corrupted data. Any detected changes will be documented and the depositor will be notified both of the changes and any resulting actions taken. A trusted digital repository is responsible for a range of interrelated tasks and functions; it will therefore be accountable for all relevant policies and procedures. Repository practices will be documented and made available on request. Monitoring mechanisms that measure and ensure the continued operation of all systems and procedures will be in place.

Preservation strategies undertaken will be recorded and justified in the context of community-wide best practices. Feedback mechanisms will be in place to support the resolution of problems and to negotiate the evolving requirements between archive providers and consumers. The prospects of preserving digital information relate directly to the framework of trusted repository attributes outlined above: administrative responsibility, organisational viability, financial sustainability, technological suitability, system security, and procedural accountability. Unfortunately, no certification program or process covers these aspects, in total.

Libraries and archives are left to hope that potential third-party archiving services adhere to relevant standards for data centers and computer rooms, but even those best practices lack crucial elements for trusted systems. Libraries and archives need a set of standards and/or best practices, criteria for assessment and measurement, and mechanisms to certify repositories of digital information as archives. At least two viable models for certification are in use and well known within the library and archives community: the audit model and the standards model. The audit model is applicable to depositories holding government records, especially electronic records.

In the US, such depositories must meet guidelines created by governmental agencies such as the Department of Defense or legislated by government. The standards model operates in a variety of places throughout the library and archival community. Two examples of the standards model for certification would be guidelines for producing preservation-quality microfilm and ISO interlibrary lending. Institutions involved in preservation microfilming or interlibrary loan adhere to standards that appropriate agencies have certified as valid and appropriate. Peer institutions then "certify" the product or service by their acceptance and/or use of it. While both models work well, neither can completely address the range of activities, functions, and responsibilities associated with digital repositories. In 1999, experts gathered at the Archival Workshop on Ingest, Identification, and Certification Standards (AWIICS) to begin developing standards specifically appropriate to the needs of digital repositories.

In the context of traditional archival settings, certification of archivists is possible through a combination of education, work experience, and a competencies examination administered by the Academy of Certified Archivists (ACA). Nothing equivalent exists for electronic archiving or digital repository management. Certification of a program or institution can be achieved through a combination of selfevaluation using standardized checklists and criteria and site inspections typical of program accreditation. Process certification assesses methods and procedures that can be subjected to either quantitative or qualitative guidelines to guarantee adherence to all internal and external requirements. Data certification is concerned with two main aspects of the stored data: data persistence or reliability over time and data security.

Issues related to data security have been addressed by the Public Key Certification Policy and Certification Practices Framework—because of the e-commerce boom, however, not because of the needs of digital archiving. This framework, which was established to deal with user authentication and user communication in ecommerce transactions, handles access control issues for repositories and removes the need for additional data security certification. A Framework for Developing a Certification Programme Representatives from interested communities and expert stakeholders can and should develop a program for certifying trusted digital repositories. One way to frame the necessary development work is to break down the identifiable steps and illustrate each with examples from related fields and disciplines. Some certification programmes are based on self-assessment while others depend on third-party examiners.

Advantages and disadvantages of both should be weighed and a determination made as to which is most appropriate to this particular need. For most ISO standards, certification combines third-party examination and self-assessment. ISO does not check on implementations of their standards. Instead, partnerships are established with relevant communities and/or professional organisations and guides are jointly developed to assess conformance to standards. Depending upon the standard, self-assessment may be all that is needed to judge compliance.

Community representatives and expert stakeholders interested in the long-term survival of preservation microfilm worked together to create national standards for its storage. In the US, these standards require that storage facilities are to be inspected at two-year intervals. If deviations are detected or have occurred in the past, inspections are to be more frequent. If the future of scholarship is to be secured, repositories need to understand fully what responsibility they should assume for the preservation of digital materials. Digital materials for libraries and archives range from simple digital files to complex multimedia and database resources.

The sheer variety of digital materials and the role that they play in the collection make development and application of collections policies very challenging. The existence or lack of a physical equivalent or counterpart influences decisions about whether and how the digital resource is preserved. For materials that have a physical counterpart, preservation decisions take into account considerations such as the condition of the original materials and the reason for digitizing. Materials that are "born digital" can present more challenging problems because their "being digital" is not only a method of access, it represents their value as an information artifact.

For many born-digital resources, effective preservation will rely as much on preservation of the object's digital characteristics or properties as on preservation of its basic intellectual content. More importantly, when a library or archive digitises its own collections, it can control decisions about standards, formats, quality control, and documentation. The preservation of materials generated outside may not include this degree of control. Preservation decisions for digital items cannot wait until continued use of the materials has proved they are worth keeping. Postponing preservation decisions can and most often will result in preservation actions that are more complex, more labor intensive, and more costly.

A resource can even be held hostage by an obsolete piece of software. It is also important to accept the fact that digital information is more transitory and mutable, so there is little likelihood of its surviving through benign neglect. Preservation requires active management that begins at the creation of the material and depends on a proactive approach by digital repositories and the cooperation of the stakeholders, including data providers. The Wide Range of Stakeholders Content creators, systems developers, custodians, and future users are all potential stakeholders in the preservation of digital materials, and this complicates the determination of responsibilities-who, when, and for how long.

Often, those creating digital materials or designing digital content management systems do not take great interest in their long-term preservation. Responsibility for preservation has traditionally been considered alongside ownership of the materials; that is, the owner of the materials was responsible for determining their lifespan. However, ownership of digital materials is not often straightforward. While a book can be taken into the collection and set upon the shelf, digital materials are less tangible.

For a growing number of digital materials considered "integral" to research collections and archives, access is provided through licensing arrangements-often through a "deal" with a regional or national consortium. Licensing arrangements can apply to either the digital content itself or to software necessary for specific functionality and access to the content. Although the organization may own the right to access material or use the software for a specified period, there is often no guarantee of rights beyond the terms of the license.

While commercial publishers are beginning to provide some guarantee of continuing access, most licensing agreements are still perilously vague about how the digital repository will be maintained and how long-term access will be ensured. Reliance solely on creators or producers of digital materials for long-term preservation is potentially risky, not least because digital resources are not generally created or engineered with long-term preservation in mind. It will require increased cooperation and effective communications with publishers, software suppliers, and other producers to ensure that what is deposited is a copy of the data object in the format most suitable for preserving the materials over the long term.

In this situation, understanding the important difference between long-term preservation and short term access-particularly while materials are still commercial viable-is critical. Libraries may require different license arrangements for long-term preservation than for end-user access. Often, rights that relate to the software and systems used to create the material impinge on its preservation. Very little, if any work, has been done with software vendors to raise awareness about the longevity of their materials in the interests of future scholarship and research.

Digital preservation has even wider legal implications. How preservation infringes on copyright remains unclear. The content creator does not usually own the rights to the software and systems used to create the digital file. This raises legal issues when access or changes to those systems are necessary. In such cases, at best, a repository will need to arrange separate rights clearance for long-term maintenance; at worst, preservation will be compromised because rights clearances for access cannot be obtained.

Some work has been done on the establishment of repositories for software to help address these concerns, however the research repository community will need to make an appeal to have this conflict taken into consideration in the creation or renewal of national deposit legislation. Although not a great deal is known about the costs of preserving complex digital objects over time, there is an accepted wisdom in the library community that digital preservation will require ongoing resource commitments-potentially more than for traditional materials, but certainly different. Traditional and digital preservation should be compared with some caution, because the complex dependencies between long-term maintenance and continuing access make comparison problematic.

Indeed, for digital materials that have no analog equivalent, comparison is meaningless. Although it may be too early to compare the costs of digital and traditional preservation meaningfully, one thing is certain: preserving digital materials will require resource commitments over time. While traditional materials, for example, may have ongoing costs for stable storage environments, digital materials will also require periodic analysis and the application of new technical strategies to ensure continuing access.

Digital preservation is also likely to draw on resources longer than traditional preservation does, and it may be the case that different technical strategies will prescribe quite different costing timeframes and schedules. The lack of standardization in both the resources themselves and the licensing agreements with publishers and other data producers, making economies of scale difficult to achieve. The as yet unresolved means of reliably rendering certain digital publications so that they do not lose essential information after technology changes. That, for some time to come, the costs of digital preservation may be added to the costs for traditional collections, unless cost savings can be realised. Digital technologies and applications shift rapidly; strategies to preserve objects resulting from new approaches must keep pace.

The inherent mutability of digital preservation therefore makes it difficult, if not impossible, to establish concrete costs for all associated activities. Further, the uncertainty of the financial commitment represented by digital preservation makes assuming preservation responsibilities more complex. However, although work can be done to understand how costs will play out and where saving can be made, the preservation of digital materials cannot wait for exact information because it may never appear. What will be important is an understanding of where the main costs are likely to fall and how, within existing practices, these can be incorporated to achieve economies of scale.

In addition, that ways that other stakeholders (e.g., content providers) can decrease costs (e.g., by changing the way they supply materials for deposit-in specific formats or with better descriptions) should be explored. Repositories that currently provide guidelines for depositors include the Cornell University Library, Arts and Humanities Data Service (AHDS), and the National Library of Australia. Repositories will also need to understand more about the advantages of collaborative approaches. Although, if all participants' costs are totaled, distributed archiving is unlikely to cost less than using a single, centralized repository, a shared operation will cost less per organization; that is, the costs may be easier to absorb across multiple institutions.

Integrating digital preservation into the everyday management and organization of the library or archive will help ensure that the necessary skills and knowledge are embedded within the organization for the earliest and most effective savings or economies of scale. The functions of a digital repository parallel those of traditional repositories. Broadly speaking, these functions describe how materials are submitted to the repository, how they are organized and managed within the repository, and, how continuing access to them is provided.

Some repositories require content creators to conform to specific restrictions on the type or format of materials, while others exert little or no influence over the creation of materials. In most cases, some activity to prepare the materials for submission will be required. In a few cases, "aggressive rescue" or salvage measures will need to be taken. Long-term preservation may be jeopardized if submission of materials is based solely on negotiations for current access, which can be more restricted to protect the commercial interests of the content provider. Preservation metadata based on agreed-on specifications.

A repository has to ensure that agreements are in place with content providers about the bibliographic and technical metadata that accompany the submitted materials. Authenticity checks, confirming that the digital materials submitted to the repository are exactly what the content provider intended. Record keeping, with adequate documentation for the transactions between the repository and content provider. Digital repositories can store a digital object and its associated metadata in two ways: as a single bytestream or separately. For practical reasons, repositories may prefer to store the digital object within the repository and provide only pointers or references to the associated metadata in different systems within the organization, such as bibliographic data stored in the library management system.

Although such fragmentation of digital object and metadata may present problems in the future, many organizations are choosing "virtual encapsulation" to avoid duplicating metadata. However, some experts feel that, despite the increased costs of duplicating metadata, long-term preservation may be best served by storing the digital content and all of its relevant metadata as a single file within the repository. The repository needs to ensure that mechanisms are in place for verifying the digital object, including all associated metadata. The repository should verify that the digital object can be rendered from the encapsulation back into its original form as it was submitted to the repository.

Preservation takes place for the designated community: whether to preserve an object or class of objects is initially determined by how the repository's designated community values its content. Likewise, the creation of the technical infrastructure to ensure access to the object depends entirely on the community's technical capability or knowledge base. In particular, the knowledge base determines the minimum level of associated technical metadata for long-term access. "Knowledge base" in this context does not necessarily imply any specific technical expertise on the part of the user; it is an assumption about the technical capability users will have available to them either as actual technical knowledge or through access systems.

Traditionally, knowledge of a library's designated community was gleaned through face-to-face interaction. Generally, the user community was assumed to fit within a broadly defined "research" or "academic" community. These assumptions may not have been documented explicitly as part of the library's policy; if they were, it was not to influence the preservation or long-term retention of materials. Digital repositories, however, rely on a thorough understanding of their designated communities and a federation of repositories that distributes responsibilities, identifying and understanding the designated community is critical, especially if the repositories have divided their collecting and archiving responsibilities along specific lines, such as particular data formats or subject areas.

Research libraries and archives may find it difficult to identify the designated community because their users typically represent a wide variety of backgrounds and interests. Making digital information independently understandable poses formidable challenges because it is not itself humanly readable at any level-it relies on further digital information to make it meaningful. However, it is possible to stipulate that the technical metadata required for rendering binary data into meaningful digital objects correspond to the lowest common level of technical knowledge or capability in the designated community. For example, in the current technical climate, one might assume that any user could use a Web browser and an HTML file.

Access and dissemination of objects from the repository will also need to reflect changes in both the technology and in the knowledge base of the designated community. It may be necessary to provide different migrated versions of objects as technologies change; whether this is also reflected in changes to the digital object and technical metadata will be determined by the organization's policies. Many repositories may change their continuing access methods without changing the stored object itself. In other words, "on-the-fly" migration may be provided for materials just for access, but the migrated version itself being not stored. Clearly defining the designated community and its level of technical capability will help limit the resources necessary to support this "lowest-common-denominator" approach.

Role of Metadata in Digital Libraries

Metadata is crucial in the field of digital libraries as there is a necessity for describing the digital documents for various purposes such as searching, indexing and presentation of spatial objects. The importance of metadata with respect to geoinformation resources has been described as "... probably the single most important action immediately needed ..."

Several metadata standards have already been proposed such as the American FGDC/Content Standards for Digital

Geospatial Metadata [FGDC] and the European Catalogue of Data Sources (CDS). When the use of spatial data repositories is considered from a global perspective, the problem of web-based access presents additional challenges. It is assumed at this level that geographic information users will cluster into communities with shared interests and perspectives as suggested by the OpenGIS Consortium [OGC]. Metadata for use in spatial digital libraries has been categorised in various ways: 'content based' or 'content independent', 'domain dependent' or 'domain independent' or 'data driven' or 'application driven'.

Metadata may be required to encompass other pertinent information such as the processing lineage of satellite images, estimates of data accuracy or administrative details for acquiring and downloading subsets of the data. These classifications of metadata type reflect the various purposes for which metadata are extracted and compiled. The approach to metadata reflects the resource discovery and retrieval process from the users' perspective. At the most abstract level, metadata captures the concepts and terminology which are common currency within a particular user community.

For example, marine scientists may refer to 'sea surface temperature', 'chlorophyll levels' and 'plankton distributions'. Additional metadata may be pertinent for more focused retrieval. For example, the users' search may be concentrated on a specific temporal interval, or specific types of data and associated attributes. Moreover, in cases where metadata generation involves a resource intensive process, the underlying functions may be invoked on input (eager evaluation mode) or only on retrieval or query of the associated object (lazy evaluation mode).

The main aim of classifying metadata as explained above is to partition the search space thematically and spatially in a multi-level hierarchy of abstraction. Different metadata objects are attached to the appropriate level of the data repository according to their purpose and function. This partitioning enables an efficient mechanism for browsing and indexing which promotes stepwise retrieval of data and closely mirrors the users search process.

This hierarchical approach guides user queries to a narrower number of interesting data sets which can be explored in greater detail to determine whether they should be downloaded for further analysis. Hence, the searches usually start at the top level of the hierarchy, and are progressively refined, from a high level of abstraction (domain dependent and application driven metadata) to a lower level of abstraction (domain independent and data driven metadata). The use of domain dependent vocabularies structured in ontologies reduces the gap between the implemented model and user reality.

The Conceptual Metadata Model: This model was designed based on a three-level hierarchy of metadata abstractions. The first level contains the ontologies, collection and spatial domain dependent classes. The ontology classes contain vocabulary specific to a particular domain and the relationship between associated concepts such as synonyms, alternative terms and translations between languages. For example a data repository which consists of information about environmental disasters could include semantic hierarchies dealing with land-cover and forest fires.

Semantics hierarchies pertaining to land cover could be based on the CORINE and USGS land use and land cover classifications. Data providers can specify new ontologies depending on their interest. The spatial dimension classes contain geographic names with their respective coordinates. They allow users to specify the region they are interested in without requiring detailed specification of the exact spatial coordinates.

The collection class contains structural and administrative information about different collections of data maintained in the SDL. A collection can be viewed as a cluster of objects (maps, satellite images, photographs, reports, video, audio) relating to a specific theme under a spatiotemporal dimension. The classification of data sets into collections is determined by the data provider.

Metadata attached to collection include the title, a descriptive annotation, the creator and the overall spatial and temporal footprints of the underlying data sets. Collections are composed of geoobjects which are described in the subsequent levels of the hierarchy. The subsequent metadata levels are more closely linked to the objects in the data repository. The objects themselves are specific data types such as image, text, video, audio and vector map.

Each elementary data type will have appropriate metadata attributes associated with it. For example the metaobject of a satellite image (metaimage) will contain attributes such as sensor, resolution and lineage, the metaobject of a report (metatext) will contain attributes such as format, length and author. An interesting feature of the model is the provision for complex spatial objects which may be composed of several objects of different base types (e.g. video and text), implementing the part of relationship. The metaobjects at the second and third levels form an is a hierarchy, data type independent attributes are abstracted at the metageoobject level and type specific attributes are represented at the base type level.

Another interesting feature is the possibility of objects being stored outside the SDL borders and referenced via a URL Thus, the indexing mechanism operates at different levels. At the top level of the hierarchy users can pose queries by concepts, spatial footprints, time and collections. Alternatively, users can pose a query using the second level of the hierarchy. In this case the user can specify a narrower spatial bounding box, use a specific temporal interval or even query the annotation keywords.

At the bottom level, users can pose queries using the attributes associated with specific base data types. Moreover, users can use data type specific indexes such as textual index: for instance look for keywords in the text, or content-based retrieval, such as looking for images similar to the query image considering different features such as colour, texture and shape. At the ontology level concepts like fire, rain forest, tribal reservations are relevant to this collection. At the base level, text objects are indexed based on keywords providing a semantic level of information which describes them.

Images (e.g. photographs and satellite images) are indexed using the content-based index which allows query by example such as 'show me images similar to this particular one'. The software at the server end consists of a component for content-based multimedia information retrieval (CBMIR) and the object-dependent manager.

A Formal Model of Digital Library: The proper concept of a digital library seems hard to completely understand and evades definitional consensus. Different views and perspectives have led to a myriad of differing definitions. Digital libraries integrate findings from disciplines such as hypertext, information retrieval, multimedia services, database management, and human-computer interaction.

The need to accommodate all these characteristics complicates the understanding of the underlying concepts and functionalities of digital libraries, thus making it difficult and expensive to construct new digital library systems. Designers of digital libraries are most often library technical with little to no formal training in software engineering, or computer scientists with little background in the research findings about information retrieval or hypertext.

Thus, digital library systems are usually built from scratch using home-grown architectures that do not benefit from digital library and software design experience. Wasted effort and poor interoperability can therefore ensue, raising the costs of digital libraries and risking the fluidity of information assets in the future. The broad and deep requirements of digital libraries demand new models and theories in order to understand better the complex interactions among its several components.

However, though the necessity for such an underlying theory has long been perceived and advocated, little if any progress has been made towards a formal model or theory for digital libraries. Formal mathematical models strengthen common practice. Their lack leads to diverging efforts and has made interoperability one of the most important problems faced by the field. As a matter of fact, it is not surprising that most of the disciplines related to digital libraries have formal models that have steered them well: programming languages, relational databases, hypertext, multimedia, and information retrieval. There are five formalisms—streams,

— structures,

— spaces,

— scenarios, and

— societies

These formalisms are important for making sense of complexity and can ultimately serve as an aid for designers, implementers, and evaluators of digital libraries. These abstractions work with other known and derived definitions to yield a formal, rigorous model of digital libraries.

A formal model abstracts the general characteristics and common features of a set of systems developed for similar problems, and explains their structures and processes. Furthermore, formal models for information systems can be used as a tool for the design of a real system while providing a precise specification of requirements against which the implementation can be compared for correctness.

The relational model is the most established formal model for databases. In this model, entities of the real world are modeled as fixed sequences of attribute values, called relations, which are actually subsets of the Cartesian product of the domain set of each attribute. Normalization encompasses a set of operations designed to divide complex relations into ones with simple domains. A specific algebra describes operations in this model; the relational calculus provides an alternative formulation.

Object-oriented databases have become the focus of much current database research and development efforts due to the limitations of the relational model regarding more complex applications, like multimedia and geographic information systems. One of the first developments of a formal framework for object databases explicitly divided them into a structural object model and a behavioral layer. The structural model is described as a directed graph whose nodes can be simple values or other abstract objects.

Formal models for information retrieval (IR) have arisen since the mid-sixties to undergird a primarily empirical approach. The three classic models in information retrieval are called boolean, vector, and probabilistic. The boolean model is set theoretic and is the basis for many IR systems. Documents are seen as sets of terms. A query is represented as a logical expression built on terms and some combination of the logical operators AND, OR, and NOT. Searching is carried out by returning documents that have combinations of terms satisfying the logical constraints of the query, with supplementary facilities that allow proximity and truncation searching.

The boolean model, in its pure form, has inherent limitations for searching textual documents: boolean queries are notoriously difficult to write and modify; allow little control over the size of the result set;and more importantly disallow the production of ranked output. In the vector space model, terms used to index documents are considered as coordinates of a multi-dimensional space. Retrieval involves ranking the document vector space with respect to the query based on some similarity function such as the cosine measure between vectors.

Hypertext systems provide the foundations for a complementary activity of retrieval called browsing, characterized by the lack of clearly defined objectives and whose purpose can change during the interaction with the system. Hypertext systems have increasingly incorporated multimedia content, leading thus to the concept of "hypermedia systems".

Multimedia and hypertext/hypermedia information systems also have received formal treatments. Lucarella and Zanzi present a formal graph-based object model of a multimedia database and describe both the underlying theory and the design and implementation of the Multimedia Object Retrieval Environment (MORE) system.

The Dexter model for hypertext abstracts the dynamic and run-time aspects of hypermedia systems as well as the data storage layer. Nevertheless the Dexter model has been shown not to be sufficient to handle the so-called "hypermedia-in-the-large," required when systems are integrated and expanded through time. The Dexter model also is not sufficient for multimedia, and was extended and implemented as the Amsterdam model by adding temporal logics, events, and activations. These models are important to digital libraries because the DL itself, especially in "browse" mode, can be presented as a large hypertext of nodes that are the documents contained by the library.

Dynamic streams facilitate communication in digital libraries, and are thus important for representing whatever communications take place in the digital library. Examples of dynamic streams and their applications include video-on-demand, filtering and routing of streams of news, and transmission of messages. Typically, a dynamic stream is understood through its temporal nature. A dynamic stream can then be interpreted as an defnite sequence of clock times and values that can be used to define a stream algebra, allowing operations on diverse kinds of multimedia streams. Types of stream include text, video, and audio.

The type of the stream defines its semantics and area of application. For example, statically thinking, any text representation can be seen as a stream of characters, so that text documents, like scientific articles and books can be considered as structured streams. A structure specifies the way in which parts of a whole are arranged or organized. In digital libraries, structures can represent hypertexts, taxonomies, system connections, user relationships, containment, data flows, and work flows, to cite a few. Books, for example can be structured logically into chapters, sections, subsections, and paragraphs; or physically into cover, pages, line groups, and lines. Structuring orients readers within a document's information space. Indeed structured documents often rely on markup languages.

Relational and object-oriented databases impose strict structures on data, typically using tables or graphs as units of structuring. Indexing in information retrieval systems by a manual or automated process serves not only to improve performance but also to cluster and/or classify documents to support future requests, generating an organizational structure for the document space. With the increase of heterogeneity of material continually being added to digital libraries, find that much of this material is "semistructured "or "unstructured".

Such "semistructured data" refers to data that may have some structure, where the structure is not as rigid, regular, or complete as the structure used by structured documents or traditional database management systems. Query languages and algorithms can extract structure from these data. Although most of those efforts have a "data-centric" view of semi-structured data, recent work with a more "document-centric view" have emerged.

In general, human and natural language processing routines can expend considerable effort to unlock the interwoven structures found in texts at syntactic, semantic, pragmatic, and discourse levels.

Spaces are extremely important mathematical constructs. The operations and rules associated with a space define its properties. For example, in mathematics, a fine, linear, metric, and topological spaces define the basis for algebra and analysis. Spaces can be generalized into "feature spaces," sometimes used with image as well as document collections and suitable for clustering or probabilistic retrieval. Document spaces are a key concept in those theories. Human understanding is captured in conceptual spaces. Various spaces or subspaces can handle metadata like author and date, or relationships like citation-based links.

Multi-media systems must represent real as well as synthetic spaces in one or several dimensions, limited by some presentational space and transformed to other spaces to facilitate processing such as compression. Many of the synthetic spaces represented in virtual reality systems are analogs to real spaces, or to information spaces of various types.

Digital libraries may model traditional libraries by using virtual reality spaces or environments. Also spaces for computer-supported cooperative work provide a context for virtual meetings and collaborations. Again, spaces are distinguished by the operations on their elements. Digital libraries can use many types of spaces for indexing, visualizing, and other services that they perform. The most prominent of these for digital libraries are measurable spaces, measure spaces, probability spaces, vector spaces, and topological spaces.

Scenarios are useful as part of the process of designing information systems. Scenarios can be used to describe external system behavior from the user's point of view; provide guidelines to build a cost-effective prototype; or help to validate, infer and support requirements specifications and provide acceptance criteria for testing. Developers can quickly grasp the potentials and complexities of digital libraries through scenarios. Scenarios tell what happens to the streams, in the spaces, and through the structures. Scenarios help us visualize the spaces, by setting up streams from views of structures.

Thus, taken together the scenarios describe services, activities, tasks and operations and those ultimately specify the functionalities of a digital library. User scenarios describe one or more users engaged in some meaningful activity with an existing or envisioned system. This approach has been used as a design model for hypermedia applications. Human information needs, and the processes of satisfying them in the context of digital libraries, are well suited to description with scenarios, including these key types: fact-finding, learning, gathering, and exploring.

Additionally, scenarios can aid understanding of how digital libraries affect organizations and societies, and how challenges to support social needs relate to underlying assumptions of digital libraries. Scenarios also help us consider the complexities of current publishing methods, as well as how they may be reshaped in the era of digital libraries, considering publishing paths, associated participants, and publication functions. The concepts of state and event are fundamental to understanding scenarios.

Informally, a state is determined by what contents are in specified locations, as, for example, in a computer memory, disk storage, visualization, or the real world. An event denotes a transition or change between states, executing a command in a program. Scenarios specify sequences of events, which involve actions that modify states of a computation and influence the occurrence and outcome of future events.

The entities are hardware, software, and wetware that are somehow related to the digital library. The activities are what the entities have done, do, and expect to do with each other. The relationships make connections between and among the entities and activities of the society. Societies are necessary to describe the context of use of a digital library, since societies are the reason why libraries are built and maintained. In this sense, digital libraries are used for collecting, preserving and sharing information artifacts between society members.

For example, digital libraries help to grow the relationship between library patrons (society members) and the information they seek. A society is the highest-level component of the library, as a digital library exists to serve the information needs of its societies. Cognitive Models for Information Retrieval, for example, focus on user's information-seeking behavior and on the ways in which IR systems are used in operational environments. In digital libraries, specific human societies include patrons, authors, publishers, editors, maintainers, developers, and the library. There are also societies of learners and teachers.

In a human society, people have roles, purposes, and relationships. Societies follow certain rules and their members play different roles-participants, managers, leaders, contributors, or users. Members have activities and relationships. During their activities, society members have created information artifacts-art, history, images, data-that can be managed by the library. Societies are holistic-substantially more than the sums of their constituents and the relationships between them. Several societal issues arise when consider them in the digital library context. These include policies for information use, reuse, privacy, ownership, intellectual property rights, access management, security, etc.

Therefore, societal governance is a fundamental concern in digital libraries. Language barriers are also an essential concern in information systems and internationalization of online materials is a big issue in digital libraries, given their globally distributed nature. Economics, a critical societal concern, is also key for digital libraries. Collections that were "born electronic" are cheaper to house and maintain, while scanning paper documents to be used online can be prohibitively expensive.

Internet access is widely available and is inexpensive. Online materials are seeing more use, including from exceedingly remote locations. With circulation costs of electronic materials very low, digital delivery makes sense. However, it brings the problem of long-term storage and preservation such that the myriad of information now being produced can be accessible to future generations. Modeling a society to the extent that it can be predicted reliably is not possible, due to its sensitivity to its inputs that gives it its chaotic nature. However, understanding certain aspects of societies as sets of entities, activities, and relationships can be beneficial.

In sum, a society is composed of individuals. Individuals have an intrinsic identity and are grouped into communities indirectly by way of descriptions that apply to all members of a community. Individuals are related to each other through relationships. Relationships specify interconnections and communications among individuals. Informally, a digital library is a managed collection of information with associated services involving communities where information is stored in digital formats and accessible over a network. Information in digital libraries is manifest in terms of digital objects, which can contain textual or multimedia content (e. g., images, audio, video), and metadata.

Metadata have been informally defined as data about other data. Although the distinction between data and metadata often depends on the context, metadata commonly appears in a structured way and covering different categories of information about a digital object. The most common kind of metadata is descriptive metadata , which include catalogs, indexes and other summary information used to describe objects in a digital library.

Another common characteristic of digital objects and metadata is the presence of some internal structure, which can be explicitly represented and explored to provide better DL services. Basic services provided by digital libraries are indexing, searching, and browsing. Those services can be tailored to the different communities depending on their roles, for example, creators of material, librarians, patrons, etc.

Activities in Digital Libraries

Activities of digital libraries-abstracting, creating, collecting, disseminating, evaluating, modeling, organizing, preserving, personalizing, requesting, and selecting all are services that follow scenarios. Furthermore, these activities make and characterize relationships within and between societies, streams, and structures. Each activity happens in a setting, arena, or space. The relationships developed can be seen under the optics of larger structures. Digital libraries can contain repositories of knowledge, information, data, metadata, relationships, logs, annotations, user profiles, and documents, all which can be interpreted as distinct forms of digital objects, according to their particular structures, metadata, and streams. They can contain structuring and organizational materials: term lists, classification tools (e. g., subject headings and taxonomies), thesauri, ontologies and catalogs.

DLs are served by a substrate a foundational complex amalgamation of different combinations of Ss that involves computers, network connections, file and operating systems, communications links, and protocols. This facet is mainly related to the societal aspects of the DL and their relationships and interactions, including regulations, measures and derivatives. It abstracts aspects surrounding the other DL issues and involves policies, economic issues, standards, and qualities. Most of those are generally established by normative structured documents.

Policies and quality control can be enforced by specific services, for example, authentication, authorization, cryptography and specific practices or protocols, which can involve other communication services and serialized streams.

The environment is the space that defines the use and the context of a DL. It involves again the society that set up the DL, uses it, and keeps it going. But it is also how the DL fits into the structure of community and its organization and dictates the scenarios by which its activities are performed.

Networked Digital Library of Theses and Dissertations (NDLTD) is an international federation of universities, libraries, and other supporting institutions focused on efforts related to electronic theses and dissertations (ETDs). Many libraries and universities run their own programs and services, but there also are consortia activities at the state, regional, and national levels. NDLTD allows institutions to cooperate and collaborate in a federated fashion, in a scalable and sustainable effort, especially since automation affords savings to both students and their universities relative to old paper-based approaches.

The NDLTD aims to enhance graduate education, particularly of those students who prepare either a thesis or dissertation. Consequently, a second society is implicated, namely those involved in administering graduate programs. Those who are deans or associate deans of graduate schools, and their supervisors (e. g., associate provosts or associate chancellors) as well as the members of related associations, are key members of this important society, that often decides if a university will join NDLTD. Because some universities have distributed these responsibilities to colleges or faculties, or because some involved in graduate program administration are too busy to carefully study NDLTD, expanded this second society to include those in colleges or departments that administer graduate programs, allowing them to have their respective units join NDLTD prior to an action by the entire university. The third society related to NDLTD includes those involved in related activities in university libraries.

This often involves the director or dean of the university library, as well as those involved in automation, support of multimedia development, training, cataloging, preservation, or other similar roles. A fourth society involved in NDLTD is that of faculty. They may encourage students to start early to experiment with electronic theses and dissertations (ETDs), and to prepare expressive works, using multimedia. They may assist by providing tools in their laboratories that help with production of an ETD. They may guide students to produce high-quality works; that, in turn, may encourage and help large numbers of potentially interested readers.

From a hypertext perspective the field of digital libraries could seem like a particular application of hypertext technology. From a wide-area information service perspective, digital libraries could appear to be one use of the World Wide Web. From a library science perspective, digital libraries might be seen as continuing a trend toward library automation. There is some truth to these perspectives but none address the field as a whole and its research agenda. The field of digital libraries will be limited if viewed only as a subfield of prior research interests. To realize its full potential, the field must be viewed as a union of subfields from a variety of domains combined with additional goals, and thus new research issues.

Digital library research must both respect the existing tradition of our physical libraries and transcend current practice in developing a new, broader research agenda. Why is a digital library called a library at all? This question has been addressed by various members of this research community. Miksa and Doty discussed the notions of collection, information sources, and place with respect to physical libraries and how these notions might carry over into the digital realm. Levy and Marshall considered how work practices in physical libraries might be used in the design of digital libraries. The physical library can provide the starting point for discussing the elements and domains of digital libraries.

An element of a library is a constituent part of the library. A domain of the library is the universe from which the library materials are drawn. There are three broad classes of library elements: data, metadata, and processes. Data are library materials. Metadata are information about the library and its materials. Processes are active functions performed over library elements. For example, a book in a library may be thought of as being data of that library. An index over book titles may be thought of as library metadata.

The act of a librarian helping a patron find a book by suggesting the use of the card catalog may be thought of as a process. This classification is vague, in the sense that it may be difficult or impossible to classify any given library element as distinctly belonging to a particular class. It may be possible to view a single element as belonging to all three classes. However, this classification is useful since it provides a framework for discussion about library elements.

Physical library elements often fulfill some role for a given library user at a given moment. These roles often can be assigned in specific cases in a meaningful way. Because this classification concerns elements in the library, it ignores differences in roles played by people interacting with the library, the various ways in which these roles are being reassigned in the digital library, and the different high-level tasks people fulfilling these roles perform. These are of course all important issues, but will not be considered here. This classification of physical library elements can be applied to digital library elements as well, with the same understanding that a given element may be thought of differently by different users at different times.

Of course most modern libraries deal with both, but it is useful for sake of discussion to consider hypothetical "all-physical" and "all-digital" libraries as foils. If physical libraries primarily contain physical data and digital libraries primarily contain digital data, then how can digital libraries preserve and disseminate the vast amounts of existing physical data? Instead of containing the physical data itself, digital libraries will contain digital translations of this data. The term translation is used, because the process of generating these digital representations of physical data is not necessarily a completely meaning-preserving process.

The product may not be perceived by users in the same way that the source is perceived since their media of presentation are necessarily different. It might be tempting to think that if there are differences between analogous physical and digital objects, they have no practical consequence. This would imply, however, that all such differences are already known. Not only is this not the case, but it is not even clear that all such differences can ever be known, because one cannot know, a priori, all the important characteristics of an object in any situation. The magnitude of differences between physical and digital analogs may be related to the accuracy of the physical/digital translation. A spectrum of translation quality certainly exists.

Without more research into the effects of translating material between physical and digital form, it is difficult to know the accuracy of such translation. The difference between the physical and digital domains also has implications for translating the metadata and processes of physical libraries. Some of the metadata and processes of a physical library are themselves physical elements. However, even those elements of the physical library that have no direct physical reality are often inextricably tied to the physicality of data and the library itself.

Digital libraries will deal with translated physical elements, conceptual elements of the physical library adapted to the digital realm, and completely new digital elements with no apparent physical library analog. Differences between physical library and digital library elements have created many open problems concerning how to adapt the tradition of the physical library into the digital realm. A central problem in translating physical library data is deciding which aspects of the original merit consideration in the translation process.

Many characteristics of physical data, such as size and shape of a book, may be meaningful only to some people or in only some circumstances. Consider how grease smudges on the sides of auto parts manuals aid people in finding desired pages. It is impossible to include every characteristic of a physical data object that may ever be deemed meaningful to any person, but ignoring meaningful aspects of an object during translation has important implications for the preservation of function in a digital library.

7

Challenges of Electronic Library

Digital information and electronic resources have transformed academic research fundamentally. As the price of print materials, such as scholarly journals continues to rise, the accessibility and functionality of electronic versions become more attractive, and libraries invest more heavily in new technologies. A related issue in the need to preserve digital resources is a growing reliance of libraries as service providers on digital technology, which must impact on our institutional goals. Digital technologies find their place in the preservation strategies of research libraries in the opportunities presented to one such goal - in improved public access to on-line digital surrogates.

By limiting the handling of rare and fragile original materials, their rate of physical deterioration is considerably slowed. Digitisation is now a mainstream activity of the Campbell Collections of the University of Natal, aimed at collecting, preserving and organising historical material of national and international importance in a manner that is widely accessible. The upgrading of our information management system from a text-based to a multi-media database management system is aimed primarily at making our unique range of resources widely available over the Internet.

The retrieval of digital images offers a significant technological advance as a vehicle for integrated access to visual representations of historic photographs, art and ethnographic artefacts - together with traditional library resources. Preservation digitisation has focussed on reformatting rapidly deteriorating materials, with the aim of preserving the intellectual content, as separate from the medium or carrier.

Because one is able to make repeated copies of digital files without the informational loss associated with analogue copies, the impact of the technology is beguiling. No longer does the life expectancy of materials seem limited to the durability of the medium, since the digital data can be copied repeatedly without loss. The separation of the information and the object however, takes on a new meaning in the digital environment.

Complete digital conversion comprises two process, the capture by scanning of digital data, and that of the associated metadata, wrapped as a digital object and stored using containers to hold the objects and related software modules. The integrity of the digital file is threatened by alterations to the contextual data file, and the loss of the linking mechanism between the two is the same as deleting the contextual information.

When preservation strategies have not been applied to systematic digital archiving and all else fails, it may become necessary to work out how to read the stored bits. Because of the manner in which magnetic media are written, it is possible, given sufficient resources, to recover much material believed lost. The cost of large scale data recovery however, renders digital archaeology an untenable strategy for digital preservation. Long term preservation of digital resources is feasible through the implementation of sound policies at the inception and in the development of digital libraries.

The challenge lies in the need for libraries to move pro-actively in establishing digital collection development programme in an electronic environment that is conducive to preservation. The interaction between library, archive and museum professionals, together with information technology specialists, helped to clarify the myriad technical issues. There are digital imaging projects underway at some libraries in South Africa, and a number of problems have been encountered that are difficult to overcome in isolation. The equipment is expensive, especially if it is state-of the-art, software varies in quality and local support is often lacking.

Standard Generalized Markup Language (SGML) an international standard designed to promote text interchange, provides a definition of a document structure that can be used to encode the logical structure and content of any defined document and known by any remote system. Extensible Markup Language (XML), a simpler dialect of SGML has since been adopted, using the information community-based document type descriptions of the Text Encoding Initiative (TEI) and Encoded Archival Description (EAD), to build an infrastructure that enables interoperability between heterogeneous systems. The most comprehensive preservation strategy currently evolving is that of a collection-based persistent archive system.

A persistent archive operates in two phases, the first comprising capture of digital data wrapped as XML digital objects and ingestion to archival disk storage, using containers to hold objects along with relevant metadata and software modules for future emulation. The second is in the opposite direction, with containers brought out of storage and loaded onto new possibly new information management systems, and returned to a new, and possibly new archival storage system. The result is a product with the ability to scale its capabilities by adding resources when required.

By differentiating between the storage of the bits that comprise the digital object and the related information carried by the metadata it is possible to create an infrastructure for life cycle management for digital preservation. Electronic commerce is the ability to perform transactions involving the exchange, or use, of goods or services between two or more parties using electronic tools and techniques. The goods exchanged could be electronic documents and digital objects (e.g. text, data, images, videos, software programs, and composites of all of the above) - the stuff one finds in Digital Libraries.

In fact, information products, like electronic documents and digital objects are particularly important because they represent the purest form of Electronic Commerce. Indeed Electronic Commerce, with its greatly reduced cost of production and distribution makes many new knowledge businesses practical that were previously impractical. For example, a fully realized infrastructure for Electronic Commerce would make it practical for authors to charge pennies for paragraphs and still make a profit - because the author can reach millions world-wide over the Internet, who can pay and download the paragraph at little or no cost to the author.

The storage and distribution of electronic documents and digital objects is reduced dramatically. It enables, through automated information, production of a reliable, "shareable" historical database of design, marketing sales, usage and payment information. The following key activities are common to both digital libraries and to electronic commerce, they are: i) searching and advertising, ii) negotiating, iii) contracting and ordering, iv) billing, v) payment and settlement, vi) production vii) distribution and receipt, viii) accounting, ix) customer service, and x) information and knowledge processing. All of these activities are performed in every transaction; nor are they necessarily performed in this order; indeed, they may be performed in parallel.

A major problem associated with the advertising and shopping activity is the cost and time expended in developing, maintaining, and finding relevant information, products, and services, given the plenitude of available information. Obviously, this problem will become increasingly complex as more data and services become available on-line, and the choices and possibilities multiply exponentially. Buyers and sellers may elect to negotiate the terms of a transaction—i.e., the terms of exchange and payment.

These terms may cover right to copy, copyright or license agreements, usage rights, distribution rights, refund policies, and terms of payment. These terms can be standardized for routine commodity use, or customized to suit more unique individual situations. Often, in the case of two parties with a well-established business relationship (e.g. a library membership agreement) the terms of exchange are prenegotiated as standing contractual terms for all their future exchanges. Often, this process will also include authentication of the two parties. The buyer eventually issues a contractual agreement of the terms of exchange, or usage, and payment.

This contractual agreement is generally issued as an order, which sets forth the price and other terms of the transaction. The order may be verbal, in writing, or electronic. It usually includes an acknowledgment of agreement by the various parties in order to help prevent any future repudiation. This agreement can be confirmed electronically through cryptographic techniques such as digital signatures. A bill can be sent to the user, either before delivery of the electronic document, with the delivery, or after the delivery.

The bill generally includes remittance information—who, where and how to pay. Even when the electronic document or digital object is provided free of charge, it is desirable to provide usage data as important feedback information to the librarian and author, which can be obtained by having the user complete order or request forms. The buyer, or some financial intermediary, eventually sends some form of electronic payment, usually along with some remittance information to the seller. This payment may occur for a single item, on a usage basis, or with a single payment for multiple items or usage.

Settlement occurs when the payment and remittance information are analyzed by the seller or the seller's agent and accepted as valid and the an actual transfer of funds is accomplished. Electronic commerce does not completely address collaborative design and manufacturing activities, although they do share many of the same sorts of activities. The publication of compelling electronic catalogs, advertisements, and product information requires the same set of electronic publishing tools, as the author of an electronic document or digital object for a digital library.

In the ultimate "wired" society; collaborative design and manufacturing could decompose to hundreds of specialty firms that meet, negotiate and contract with each other over the network, which they would then use to purchase, sell, distribute, and assemble the various components that make up a product or service.

Customer service also involves providing general cash management advice, including addressing foreign exchange imbalances and risk exposures, collection of delinquent payments and late fees. A key activity in electronic commerce is the collection, management, analysis, and interpretation of the various data to make more intelligent and effective transaction-related decisions. Performance of these tasks often involves the use of advanced information management techniques, including models and simulations and collaborative computing technologies to support conferencing and distributed workflow processes. These tasks will become more difficult as the sources of information grow in number and are of increasingly diverse and uncertain quality.

Additionally, the use of this information may raise significant privacy concerns and issues, that will result in the imposition of significant limitations on the use of this data, and conceivably encryption of selected portions of the transaction information. In the information age, a large percent of the commerce will never be embodied physically. Information products are enabled by information technology and not just distributed more efficiently by it. These products can consist not just of electronic publications, catalogs, videos and the like, but can include interactive video games, software programs, electronic keys and tokens, customized design specifications, even electronic keys that can open to hotel rooms, cars, storage compartments, and airport boarding gates.

Furthermore, these information products are not just created entirely by the service provider, but can be designed or customized by the customer, adding a customer-driven activity call "design" to the purchase cycle. Indeed, information products can be continuously added to, modified, and morphed, as they pass along a chain of users. It is also likely that for these products ordering, billing, payment, and distribution would likely all happen simultaneously. The electronic commerce infrastructure will need to support advanced types of revenue collection, in addition to traditional methods.

Some micro-payment schemes for use over the Internet have been proposed that are significantly weaker than those being proposed for the more traditional payment schemes. The argument is that one can safely sacrifice security for processing efficiency when the transactions are low value enough. The argument is that it is much more important to minimize the amount of computational and communications resources needed to effect payment than to ensure the integrity of the transaction—that the loss of a penny here or there will not be consequential enough to matter.

But, the complexity of these bills certainly pale by comparison to the sorts of bills that users might expect to see in some future "wired" world of micro-payments. Imagine sitting down to reconcile a bill comprised of thousand of penny items. Each item is small enough, but the total will probably be large enough to command attention. Also, these all these examples of usage billing are coming from businesses that have been run as a monopoly - the user has had no other alternative offered them. When given the choice, users have often opted for a more certain, fixed flat fee, even if that fee is slightly greater than their historical usage pattern.

The cost of usage billing and accounting may be unacceptably high in the future economics of the "wired" society. For example, it has been argued that a significant portion of the cost of operating the telephone and utility infrastructure today is due to the imposition of usage metering and accounting hardware and systems, and that more nimble companies offering equivalent services based on a flat fee, could operate equivalent service at much lower cost. Electronic commerce transactions currently involve all manner of devices (e.g., phone, fax, POS - point-of-sale device) and media (e.g., electronic data, image, voice, paper), and networks (cable, wire, satellite, cellular) over which they will be delivered, so the system infrastructure must accommodate all of these devices, media and communications networks, without degrading them to the lowest common denominator.

Opening up digital libraries to all these devices, at of course a greatly reduced functionality on some of the less capable devices, might still be a capability worth looking into. It would better bridge the gap between the real physical world and the future "wired" world, and it would dramatically increase the accessibility of the digital library to a much wider population faster, including the more disadvantaged citizens. The electronic commerce domain has a large quantity of legacy systems which it needs to interface to, and ultimately phase-out, as it evolves to more modern systems, applications and processes.

These legacy systems and processes will not go away overnight, and a successful electronic commerce infrastructure must allow the user to easily and transparently transfer between and switch back and forth between the new all electronic, and the older, hybrid legacy systems and processes. Digital Libraries also need to deal with similar legacy issues. A convergence of several factors has recently lifted digital libraries and electronic commerce to the promise of a new level of utility and viability. These factors include the increased availability of communications and communications bandwidth, the reduced cost and increased user-friendliness of computers and communications, the growth of the Internet and on-line services, and the drive toward global competitiveness.

There are however, a number of standardized services that are needed to fully realize their complete potential. Most of these services are common to many different applications, including electronic commerce and digital libraries. Each application domain could address these issues separately, but the cost and accessibility of these services would be greatly improved if all applications utilized the same set of services, much the way they now are all utilizing the same communications networks.

All of these initiatives must be developed within a common framework, or we run the risk of creating isolated, non-interoperable implementations that will inhibit progress toward truly free, open, and spontaneous electronic commerce and digital libraries. Most of the current solutions being prototyped over the Internet, all vary in their approach to security and privacy, their ability to handle micro-payments, and their applicability to various types of transactions. They also differ in their business models - for example, in their pricing strategy and in their assumptions as to who bears the risk in case of insufficient funds or disputes. The electronic commerce infrastructure therefore must achieve the following goals:

A truly interoperable common infrastructure, for applications such as electronic commerce and digital libraries, would allow parties to conduct their transactions in private, without paying any fees to intermediaries unless they provide some real added value, such as credit or search services. This infrastructure would make it easier for any and all interested persons to become service providers as well as consumers. The infrastructure must be based on a common set of services and standards that ensure interoperability.

As the Internet and its successors evolves, it will grow and mature significantly - possibly in ways not even imagined today. New services and businesses will emerge. For example, NII's electronic marketplace will provide new opportunities for narrowcase marketing and publishing to very short-lived niche markets. Also, existing services and products will be redefined and modified. The common infrastructure will have to be sufficiently flexible to accommodate all of these changes and be able to address new applications and new requirements as they arise. The consumer cannot usually communicate or transact with vendors in a simple, direct, freeform environment in today's electronic commerce applications.

For example, to access most electronic shopping services, a consumer must subscribe to an on-line service which then provides proprietary hardware and/or software with which to communicate with the vendors that have also registered with that service. The lack of personal contact and the anonymity associated with conducting transactions over a telecommunications network make it difficult to authenticate parties and detect intruders; this in turn makes the system vulnerable to fraud and increases the need for security services.

Additionally, the speed with which transactions can be conducted leaves parties with less time to react, check, and respond appropriately - again creating the potential for system fraud and abuse. Lack of sufficient security inhibits the introduction of direct, secure, real-time electronic payment and settlement systems that can support secure exchanges without pre-arrangements or third parties.

Intellectual Property Conservancies (IPCs) are a new idea, being conceived as a means to provide public benefits by making digital content donated, or licensed to them, freely available and by ensuring its long-term preservation. IPCs are digital libraries and therefore have all the problems associated with digital libraries. In addition, IPCs face a large number of challenges that most digital libraries do not confront. Content owners may, or may not, be ideologically committed to free-to-read. Those who are persuaded in principle that free-to-read is a good idea probably need only to be given a way to do it.

The challenge with these owners will be to make the opportunity known and make contribution methods convenient to use. An IPC will also need to attract those who would not be inclined to give away access rights without persuasive arguments of the benefits to them. Several strategies can be employed to convince them. Tax benefits are central to land conservancies and historic trusts, but it is not clear whether meaningful tax benefits will, in fact, be available for Intellectual Property Conservancies.

If the original creator of the intellectual property (an author, artist or inventor) donates it, current tax laws restrict them to writing off the value of the raw materials that were consumed in its creation. If the donor is an owner (such as a publisher, music label or employer) who has paid to acquire an intellectual property right, outright donation of the intellectual property should be eligible for a tax credit. Concepts such as 'easements', however, though well established in tax law for real property, are novel ideas in intellectual property law and will, at the very least, need to be tested with tax authorities.

They may well need to be legislated. Providing public access to free-to-read content is a way to promote value-added content. In the physical bookstore, we often browse a book, or listen to a few tracks of a CD, before making a purchase. Free-to-read online content may serve this same purpose. One challenge to an IPC will be to develop a model for free-to-read functionality that is accepted by publishers as not unduly competitive with their value-added products, and by online readers as useful in its own right.

The IPC concept will be viable if at least some publishers are willing to provide a level of free-to-read access as a means of promoting their value-added products. The IPC will need to protect the publishers' interests in order to obtain an early donation of limited rights and, as the threat to a publishers' commercial interests subsides, the promise to make more valuable access available over time. Individual IP owners will readily appreciate the benefits of making a gift of rights to an organization that ensures their work a sort of immortality.

But an IPC can also attract publishers with the benefits of perpetual access.

Publishers who provide free-to-read content on their web sites (and this is increasingly going to be necessary for competitive reasons) are faced with a new liability—either they have to keep their digital content online and free (which costs them money if it doesn't continue to sell) or they need to take it down. It makes sense to give the limited rights-to-read to an IPC early in the life of the intellectual property, thereby avoiding the liability and reaping the reward of public service. Since the mission of the IPC is to make content to which it has rights easily available online, and its promise to the owners of that IP is to make the free-to-read content easy to find, an IPC needs to invest in rich descriptive metadata to make its content readily discoverable on the web. IPCs, like other non-profits seeking donations from the general public, will need to provide concrete benefits to supporters in order to maintain a sufficient stream of financial contributions.

A "membership" organization gives public supporters a sense of belonging and of receiving concrete, perhaps even personal, benefits. A newsletter and the web site that communicate news of the success of the IPC and review recent additions to the properties it holds, would be attractive to many such general members. An IPC may also need to solicit cash donations from intellectual property owners to help pay the costs of digitizing, transforming, or cataloging gifts of intellectual property that are not suitable for digital delivery or preservation in their current form. Individual IP donors, in particular, may need to help bear these costs since metadata creation for their donations will be a one-off cost and the transaction costs are likely to be higher.

But even donors of large quantities of IP may need to be asked to contribute financially for an IPC to absorb a sizable gift (ten thousand articles from a magazine publisher for instance) in a reasonable time. The most critical issue in the success of an IPC is probably the technical characteristics of the Intellectual Properties it acquires. If selective, the IPC could obtain content in a way that enables it to deliver the content in the future without substantial additional investment and to offer a range of value added views without requiring costly intervention. Without careful selection, an IPC could be saddled with overwhelming costs to initially capture the data in usable formats, transform what it receives, or to manage the digital data over time. Its presumed digital assets would instead become liabilities that could far exceed its likely resources.

One of the most costly factors in acquiring content is negotiating the terms and conditions for its donation and subsequent use. But depending on what those terms and conditions are, the cost of administering access could also be very high. Contractual terms that define a limited number of concrete levels of rights (for example, rights to provide free public access one page at a time and print the page being viewed) must be easily translated into levels of functionality.

With such fixed levels of rights, a donor could agree on a sequence of further future rights releases. It is critical that the donation of different levels of functionality, and the progressive release of further permissions over time, not result in additional operational costs for an IPC. Metadata captured up front must interact with the format captured up front to dictate levels of functionality. Some formats of donated content will require substantial investment to make them usable online, or to be kept online in perpetuity.

Hence, an IPC needs to consider the risks involved in selection, based on decisions about what formats to acquire. Text and image can be delivered with layered public-access-level functionality using existing web-based distribution servers. An IPC must have defined rights adequate to make content available to users under some terms, but it need not own the IP to do so. If a donation with some access or development limits is accepted by the IPC, the donor is brought into a relationship with the Conservancy that might also be translated later into donations of further public rights. Conditional agreements and agreements to release content for free public viewing at a future date, are common in archives.

In such a case, the property owner would provide the IPC with a copy, but the specific rights granted to the IPC would only come into effect at a designated time or under specific conditions. One of the benefits of an IPC is that it promises to keep IP always available, while the current system of publishing makes much IP difficult to obtain. Metadata management will be critical to an IPC's success. Like any Digital Library it needs to invest in discovery (content description) metadata. An IPC must additionally invest substantially in rights management metadata and technical (migration specification) metadata.

While the IPC can rely on natural partners in the library community to help provide descriptive metadata for simple resource discovery (such as Dublin Core metadata), it also needs to be able to incorporate metadata conforming to standards in the publishing community. An IPC will need to determine the requirements for rights metadata linked to delivery functionality, as discussed above. Finally, an IPC needs to manage a digital artifact over time. As such, it needs to determine what metadata will need to be acquired and kept for long-term preservation.

IP owners prefer that the digital data be located on their own servers; the terms of the gift would ensure that, should the IP owner fail to keep it available, the IPC can shift access to its own servers. The benefits to the IPC suggest that an architecture enabling this kind of distributed access will be necessary. The fundamental objectives of an IPC are to offer free access to its catalog of intellectual property in perpetuity. For this, the IPC does not need to be the archival repository of the authentic, verifiable, record copy.

Like a digital library, which holds a copy of a work and makes the accurate and full content available to users, the IPC doesn't claim to preserve contextual or structural authenticity. Both an IPC and a digital library focus on preservation of content as required for preservation of public access and the right-to-read. Therefore an IPC need not preserve the initial delivery format, nor any particular subsequent delivery format. Instead, the IPC can return to its escrowed copy to generate a delivery copy in a new format, or move from one delivery format to the next, depending on cost and technology availability.

Of course, an IPC still must make strategic decisions about when and how to convert data from one delivery and or long-term storage format to another, to keep the content accessible over time. A Digital Research Library (DRL) is a collection of electronic information organized for use in the long term. To meet user needs, the founders of a DRL must accomplish two general tasks: establishing the repository of electronic scholarly materials, and implementing the tools to use it.

More important, long-term commitments are needed if scholarly information is to be available over periods longer than human life: organizational commitments, fiscal commitments and institutional commitments. The mission of research libraries is to acquire information, organize it, make it available and preserve it. This has been their significant, distinctive and successful role with print and other artifactual materials for the past several hundred years. An implicit mission of computing science has been to make the benefits of computing technology of use to society at large.

Missions, needs and capabilities now come together so that information users can have added assistance in performing research and in assuring the continuity of scholarship, today and in the future. It will take conscious, planned efforts by both librarianship and computing to make this happen. Many libraries are now trying to provide the increasing volume of scholarly electronic information to their clienteles. Current information needs are being provided in electronic form with varying success in public, college and research libraries around the country and the world.

Research libraries have only begun to take on the provision, organization and preservation of information with the same long-term commitment they have made for print materials. It is an expensive, uncharted and difficult task. But until the long-term commitments are undertaken, many currently proposed solutions will have only temporary effects. For example, discussion of cataloging network resources will remain tentative, for until resources being cataloged have a permanent network presence, the cataloging that points to them must also have an ephemeral quality.

Similarly, the expensive products of recent valuable digitizing demonstration projects, from microfilm to digital form and vice versa, will be at risk after only a few years if tools and commitments are not in place for the preservation of what has been achieved. The ability of the scholarly community to give serious weight to electronic information depends upon their trust in such information being dependably available, with authenticity and integrity maintained. Looked-for changes in scholarly publishing to help alleviate the serials crisis, for example, are usually thought to be bound up with the prestige of electronic journals in the academic tenure process.

The ability of the academy to count on long-term, secure existence of electronic scholarly work will be an important determinant of the success of academic electronic publishing. Libraries and universities have a stake in helping electronic publishing to succeed, and therefore have an interest in establishing secure digital research libraries. Users' needs will continue to be what they long have been. Users will want information reliably locatable, so that when they go there, they can expect to find what they're looking for. Users will want information easily accessible: the cataloging must be clear and accurate, and the information must be promptly retrievable.

In the electronic environment the need for access tools will be more evident, and users will expect appropriate and standard software to be readily available. Users will expect information to be available that was placed in the library's care a long time ago; and they will expect that the integrity of the information they get from the library will be assured. Implementation of a Digital Research Library will require several specific tasks, broadly familiar to a computing audience, and three kinds of new commitments.

A Digital Research Library will be manifest to users as collections of information existing in various places and accessible through the use of widely available tools. The locus of information may be called the electronic storage repository; the access tools will be described below. Over time, we will learn how collection development plays out in an access environment as well as in an ownership environment. It is sometimes loosely proposed that libraries need not acquire electronic information, for it will be available somewhere on the network.

Such proposals ignore the obvious truth that some institution must still, in the end, take responsibility for the information. That has always been a definition of the library responsibility. There will be many electronic storage repositories, responding both to requirements of redundancy and to the individual needs of institutions. In contrast to print collections, it is unlikely that there will be a high degree of content duplication across many electronic repositories, since for most purposes existence in a single place allows world-wide access.

Aside from their actual contents, however, repositories that are part of a DRL will have many common characteristics. Some of these are described here; in some cases, open questions are noted that need to be explored in early implementations. Even an initial repository will comprise many gigabytes of information, growing quickly to millions of electronic documents. The medium itself is cheap and the possible resources are plentiful.

There will be organizational and bureaucratic issues in addition to the simply technical. If information is copied from magnetic to optical disk, copyright issues must be recognized. Automation will be necessary to reduce labor costs. Other issues include workflow and record-keeping, migration techniques, and standards and techniques that will apply independently of technology. It may be possible to link refreshment to backup techniques for expedience and economy.

Major institutions may separately or consortially establish repositories. It is not yet clear how much redundancy of their components will be desirable among them. Aside from assuring longevity, other issues come to bear on decisions to provide multiple permanent copies of electronic information. Informed decisions will be made about the dynamic interplay between costs of network bandwidth, response time and costs of storage. It seems likely that many library consortia will be formed on the basis of joint contracts with information vendors.

Providing access to voluminous information is an intellectual problem that historically has been solved in the print environment by abstracting and indexing services and by library cataloging, with attendant rules and procedures to insure consistency and accuracy. These tools, adapted to suit new needs, will work for electronic information as well. They should be linked to the new retrieval mechanisms so that users can smoothly navigate from location of information to retrieval of it without having to shift their mode of use.

Early mechanisms will probably link catalog records to documents using tools such as the WWW, the Uniform Resource Indicator (and Locator) or URI/URL, and the recently proposed MARC 856 field. SGML may offer other possibilities for linking of certain documents through its document description techniques. In any case, there eventually will need to be consensus both for the representation of physical electronic locations in bibliographic records and for representation of virtual locations.

If the DRL's catalog system works well, users will be able to search for information, locate bibliographic records for desiderata, and use those records directly to draw the desired information to their workstation. Where an authentication technique is used, means for including and testing the certification must be provided. Standards for such cataloging and remote access still need to be developed, particularly for providing catalog access to non-owned materials.

Internet-wide access should generally be possible. In early pilot implementations it may initially be advisable for a few libraries to plan and development catalog and access mechanisms that integrate the individual libraries' collections with that of the DRL. Procedures for dissemination of such catalog records will be needed; it will be not only a technical matter but a policy matter for libraries associated with the DRL to provide non-local access to their local patrons.

More difficult will be the social compacts, that is, the agreements on standards, intellectual property and access modes. Most difficult of all to achieve, if electronic preservation and access are to be accomplished on any significant scale, will be the long term commitments to these goals by institutions. Nothing makes clearer that a library is an organization, rather than a building or a collection, than the requirement for institutional commitment for electronic information to have more than a fleeting existence. The organization of libraries is already changing as electronic information increasingly becomes part of their charge. Most research libraries now have substantial systems departments.

Some libraries locate the responsibility for electronic information distinctly from that for print. Other libraries see the forms as inseparable and include electronic responsibilities along with artifactual responsibilities in assignments for collection development, cataloging and public service. What is new will be the permanent assignment of staff responsibility for the long term maintenance of electronic information within a library.

Impact of World Wide Web

Web libraries can consist of native documents linked to the library, which provides access to the document but do not exercise control or ownership over the document. Web libraries can also "collect" Web documents through caching or archiving, thus creating a local electronic record on an historical Web document. Digital libraries, including Web-based collections, are redefining both the role of electronic information storage and retrieval as well as the role of traditional libraries.

Digital libraries include collections of books, journal articles, graphics, newspapers, and other material in digital format; in sum, collections of digitized content. To be a library, that collection should be organized according to some standard. There are many examples of digital libraries. On one level, the Web can be seen as an extension of and as a tool for libraries. If the Web is a tool, it is a complex tool serving to modify the information management and retrieval functions of both librarians and libraries. The Web can be employed as a transfer and distribution mechanism for the digital and digitized collections of libraries. The Web as communications medium has become an interface, if not the major interface to any number of database vendors including Dialog, Lexis/Nexis, Thomson and Thomson, and FirstSearch.

Many academic and public libraries provide Web access to their OPACs. Document delivery can be accomplished over the Web, and may include both native Web documents as well as digitized print material. Some, like the US Library of Congress, are beginning to provide Web access to their digitized collections. Web users can organize Web documents into document clusters that can be managed, searched, and accessed. These clusters or libraries have taken many forms.

The vast majority of these attempt an in situ organization and categorization of Web content. Perhaps the most common are the jumppages, or Web page collections of hypertext links that point to other Web pages or Web sites with a defined content. NetFirst, a part of OCLC's FirstSearch family of databases, employs a MARC format, catalogues Web pages, abstracts and indexes them, and applies a Dewey Decimal Classification for the document. There are also a growing number of limited area search engines (LASE) that are restricted to development of indexes for Web documents with specific content. These include Argos, the Limited Area Search of the Ancient and Medieval Internet LASE, the Ananzi LASE providing access to material from or about South Africa, or the directory of LASEs provided by Internet Sleuth. The Web differs from the more traditional information media in several substantial ways.

The Web as a whole may not be organized to the degree that Chen might want it to meet the standard of a library, but neither is the entire corpus of print or electronic media so organized either. Part of the problem lies in part in definition of the Web: sometimes process and sometimes content. The Web lacks authority and quality control, but so do many print publications. Much of the Web is reminiscent of the political and religious pamphleteering so prevalent in Europe and North America over the past 200 years. The Web can resemble that archetypal forgery in print

The Protocols of the Elders of Zion raised to some major order of magnitude. It can be an intentional or unintentional vehicle for poor or wrong information. It is a conduit for pornography. It can also provide effective and timely access to useful and accurate information. One difficulty with the Web is that it is today far more difficult for third parties to assess quality and authority using methods developed for more traditional publications. There are six approaches to bring quality control to the Web. These are the programming, procedural, structuring, bibliographical, evaluative or indexed, and organizational approaches.

Variations and additions to these approaches have been offered as well. Bibliometric or Webometric approaches may provide additional quality control. These include citation analysis, link following and word counts. Others have adopted bibliometric approaches by following hypertext link trails to authoritative or substantive sites. Recent work suggests that following link trails to clusters of clusters can identify authoritative Web sites. There is no doubt that the indexes of the major search engines and directories are inadequate. The fact is do not even know how big the Web is much less how to define big. The Web contains many documents, pages, sites, and objects. Sizing the Web has proven to be a complex and uncertain enterprise.

Some Web resources are trash as is some print. But even trash (a highly subjective subject) needs at times to be classified or catalogueed. Their other two observations are more telling. Others recognize that Web document changes are important to their bibliographic control and still others have found it necessary to modify practice in response to those changes. Much attention has been paid to Web size and growth, as defined by server and host counts, packet traffic (MIDS) and other indicators. Libraries are collections of these information products, organized in some useful fashion, and made available to the appropriate client or patron pool. Perhaps not or perhaps it does not matter, for libraries can be libraries if their collections either are not universally comprehensive or if their collections do not address all points of view concerning a specific issue.

In fact, no library can ever fully meet the "access to all information" test. It can also be argued that in time the Web may more likely provide access to all points of view than print because of the very ease of publication to the Web. Like other information streams, the Web can be organized, collected, and managed. Libraries, necessarily digital libraries, can be and are constructed from Web resources. The Internet is a moving target in two ways. First, there is a constant stream of technical change and computing upgrades and improvements. New capabilities, concepts and terminology challenge the practitioner, but these are manageable.

The other change is, from the perspective of managing

Web content, far more profound. Web pages and Web sites undergo constant modification. These changes take two general forms. The first is existence. Both Web pages and Web sites exhibit varied longevity patterns. The second is content modification. Efforts to organize, categorize, index, or catalogue the Web all contain one inherent and fatal flaw. Before one can successfully organize Web content, one must recognize and compensate for the dynamic nature of the Web. Just as the Web is much easier to publish to than the traditional media is; it is also much easier to unpublish to, and to edit and modify than those same traditional media are.

Conceivably, Web documents are not subject to physical deterioration but they are subject to the technological. There is an even more important difference between Web documents and traditional ones. Once an author or publisher ceases to support a traditional publication, so long as copies are maintained in libraries, the document continues to exist and more often than not continues to be available for use. This is not so with the Web. Moreover, when a Web document is edited or updated, the edited version replaces and erases the earlier edition. New traditional editions may update older ones but they do not erase them. Creating Web document archives and caches can solve some of these issues.

A Web cache may be considered a very short term Web archive. In caching, Web documents are stored then accessed at some location closer to or faster for the end user than the original host is. Caching creates ethical, legal, as well as timeliness concerns. Archiving raises additional problems including what to archive and how often should the archive be updated. Storage and retrieval can quickly become a major problem. The library of native documents rather than with the library of cached documents.

The organization of Web sites may help predict document longevity. Web pages located at the server-level domain are zero level pages, those one file removed are at the first level, and so on. This is not particularly surprising in that many zero and first level pages are navigational and will necessarily change as the Web site as a whole changes, while those pages located deeper on the file structure are more likely to be content in nature.Web sites and Web pages undergo content change and attrition. While content and structural changes can and have been measured the limits its focus to Web site and Web page persistence.

Persistence is the most fundamental form of change. Either a document exists or it does not. Both Web pages and sites manifest one of three forms of persistence behavior. They may persist of a given period of time - which is to say each time the URL is queried, the specific page addressed is accessed, it responds. The Web page may fail to respond. Any Web page that fails to respond, but subsequently responds after one of two additional queries in a forty-eight hour period is considered present. Web page data are collected on a weekly basis. A Web page is defined here as comatose if on the sixth and subsequent weekly queries including the most recent when data were taken, that Web page failed to resolve.

The term comatose is chosen purposefully, for as the data which follow demonstrate, once a Web page goes comatose, this in itself is no guarantee that a Web page will not return at some time to the same URL. If a Web page were to return after the sixth collection period or five weeks, it would no longer be counted in subsequent assessments as comatose. Web pages that fail but return are labeled intermittent. Two forces effect library collection development from the Web. In order to provide patrons with both broad and exhaustive resources libraries will necessarily have to turn to digital and Web resources to expand and augment their collections.

In the end, digital and hybrid libraries, will have to incorporate native Web documents into their collections to a degree far greater than is now the practice. The Web and for that matter traditional publishing are in constant flux. New Web documents are constantly being added to the available resource pool, just as new print and digital materials are. This offers no original challenge to libraries. The original challenge to libraries brought by the Web lies in its ephemeral nature. Both Web pages and Web sites undergo metamorphosis, attrition, and return. Any library that seeks to incorporate Web materials into its collection must take into account this dynamic or the quality of the bibliographic representation as well as of the collection itself will rapidly erode.

If indeed the half lives of Web sites and Web pages are about two years, information managers must pay attention to the process. Document death is never trivial, for in the absence of an archive, the information contained in that document is lost. Comatoseness is not necessarily as tragic as document death in that some documents are intermittent and do return. This may not be unique to the Web, librarians have had extensive experience managing changing technology, changing media, and controlling for document demise. The document lifecycle is far more prevalent on the Web than for print; it is in fact an accepted norm.

If this lifecycle is both ubiquitous and normal, those who seek to manage Web content must develop new systems and adapt old standards that specifically address it. To manage the lifecycle, the digital library community has begun to address the dynamic and the impact that change has on the quality of collections; indexing. search, and retrieval algorithms, end user and intermediary behavior; document storage, caching, and archiving; and other related issues. At OCLC Research, any service that uses the HTTP protocol and returns XML as a Web service. There are two main approaches to providing Web services: the Simple Object Access Protocol (SOAP) and Representational State Transfer (REST).

REST is the simpler of the two. It is a codification of the style of interaction that has formed the basis of the Web over the last decade. REST, whenever possible uses existing mechanisms to communicate, such as HTTP put and get. The main advantages of this approach to us are the simplicity of REST services and the ease in which they can in turn be used within other services. Since REST services can often be invoked directly from a Web browser, this offers additional possibilities for interaction with services. SOAP takes a more procedural view of Web services. Functions, their parameters and return values are defined, often using an XML language called Web Services Definition Language (WSDL).

This enables a very formal and easily portable description of the Web service that makes it fairly easy for a programmer to create a client that will make use of it, or a server to implement the service. The main disadvantage of SOAP is more complication and overhead in the messages compared to REST. This can be a factor in efficiency and ease of integration for those not conversant with SOAP. REST advocates also feel that SOAP hides too much within opaque function calls that would be better exposed using standard HTTP functions whose semantics are well understood. REST takes a very simple approach: requests are sent in as HTTP requests, often as simply a URL.

The response is sent back in XML. In some of the services now include stylesheets to format the XML so that someone coming to the service through a Web browser will see a nicely formatted page rather than the raw XML. To a great extent, this is how the whole Web works, except that HTML (or now XHTML, the XML variant of HTML) is used in replies. SOAP is complex enough that including even one simple SOAP example in its full XML within a paper is difficult. SRW (Search and Retrieve on the Web) is a good example of a digital library SOAP service, offering the same functionality as SRU, but using SOAP wrappers to move the data. This brings with it a WSDL definition of the service that can ease the implementation of a SRW server within an HTTP server such as Apache.

The WSDL definitions and software such as Apache Axis 9 hide much of the complexity of SOAP from the implementer. There are a number of classifying digital library Web services. Users and systems need to register different types of objects, search for them, resolve references, navigate hierarchies and other types of links, decompose objects into simpler objects, enhance objects, and transform objects from one format to another. Registration services provide persistent identifiers to concepts or objects. They often serve up metadata about metadata. Examples of this include Dublin Core extensions, and the OpenURL formats of digital objects. Physical or digital items can also be registered, and cataloguing services such as OCLC's offer that sort of registration and control.

Search services are all familiar to us. Some sort of search string is typically mapped to a list of records. Searching Web services put this basic functionality in XML wrappers to make it available to higher-level programs the user interacts with. The leading example of this in digital libraries is the Z39.50 work on SRU/SRW. Rather than having to understand BER and ASN.1, programs interact in XML over HTTP. In this case, the main reason not to change over from classic Z39.50 is probably the investment in the current systems. Newly designed systems would find SRU/SRW much easier to implement and use.

Slightly outside the library world, systems such as Google are making their services available using SOAP, and finding many different institutions integrating Google in their applications. Resolution services come in many different flavours. Typically, they map from identifiers to data. An example might be a service that accepts an ISBN and returns bibliographic data about the items that ISBN is associated with. Other examples include mapping controlled names to metadata about the people identified, and mapping a subject class number to a textual description of that class. It is possible to create Web services that facilitate the navigation through a set of links.

Of course, the Web itself is an example of general

network movement using links, but more specialized services may also be of use. There are a number of decomposition services appearing. Decomposition services offer the possibility of applying concentrated knowledge and expertise to these problems and making them widely available. These services might be as simple as identifying individual names from a list of names or breaking a class number into its constituent parts, to the more complex problems of exposing the structure of a document or identifying letters/words/sentences within an image. Digital library systems could use any number of enhancement services.

An important enhancement are normalization services, such as adding controlled forms of names to metadata containing uncontrolled forms, or adding classification numbers selected on the basis of the text of a document. If links can be identified within metadata records it would also be possible to expand incomplete data. OCLC does that now internally in some of our online services where tables of contents and cover art are added to book catalogue records for display.

Web services are a way this type of information could be integrated into distributed and disparate services at less cost than maintaining and integrating all the data locally. Many of the above services offer some sort of 'transformation,' so there is overlap between types of services. Transformation services operate at a higher level than many of the other services, e.g. translating the syntax of metadata records from MARC21 to MARC-XML. Library web pages are focused mainly on individual libraries and the resources and services they offer. Consequently, with rare exceptions web access hosted by libraries is not designed to serve as a general entry point for the larger world of web-accessible resources.

Neither are the multitude of individual library web pages equal to a single, widely known, dependable beginning place for research in the web environment. For this reason, library users and librarians in search of web-based information turn instead (and are sometimes directed through library web pages) to search engines or information services created by what may be referred to in the new parlance as information.

After all, the information.coms offer a variety of different formats and approaches to finding information, and our constituencies are accustomed to using them. In addition, developing a scholars portal would undoubtedly be a complex and expensive undertaking and would require concerted action on a scale that has been difficult to achieve, let alone sustain, within the research library community. Letting a thousand flowers bloom, it turns out, has always been easier than cultivating a garden. In addition, such services do not plumb to the depths of information ordinarily reached by researchers in subject disciplines.

Conceptually, one might say that information.coms are horizontal rather than vertical information retrieval services. So except for the most straightforward types of inquiries, their ability to facilitate what the academy considers in-depth research is extremely limited. In the best of all possible web-based worlds, the subject library of the future might be conceived of as a highly customized, narrowly focused search engine adapted to the character of publications and research habits of a discipline. This is not, however, the nature of current information.coms and there is no evidence yet that one or more will evolve in this direction. Indeed, the largest drawback of all may be precisely that information.coms in general have not been designed with the particular needs of the research community in mind.

Rather, for good business reasons, they appear focused on broad customer bases and the most common information-seeking activities of the general public. This may simply be a necessary condition for success with commercial enterprises. More limited niche markets are certainly not prohibited in the commercial world, and indeed, some are beginning to appear in the education sector. At this time, however, the information.coms with an education focus are aimed more at providing content than web searching and are still able to offer only small and basic collections as gauged by research library standards. In addition, these and other information.coms are proprietary and distinct and are themselves in some need of aggregation for portal access.

For instance, while one will occasionally find information on a university web page about how to search the Internet including a listing of search engines, never will one encounter such a listing when accessing an information.com, since it would be self-destructive to promote one's competition. Thus, ironically, the information.com world, while replete with help for web information seekers, in the final analysis adds to the overall complexity of the situation.

There are other more proactively positive reasons that ARL, along with strategic partners, should undertake to build a scholars portal. One may be simply that there is arguably no other agency with the breadth of awareness, the information, the skills, and the objectivity to succeed at doing so. This is not meant to be a grandly arrogant statement but rather to point out the unique character of the research library community: the libraries themselves, those who operate them, their not-for-profit status, and the potential resident therein for making sense of the world's largest unmanaged database, the World Wide Web.

In other words, research librarians can likely create a scholars portal better than anyone else. Perhaps less noble but still important is the growing fact that increasingly the world's business, including the business of research, is becoming web-based. Those agencies that wish to survive, let alone thrive, are busily developing new web architectures and exploring how to migrate significant portions of their business to the web environment.

In the academic community, this move to the Web includes internal administrative business functions and increasingly the core functions of teaching and learning. Similarly, in the research library environment, integrated systems and digital library experiments have migrated to web-based functions almost totally. As of yet, however, this move to the Web for research libraries does not include an effort to make sense of the Web itself. Thus, there is an opportunity for ARL both to perform a service and to heighten its visibility by playing a leadership role in designing and developing a scholars portal. Conversely, failure to create such a collective web presence and service may mean that research libraries as a collective, and ARL, will become increasingly invisible to the web generation.

Finally, perhaps the most persuasive arguments in favor of ARL undertaking this project are the magnitude of the need and the significance of the opportunity. Scholars must be able to depend upon the veracity of the results of their efforts. At the moment, there is simply no satisfactory means of certifying results obtained from the information.coms. The potential usefulness of a scholars portal is so extraordinary that it is tempting to describe such a wonderful service that it would be practically unachievable. Indeed, the real work (and the fun) will consist of creating the design of the portal, deciding what to include, and determining where to begin. The scholars portal would promote the development of and provide access to the highest quality content on the Web.

Through the efforts of a myriad number of agencies the information content of the Web is growing exponentially. What is needed, however, is the addition of information content of academically sound quality. The scholars portal would facilitate the addition of high-quality material by fostering standards, searching across databases, and offering a variety of supporting tools. As a result, libraries, corporations, and many other organizations would be empowered to contribute to an accessible, distributed digital library.

The existence and efforts of scholars portal, therefore, would accelerate the growth of high-quality material and facilitate what has been referred to as the global relational research library. Such a library could contribute to a reformation in the format of scholarly publishing and usher in access to a vast and heretofore largely unusable body of original material, specialized resources for communities of scholars, and accumulated scientific data. With the growing use of asynchronous learning methodologies, there is also an increasing need for extending certain elements of traditional library public services to the Web.

This is already beginning to happen through experiments with virtual reference environments. Perhaps the most ambitious test of the virtual reference environment today is the Collaborative Digital Reference Service (CDRS) sponsored by the Library of Congress. The goal of CDRS is to provide professional reference service to users anywhere anytime by means of an international, digital network of libraries. The service will include electronic responses to questions, including document delivery, when appropriate and 24x7 virtual access to a live librarian when necessary. To accomplish this, CDRS will utilize a cooperating group of libraries around the globe in a shared enterprise.

In addition, scholars portal would foster the extension of web-based services further into document delivery, provision of specialized supporting materials, experimental shared work spaces, and activities in support of alternative scholarly publishing. To begin with, scholars portal would provide a number of highly desirable gateway functions. These might include an explanatory guide to information.coms as well as cross-platform access to commercial databases. It might also offer sophisticated electronic thesauri to guide researchers toward areas of interest with precision. The goal would be for the scholars portal to be adopted as the place to start for anyone seeking academically sound information.

Thus, a primary function of the scholars portal would also be to provide researchers with an alternative means of retrieving dependable information beyond the capacity of the information.coms. Its goal would be to provide highly focused search engines adapted to the technical languages of the various academic specialties. By customizing search engines in this fashion and directing them to dependable sources of information, scholars portal would evolve increasingly "intelligent" automated systems and improve the success rate of query systems. The foundations for moving in this direction are already visible in the emerging capacities of OCLC'S Cooperative Online Resource Catalog (CORC). CORC represents the development of tools capable of automating the creation of metadata for web-based electronic resources, a necessary precondition for access.

Without CORC and other tools in the CORC suite, the volume of data on the Web would never be harnessed by manual techniques. Libraries are awash in contradictions. Gate counts are up; circulation is down. While one set of constituents eschews traditional library services, another group pushes statistics for catalog searching steadily upward. Inside the profession, librarians engage in spirited debates about their role. In the face of doubters, librarians argue that only ignorant or naïve individuals would believe that the Web could satisfy all their information needs, particularly in the scholarly community. At the same time, they energetically acquire or license digital resources.

With the addition of digital materials to the library's portfolio a debate about the role of the catalog has also developed. Proponents of the catalog and of libraries believe strongly that the catalog has enduring value and that it can evolve to be a useful tool for Web access, whereas critics do not foresee any role for the library catalog as a research tool for networked information. It is always humbling to learn that something you regard as a great and very contemporary problem echoes an experience from the past. In America, large libraries are getting very large. They are being run for wide constituencies on broad lines.

More and more the practical American spirit is seeking for coordination and cooperation. It is by no means certain that the card form of catalog will continue indefinitely as the chief tool of library workers. It is highly probable that selected catalogs will take the place of huge general repertories. Dimly one can see the possibilities of mechanical changes and alterations, of the use of photography, instead of printer's ink, possibilities of compression or even total change of form. Certainly present card catalogs will require intelligent direction of the highest order to make them respond to the demands of readers, to the needs of the community. Changes such as these will require an intelligent and sympathetic oversight to insure their success.

The librarians who will carry them out, who will guide and mold the development of cataloging, must perforce have been experienced and trained catalogers. Union catalogs expanded the function of the catalog to serve as an index to the holdings of multiple institutions, increasing their importance in the process. Concomitant with the emergence of the union catalog was an increase in the standardization of cataloging practice. Early in this century, The Library of Congress revolutionized catalogs through the provision of printed cards. A key catalyst for the development of more uniform cataloging was the MARC format, created in the 1960s through major leadership and innovation at the Library of Congress.

MARC enabled electronic dissemination of bibliographic records and engendered networks of libraries in such entities as OCLC and the Research Libraries Group. While initially

MARC's power was felt in the economies realized through copy cataloging, first of records emanating from the Library of Congress, and subsequently, from original cataloging contributed through thousands of libraries, large and small, in the last two decades, MARC's potency has increasingly derived from unleashing the potential of the large-scale union catalog for resource sharing. Standardized bibliographic records conveyed using the MARC format also led to the rise of local systems for the management of local library holdings.

In 2001, the information landscape appears to be considerably more complex than the one our predecessors populated. There is more information, the pace of change is more rapid, and the means and formats for communication are more diverse. The catalog, at the level of the local institution, provides the information-seeker with bibliographic description and access to content imbued with several critical features. There is an implicit assumption that the works cited in the catalog are readily available for consultation. Furthermore because libraries have generally had a commitment to preserve and maintain those items they acquired, readers anticipate that a source identified today will be available in the future as well.

Because they have been assembled according to standard practices and rules, by human intelligence, there is a high consistency in description, which in turn creates a high degree of predictability in results. This dependability generates an aura of trust. The user familiar with a catalog will have a high degree of confidence in the credibility of the sources contained in it. Another function of the catalog has been to link disparate materials. Until recently, the subject linkage has been chiefly among books, but in the past few years, catalogs have begun to incorporate a variety of formats, including manuscripts, visual images, audio recordings, and now, in great numbers, digital objects. Finally, although catalog searching is a seemingly free good, with host institutions assuming the cost of maintaining local catalogs and paying for the subscription costs. Even the titles and proprietary information referenced by the catalog are more often than not purchased or licensed by a library and made freely available to its users.

Recent enhancements in online catalogs have improved the quality of access. Some of the features found in state-of-the art catalogs are Web access, relevance ranking, more refined keyword searching, ability to limit by date or other information, and reference linking. Thus, the functionality of the online catalog is increasing, and its proponents are convinced that it can continue to remain an essential tool for the identification and location of documents and materials of importance for researchers. As libraries subscribe to more and more online journals, full text documents, and other digital materials, catalog records refer to publications accessible to a community through a variety of authorizations.

No longer are all the citations in a catalog to holdings owned by a library; pointing to materials served remotely has become commonplace. The purity of the principle that the local catalog provides access to materials held by the host institution has become diluted slightly to accommodate items selected for community use and readily accessible, although not physically controlled by the library.

On the other hand, some librarians have balked at the

introduction of certain types of electronic resources into the catalog, particularly those likely to have transient URLs or which require heavy maintenance. The catalog represents stability, dependability, reliability, and quality. Its holdings have not typically been ephemeral in nature. It goes against the grain for librarians to invest in the creation of an expensive and detailed bibliographic record if the resource for which it is a surrogate, is not likely to endure for the foreseeable future, if not permanently.

Recognizing that some patrons may prefer to connect directly with online resources without being routed through the catalog, some libraries have developed separate gateways to networked resources. These gateways facilitate access to electronic materials selected by the library by providing a single point of entry, by organizing them into categories, and using metadata, often derived from their catalog records, to assist users in locating networked resources.

Index